Selected Chapters
from the
Autobiography
of
Andrew D. White

SELECTED CHAPTERS FROM THE

Autobiography

of

Andrew D. White

Ithaca · New York

CORNELL UNIVERSITY PRESS

1939

ACKNOWLEDGMENT

THESE SELECTED CHAPTERS FROM THE *Autobiography of Andrew D. White* are published by permission of D. Appleton-Century Company, New York, and Mrs. Andrew D. White. To her and to her daughter, Miss Karin White, especial thanks are due for their generous help in forwarding the publication of this edition. It has been prepared by a committee of the English Department of Cornell University. The Committee is indebted to Professor F. C. Prescott for writing the introduction and to Professor E. A. Tenney for seeing the volume through the press.

INTRODUCTION

A S THE YEARS PASS CORNELL WILL TAKE INCREASING
pride in one advantage it has over other universities.
Others find their history running back into obscurity and fable;
Cornell is fortunate in having a record of its beginnings which
is unusually clear, full, and authentic. Andrew Dickson White
served as president of Cornell during its first twenty years,
and he was its constant friend and benefactor during the
remainder of his life. Toward its close he wrote an autobiography which contains, among many other interesting experiences and activities, an account of the founding and early
years of the University. Like Thomas Jefferson, who also
founded a university and wrote an autobiography, President
White regarded his share in the university as his crowning
achievement. "Most of all," he says, "I have been interested
in the founding and maintaining of the University, and by the
part I have taken in that, more than by any other work of my
life, I hope to be judged." Jefferson's autobiography was left
incomplete and unfortunately does not reach the founding of
the University of Virginia. Those of Franklin and Henry
Adams—to mention others with which President White's may
fairly be compared—are incomplete or partial. The *Autobiography of Andrew D. White* is hardly inferior to these in
interest, while in length, scope, detailed observation, and va-

riety, it goes beyond any of them. It is one of the notable books of nineteenth-century America.

The *Autobiography* was begun, the author tells us in the first chapter, in 1900, in his sixty-eighth year, at the Embassy in Berlin. It was completed three years later in Alassio. It was apparently revised after his return to Ithaca, and was published in 1905 in two volumes, together running to more than twelve hundred pages, hardly one of which is without interest. It begins with his boyhood and covers a long life of varied activity, extending from his first public service in 1854 as attaché of the legation at St. Petersburg, to his death in November, 1918, the month of the Armistice.

Of the sixty-one chapters of the whole only thirteen can be included here. These have been selected, not because they are for the general reader more interesting than the rest, but because they have a peculiar importance for Cornell teachers and students. In the hope of making better known these chapters which deal with the early life of President White and with the founding of the University, this volume has been prepared.

The first chapter tells of his boyhood at his birthplace, Homer, and at Syracuse—a boyhood very characteristic of the later man. It was fortunate in many ways, but, as someone has said, the one thing more fortunate than his early advantages was his use of them. Next comes his unsatisfactory experience as a student at Geneva (now Hobart) College—where he had his first vision of the future university; and his transfer to Yale—this apparently involving the unusual case of a son's setting his father right, though we have only the son's side of the story. Then, after travels in Europe, follow seven years at the University of Michigan, where he was professor of history—a subject of lifelong interest.

The chapters on Cornell treat, in general, of three subjects which are still of interest to all Cornellians, whether teachers or students. First a narration of the inception, chartering, organization, and opening of the University; the building, the formation of the first faculty, the arrangement of the courses of study, and the final admission of women to full opportunities in these. Notable are chapters devoted to early "Difficulties and Dangers at Cornell" and to "Rocks, Storms, and Peril"—chapters full of work, courage, and sacrifice; chapters which in our present success and security we may read calmly but which tell of storms threatening indeed; chapters which—to quote the book—may well "impress upon the more thinking students at least, the idea that all they see has not 'happened so,' without the earnest agency of human beings; but that it has been the lifework of men and women."

Some of these men and women—and this is a second value of these chapters—are described and characterized: trustees and professors, friends and benefactors. Most interesting is the chapter devoted to Ezra Cornell, containing the best extant portrait and estimate of this truly remarkable man. Shining through these pages also is a characterization of the first president himself. Seldom have two men worked together for an important purpose more effectively and harmoniously, or shown more intelligence, resource, and courage.

But perhaps most significant for us now is the conception we may gain of the ideas on which the University was founded. A chapter is entitled, "Evolution of the Cornell Idea." What was this idea? And what is its present importance? President White tells how, after unsatisfactory student days in two old-fashioned American colleges—narrow in their courses of study, their sectarianism, and their parental attitude toward students —and after thoughtful observation of many European institutions, he gradually formed his idea of a true American university. This idea is perhaps summed up in the sentence attributed, and, as he says, rightly attributed, to Ezra Cornell: "I would found an institution where any person can find instruction in any study." About this "legend of the University" all President White's "formative ideas" gather. He believed, first, in an institution, religious in spirit, but freed from all denominational or partisan restriction or control upon trustees, faculty, or students—an institution entirely free in its cultivation of scholarship and character; secondly, in a "democracy of studies," placing classical and modern studies—humanities, sciences, and technical arts—on an equal footing; and thirdly, in the treatment of students as men and women, and of teachers as their friends. Upon these "formative ideas"—then novel, now generally adopted in our universities—was founded President White's notable contribution to American higher education. Besides developing these he discusses in a clear-sighted way and makes wise observations on many other questions of education: academic freedom, co-education, scholarships, honorary degrees, religious education, discipline, military drill, and athletics. He tried above all to interest students in their studies. After rowing in the Yale crew and observing the good effects of rowing at Cornell he "sought to promote a reasonable devotion to athletics," as exercise and as a valuable influence on character.

President White shared the liberalism of the nineteenth-century, with its complacent confidence in progressive amelioration through reason and science; and this attitude was natural to his temperament; "I have," he says, "the faith of an optimist." If any "ruling passion" warms his work, it is that for bettering every condition which he confronted—in education, politics, international relations, the diplomatic service, or social life. He saw that times change and that universities must change with them. He was remarkably tolerant and free from the type of conservatism which attempts to hold institutions in fixed moulds. Just as clearly, however, throughout the book, appears a fondness for conservatism—perhaps due to the influence of the rather old-fashioned and "high-church" views of his mother. He was almost as happy in an old Oxford quadrangle as on the new Cornell campus. As a life-long lover of history and a sympathetic student of the past, he had strong belief in the value of antiquity, tradition, and continuity in human affairs. So his idea of a university, certainly novel and naturally considered revolutionary in its time, was based on a study of past experience and what might be called a historical insight into human nature. If later Cornellians adopt his attitude they will always be ready for reasonable change in the University, but at the same time they will consider the value of perpetuating the "formative ideas" on which the University was founded. At the present time when the tendency in education, as in many other activities, is so strongly toward conformity and standardization—when in debating any new measure professors ask first about the practice at Harvard or Chicago, when in regulating their conduct students turn for models to Yale or Princeton—it is well for us, President White would perhaps say, to learn from the experience of others, but also to remember the value of our own continuity. He would perhaps urge us sometimes to look back to a time when Cornell was far from standardized, when it stood for something very distinctive in education, when there was a true "Cornell Idea" giving vitality and impetus to every teacher and student whom it reached. Because it gives the very "form and pressure" of this time, the *Autobiography* will always be for Cornellians a valuable book.

The other activities of Cornell's first president recorded in the *Autobiography* are too numerous to be more than suggested here. He took a practical view of scholarship and of his own field of history; he thought study of the past valuable mainly as a guide to the present. He put his ideas into practice and was the true scholar in public life. His book tells of his activity in American politics from 1854 to 1918—of many meetings, conventions, and legislatures, and countless public services. It tells of his years as minister or ambassador to Germany and Russia; of his experiences on the Santo Domingo and Venezuelan Boundary Commissions; of his work as president of the American delegation to the Peace Conference at the Hague; of his effective labors for the establishing of a Court of Arbitration and in the cause of peace. It tells of his travels, investigations, observations, and reflections in many parts of the world. Its index is a roster of the men worth meeting in the world in his time, with very many of whom he had lasting and important relations. It includes all the American presidents from Buchanan to Taft; notable European kings and statesmen—William II of Germany and Nicholas II of Russia, Bismarck and Salisbury; authors, scientists, men of letters, both American and foreign—Emerson, Longfellow, and Lowell, Goldwin Smith, Tolstoi, Pasteur, Lecky and von Ranke,—and countless others. Many of these are picturesquely described and shrewdly estimated.

The best way to give an idea of the omitted portions of this remarkable book may be to quote a few of its many pages.

In 1864, after sitting as a delegate in the Republican national convention in Baltimore, which nominated Lincoln for the second time, President White went on to Washington and with other delegates called at the White House.

Shortly after our arrival, [he says], our party, perhaps thirty in number, went to the White House and were shown into the great East Room. We had been there for about ten minutes when one of the doors nearest the street was opened, and a young man entered who held the door open for the admission of a tall, ungainly man dressed in a rather dusty suit of black. My first impression was that this was some rural tourist who had blundered into the place; for, really, he seemed less at home there than any other person present, and looked about for an instant, as if in doubt where he should go; but presently he turned toward our group, which was near the southwestern corner of the room, and then I saw that it was the President. As he came toward us in a sort of awkward, perfunctory manner his face seemed to me one of the saddest I had ever seen, and when he had reached us he held out his hand to the first stranger, then to the second, and so on, all with the air of a melancholy automaton. But, suddenly, some one in the company said something which amused him, and instantly there came in his face a most marvelous transformation. I have never seen anything like it in any other human being. His features were lighted, his eyes radiant, he responded to sundry remarks humorously, though dryly, and thenceforward was cordial and hearty. Taking my hand in his he shook it in the most friendly way, with a kindly word, and so passed cheerily on to the others until the ceremony was finished. (I, 121)

During his first ministry to Germany, in 1879–1881, he saw often "the greatest German since Luther." From a chapter devoted to Bismarck come these paragraphs.

My first glimpse of Bismarck was obtained during one of my journeys through middle Germany, about the time, I think, of the Franco-Prussian War. Arriving at Kissingen junction, we found a crowd gathered outside the barriers, and all gazing at a railway-carriage about to be attached to our train. Looking toward this, I recognized the face and form of the great North-German statesman. He was in the prime of life— sturdy, hearty, and happy in the presence of his wife and children. The people at the station evidently knew what was needed; for hardly had he arrived when waiters appeared, bearing salvers covered with huge mugs of foaming beer. Thereupon Bismarck took two of the mugs in immediate succession; poured their contents down his throat, evidently with gusto; and a burly peasant just back of me, unable longer to restrain his admiration, soliloquized in a deep, slow, guttural, reverberating rumble: "A-a-a-ber er sieht sehr-r-r gut aus." So it struck me also; the waters of Kissingen had evidently restored the great man, and he looked like a Titan ready for battle. . . . (I, 574)

It was my good fortune to hear Bismarck publicly discuss many important questions, and his way of speaking was not like that of any other man I have ever heard. He was always clothed in the undress uniform of a Prussian general; and, as he rose, his bulk made him imposing. His first utterances were disappointing. He seemed wheezy, rambling, incoherent, with a sort of burdensome self-consciousness checking his ideas and clogging his words. His manner was fidgety, his arms being thrown uneasily about, and his fingers fumbling his mustache or his clothing or the papers on his desk. He puffed, snorted, and floundered; seemed to make assertions without proof and phrases without point; when suddenly he would utter a statement so pregnant as to clear up a whole policy, or a sentence so audacious as to paralyze a whole line of his opponents, or a phrase so vivid as to run through the nation and electrify it. Then, perhaps, after more rumbling and rambling, came a clean, clear, historical illustration carrying conviction; then, very likely, a simple and strong argument, not infrequently ended by some heavy missile in the shape of an accusation or a taunt hurled into the faces of his adversaries; then, perhaps at considerable length, a mixture of caustic criticism and personal reminiscence, in which sparkled those wonderful sayings which have gone through the empire and settled deeply into the German heart. I have known many clever speakers and some very powerful orators; but I have never known one capable, in the same degree, of overwhelming his enemies and carrying his whole country with him. Nor was his eloquence in his oratory alone. There was something in his bearing, as he sat at his ministerial desk and at times looked up from it to listen to a speaker, which was very impressive. (I, 598)

In a chapter entitled "England Revisited—1885" President White renewed an old acquaintance with Oxford and Cambridge. At the latter he records the following, evidently drawing upon his diary.

December 4. Visited St. John's, St. Peter's, and other colleges; in the afternoon saw the eight-oared boats come down the river in fine style; and in the evening went to the annual "audit dinner" at Trinity College, the number of visitors in the magnificent hall being very large. I found myself between the vice-master, Trotter, and Professor Humphrey, the distinguished surgeon. The latter thought Vienna had shot ahead of Berlin in surgery, though he considered Billroth too venturesome, and praised recent American works on surgery, but thought England was still keeping the lead. At the close of the dinner came a curious custom. Two servants approached the vice-master at the head of the first table, laid down upon it a narrow roll of linen, and then the guests rolled this along by pushing it from either side, until, when it had reached the other end, a strip of smooth linen was left along the middle of the whole table. Then a great silver dish, with ladles on either side, and containing some sort of fragrant fluid, was set in front of the vice-master, upon the narrow strip of linen which had formed the roll, and the same thing was repeated at each of the other tables. The vice-master having then filled a large glass at his side from the dish, and I, at his suggestion, having done the same, the great dish was pushed down the table to guest after guest, each following our example. Waiting to see what was to follow, I presently observed a gentleman near me dipping his napkin into his glass and vigorously scrubbing his face and neck with it, evidently to cool himself off after dinner; this was repeated with more or less thoroughness by others present; and then came a musical grace after meat—the *non nobis, Domine*—wonderfully given by the choir. In the combination room, afterward, I met most agreeably Mr. Trevelyan, M.P., a nephew of Macaulay, who has written an admirable biography of his uncle. (II, 407)

In pre-revolutionary Russia President White was evidently impressed by its mediaevalism and unenlightenment, and in its statesmen by an illiberality of thought, the very opposite of his own. He went, however, on the principle he somewhere recommends—that the man you don't like is the man you don't know—and found common ground. Pobedonostzeff was, he says, "under Alexander III the most influential personage in the Empire," and because of his cruelty and persecution he was regarded in western countries as a veritable Torquemada. President White found him "a scholarly, kindly man, ready to discuss the business which I brought before him, and showing a wide interest in public affairs." He goes on:

But the most curious—indeed, the most amazing—revelation of the man I found in his love for American literature. He is a wide reader; and, in the whole breadth of his reading, American authors were evidently among those he preferred. Of these his favorites were Hawthorne, Lowell, and, above all, Emerson. Curious, indeed, was it to learn that this "arch-persecutor," this "Torquemada of the nineteenth century," this

man whose hand is especially heavy upon Catholics and Protestants and dissenters throughout the empire, whose name is
spoken by millions within the empire and without it, still
reads, as his favorite author, the philosopher of Concord. He
told me that the first book which he ever translated into Russian was Thomas à Kempis's "Imitation of Christ"; and of that
he gave me the Latin original from which he made his translation, with a copy of the translation itself. But he also
told me that the next book he translated was a volume of
Emerson's "Essays," and he added that for years there had always lain open upon his study table a volume of Emerson's
writings. . . . (II, 61)

He appeared to hold our nation as a problem apart, and
was, perhaps, too civil in his conversations with me to include
it in the same condemnation with the nations of Western
Europe, which had, in his opinion, gone hopelessly wrong. He
also seemed drawn to us by his admiration for Emerson, Hawthorne, and Lowell. When Professor Norton's edition of
Lowell's "Letters" came out, I at once took it to him. It evidently gave him great pleasure—perhaps because it revealed
to him a very different civilization, life, and personality from
anything to which he had been accustomed. Still, America
seemed to be to him a sort of dreamland. (II, 66)

"Revisiting Moscow," President White says, after an absence
of thirty-five years, he found few changes, except that "for the
first time in the history of Russia a man of world-wide fame
in literature and thought was abiding there." In a chapter of
"walks and talks with Tolstoi," he describes his first visit:

On the evening of my arrival I went with my secretary to his
weekly reception. As we entered his house on the outskirts
of the city, two servants in evening dress came forward, removed our fur coats, and opened the doors into the reception-
room of the master. Then came a surprise. His living-room
seemed the cabin of a Russian peasant. It was wainscoted
almost rudely and furnished very simply; and there approached us a tall, gaunt Russian, unmistakably born to command, yet clad as a peasant, his hair thrown back over his ears

on either side, his flowing blouse kept together by a leathern girdle, his high jack-boots completing the costume. This was Tolstoi.

Nothing could be more kindly than his greeting. While his dress was that of a peasant, his bearing was the very opposite; for, instead of the depressed, demure, hangdog expression of the average muzhik, his manner, though cordial, was dignified and impressive. . . .

Naturally, I soon asked to be presented to the lady of the house, and the count escorted us through a series of rooms to a salon furnished like any handsome apartment in Paris or St. Petersburg, where the countess, with other ladies, all in full evening dress, received us cordially. This sudden transition from the peasant cabin of the master to these sumptuous rooms of the mistress was startling; it seemed like scene-shifting at a theatre. (II, 72, 73)

In a busy university perhaps few will find time to read the *Autobiography* in all its twelve-hundred pages. But a reader may select at will from its detailed Table of Contents chapters which promise interest, and he will probably not begin one of these without finishing it. At any rate the chapters in the present volume alone will give a new interest to the statue of the author standing before Goldwin Smith Hall. It is the work of Karl Bitter, a well-known sculptor in his time, and it appropriately represents President White as a thinker rather than as a man of action and affairs. It stands, as the reader of these chapters will learn, on what once was Ezra Cornell's cornfield. For the occasion of its dedication Dean Smith wrote a poem, which closes:

> Here amid the fair fulfillment of his dream
> His statue broods above the busy ways;
> Long since on this bare hill he saw the gleam
> Prophetic of these present golden days.

F. C. PRESCOTT

CORNELL UNIVERSITY
June 1, 1939

CONTENTS

BOYHOOD IN CENTRAL NEW YORK

1832–1850

A T THE CLOSE OF THE REVOLUTION WHICH SEPARATED the colonies from the mother country, the legislature of New York set apart nearly two million acres of land, in the heart of the State, as bounty to be divided among her soldiers who had taken part in the war; and this "Military Tract," having been duly divided into townships, an ill-inspired official, in lack of names for so many divisions, sprinkled over the whole region the contents of his classical dictionary. Thus it was that there fell to a beautiful valley upon the headwaters of the Susquehanna the name of "Homer." Fortunately the surveyor-general left to the mountains, lakes, and rivers the names the Indians had given them, and so there was still some poetical element remaining in the midst of that unfortunate nomenclature. The counties, too, as a rule, took Indian names, so that the town of Homer, with its neighbors, Tully, Pompey, Fabius, Lysander, and the rest, were embedded in the county of Onondaga, in the neighborhood of lakes Otisco and Skaneateles, and of the rivers Tioughnioga and Susquehanna.

Hither came, toward the close of the eighteenth century, a body of sturdy New Englanders, and, among them, my grandfathers and grandmothers. Those on my father's side: Asa White and Clara Keep, from Munson, Massachusetts; those on my mother's side, Andrew Dickson, from Middlefield, Massachusetts, and Ruth Hall from Guilford, Connecticut. They were all of "good stock." When I was ten years old I saw my great-grandfather at Middlefield, eighty-two years of age, sturdy and vigorous; he had mowed a broad field the day before, and he walked four miles to church the day after. He had done his duty manfully during the war, had been a member of the "Great and General Court" of Massachusetts, and had held various other offices, which showed that he enjoyed the confidence of his fellow-citizens. As to the other side of the house, there was a tradition that we came from Peregrine White of the *Mayflower;* but I have never had time to find whether my doubts on the subject were well founded or not. Enough for me to know that my yeomen ancestors did their duty in war and peace, were honest, straightforward, God-fearing men and women, who owned their own lands, and never knew what it was to cringe before any human being.

These New Englanders literally made the New York wilderness to blossom as the rose; and Homer, at my birth in 1832, about forty years after the first settlers came, was, in its way, one of the prettiest villages imaginable. In the heart of it was the "Green," and along the middle of this a line of church edifices, and the academy. In front of the green, parallel to the river, ran, north and south, the broad main street, beautifully shaded with maples, and on either side of this, in the middle of the village, were stores, shops, and the main taverns; while north and south of these were large and pleasant dwellings, each in its own garden or grove or orchard, and separated from the street by light palings,—all, without exception, neat, trim, and tidy.

My first recollections are of a big, comfortable house of brick, in what is now called "colonial style," with a "stoop," long and broad, on its southern side, which in summer was shaded with honeysuckles. Spreading out southward from this was a spacious garden filled with old-fashioned flowers, and in this I learned to walk. To this hour the perfume of a pink brings the whole scene before me, and proves the justice of Oliver

Wendell Holmes's saying that we remember past scenes more vividly by the sense of smell than by the sense of sight.

I can claim no merit for clambering out of poverty. My childhood was happy; my surroundings wholesome; I was brought up neither in poverty nor riches; my parents were what were called "well-to-do-people"; everything about me was good and substantial; but our mode of life was frugal; waste or extravagance or pretense was not permitted for a moment. My paternal grandfather had been, in the early years of the century, the richest man in the township; but some time before my birth he had become one of the poorest; for a fire had consumed his mills, there was no insurance, and his health gave way. On my father, Horace White, had fallen, therefore, the main care of his father's family. It was to the young man, apparently, a great calamity:—that which grieved him most being that it took him—a boy not far in his teens—out of school. But he met the emergency manfully, was soon known far and wide for his energy, ability, and integrity, and long before he had reached middle age was considered one of the leading men of business in the county.

My mother had a more serene career. In another part of these Reminiscences, saying something of my religious and political development, I shall speak again of her and of her parents. Suffice it here that her father prospered as a man of business, was known as "Colonel," and also as "Squire" Dickson, and represented his county in the State legislature. He died when I was about three years old, and I vaguely remember being brought to him as he lay upon his death-bed. On one account, above all others, I have long looked back to him with pride. For the first public care of the early settlers had been a church, and the second a school. This school had been speedily developed into Cortland Academy, which soon became famous throughout all that region, and, as a boy of five or six years of age, I was very proud to read on the cornerstone of the Academy building my grandfather's name among those of the original founders.

Not unlikely there thus came into my blood the strain which has led me ever since to feel that the building up of goodly institutions is more honorable than any other work,—an idea which was at the bottom of my efforts in developing the University of Michigan, and in founding Cornell University.

To Cortland Academy students came from far and near; and it soon began sending young men into the foremost places of State and Church. At an early day, too, it began receiving young women and sending them forth to become the best of matrons. As my family left the place when I was seven years old I was never within its walls as a student, but it acted powerfully on my education in two ways,—it gave my mother the best of her education, and it gave to me a respect for scholarship. The library and collections, though small, suggested pursuits better than the scramble for place or pelf; the public exercises, two or three times a year, led my thoughts, no matter how vaguely, into higher regions, and I shall never forget the awe which came over me when as a child, I saw Principal Woolworth, with his best students around him on the green, making astronomical observations through a small telescope.

Thus began my education into that great truth, so imperfectly understood, as yet, in our country, that stores, shops, hotels, facilities for travel and traffic are not the highest things in civilization.

This idea was strengthened in the family. Devoted as my father was to business, he always showed the greatest respect for men of thought. I have known him, even when most absorbed in his pursuits, to watch occasions for walking homeward with a clergyman or teacher, whose conversation he especially prized. There was scant respect in the family for the petty politicians of the region; but there was great respect for the instructors of the academy, and for any college professor who happened to be traveling through the town. I am now in my sixty-eighth year, and I write these lines from the American Embassy in Berlin. It is my duty here, as it has been at other European capitals, to meet various high officials; but that old feeling, engendered in my childhood, continues, and I bow to the representatives of the universities,—to the leaders in science, literature, and art, with a feeling of awe and respect far greater than to their so-called superiors,—princelings and high military or civil officials.

Influences of a more direct sort came from a primary school. To this I was taken, when about three years old, for a reason which may strike the present generation as curious. The colored servant who had charge of me wished to learn to read— so she slipped into the school and took me with her. As a result, though my memory runs back distinctly to events near the beginning of my fourth year, it holds not the faintest recollection of a time when I could not read easily. The only studies which I recall with distinctness, as carried on before my seventh year, are arithmetic and geography. As to the former, the multiplication-table was chanted in chorus by the whole body of children, a rhythmical and varied movement of the arms being carried on at the same time. These exercises gave us pleasure and fastened the tables in our minds. As to geography, that gave pleasure in another way. The books contained pictures which stimulated my imagination and prompted me to read the adjacent text. There was no over-pressure. Mental recreation and information were obtained in a loose way from "Rollo Books," "Peter Parley Books," "Sanford and Merton," the "Children's Magazine," and the like. I now think it a pity that I was not allowed to read, instead of these, the novels of Scott and Cooper, which I discovered later. I devoutly thank Heaven that no such thing as a sensation newspaper was ever brought into the house,—even if there were one at that time,— which I doubt. As to physical recreation, there was plenty during the summer in the fields and woods, and during the winter in coasting, building huts in the deep snow, and in storming or defending the snow forts on the village green. One of these childish sports had a historical connection with a period which now seems very far away. If any old settler happened to pass during our snow-balling or our shooting with bows and arrows, he was sure to look on with interest, and, at some good shot, to cry out,—"*Shoot Burgoyne!*"—thus recalling his remembrances of the sharpshooters who brought about the great surrender at Saratoga.

In my seventh year my father was called to take charge of the new bank established at Syracuse, thirty miles distant, and there the family soon joined him. I remember that coming through the Indian Reservation, on the road between the two villages, I was greatly impressed by the bowers and other decorations which had been used shortly before at the installation of a new Indian chief. It was the headquarters of the Onondagas,—formerly the great central tribe of the Iroquois,— the warlike confederacy of the Six Nations; and as, in a general way, the story was told me on that beautiful day in September a new world of romance was opened to me, so that Indian stories, and especially Cooper's novels, when I was allowed to read them, took on a new reality.

Syracuse, which is now a city of one hundred and twenty thousand inhabitants, was then a straggling village of about five thousand. After much time lost in sundry poor "select schools" I was sent to one of the public schools which was very good, and thence, when about twelve years old, to the preparatory department of the Syracuse Academy.

There, by good luck, was Joseph A. Allen, the best teacher of English branches I have ever known. He had no rules and no system; or, rather, his rule was to have no rules, and his system was to have no system. To most teachers this would have been fatal; but he had genius. He seemed to divine the character and enter into the purpose of every boy. Work under him was a pleasure. His methods were very simple. Great attention was given to reading aloud from a book made up of selections from the best authors, and to recitals from these. Thus I stored up not only some of the best things in the older English writers, but inspiring poems of Bryant, Whittier, Longfellow, and other moderns. My only regret is that more of this was not given us. I recall, among treasures thus gained, which have been precious to me ever since, in many a weary or sleepless hour on land and sea, extracts from Shakspere, parts of Milton's "Samson Agonistes," and of his sonnets; Gray's "Elegy," Byron's "Ode to the Ocean," Campbell's "What's Hallowed Ground?" Goldsmith's "Deserted Village," Longfellow's "Psalm of Life," Irving's "Voyage to Europe," and parts of Webster's "Reply to Hayne."

At this school the wretched bugbear of English spelling was dealt with by a method which, so long as our present monstrous orthography continues, seems to me the best possible. During the last half-hour of every day, each scholar was required to have before him a copybook, of which each page was divided into two columns. At the head of the first column was the word "Spelling"; at the head of the second column was the word "Corrected." The teacher then gave out to the school about twenty of the more important words in the reading-lesson of the day, and, as he thus dictated each word, each scholar wrote it in the column headed "Spelling." When all the words were thus written, the first scholar was asked to spell from his book the first word; if misspelled, it was passed to the next, and so on until it was spelled correctly; whereupon all who had made a mistake in writing it made the proper correction on the opposite column. The result of this was that the greater part of us learned orthography *practically.* For the practical use of spelling comes in writing.

The only mistake in Mr. Allen's teaching was too much attention to English grammar. The order ought to be, literature first, and grammar afterward. Perhaps there is no more tiresome trifling in the world for boys and girls than rote recitations and parsing from one of the usual grammatical textbooks.

As to mathematics, arithmetic was, perhaps, pushed too far into puzzles; but geometry was made fascinating by showing its real applications and the beauty of its reasoning. It is the only mathematical study I ever loved. In natural science, though most of the apparatus of schools nowadays was wanting, Mr. Allen's instruction was far beyond his time. Never shall I forget my excited interest when, occasionally, the village surgeon came in, and the whole school was assembled to see him dissect the eye or ear or heart of an ox. Physics, as then understood, was studied in a text-book, but there was illustration by simple apparatus, which fastened firmly in my mind the main facts and principles.

The best impulse by this means came from the principal of the academy, Mr. Oren Root,—one of the pioneers of American science, whose modesty alone stood in the way of his fame. I was too young to take direct instruction from him, but the experiments which I saw him perform led me, with one or two of my mates, to construct an excellent electrical machine and subsidiary apparatus; and with these, a small galvanic battery and an extemporized orrery, I diluted Professor Root's lectures with the teachings of my little books on natural philosophy and astronomy to meet the capacities of the younger boys in our neighborhood.

Salient among my recollections of this period are the cries and wailing of a newly-born babe in the rooms at the academy occupied by the principal, and adjacent to our big schoolroom. Several decades of years later I had the honor of speaking on the platform of Cooper Institute in company with this babe, who, as I write, is, I believe, the very energetic Secretary of War in the Cabinet of President McKinley.

Unfortunately for me, Mr. Root was soon afterward called away to a professorship at Hamilton College, and so, though living in the best of all regions for geological study, I was never properly grounded in that science, and as to botany, I am to this hour utterly ignorant of its simplest facts and principles. I count this as one of the mistakes in my education,—resulting in the loss of much valuable knowledge and high pleasure.

As to physical development, every reasonable encouragement was given to play. Mr. Allen himself came frequently to the play-grounds. He was an excellent musician and a most helpful influence was exerted by singing, which was a daily exercise of the school. I then began taking lessons regularly in music and became proficient enough to play the organ occasionally in church; the best result of this training being that it gave my life one of its deepest, purest, and most lasting pleasures.

On the moral side, Mr. Allen influenced many of us by liberalizing and broadening our horizon. He was a disciple of Channing and an abolitionist, and, though he never made the slightest attempt to proselyte any of his scholars, the very atmosphere of the school made sectarian bigotry impossible.

As to my general education outside the school I browsed about as best I could. My passion in those days was for machinery, and, above all, for steam machinery. The stationary and locomotive engines upon the newly-established railways toward Albany on the east and Buffalo on the west especially aroused my attention, and I came to know every locomotive, its history, character, and capabilities, as well as every stationary engine in the whole region. My holiday excursions, when not employed in boating or skating on the Onondaga Creek, or upon the lake, were usually devoted to visiting workshops, where the engine drivers and stokers seemed glad to talk with a youngster who took an interest in their business. Especially interested was I in a rotary engine on "Barker's centrifugal principle," with which the inventor had promised to propel locomotives at the rate of a hundred miles an hour, but which had been degraded to grinding bark in a tannery. I felt its disgrace keenly, as a piece of gross injustice; but having obtained a small brass model, fitted to it a tin boiler and placed it on a little stern-wheel boat, I speedily discovered the secret of the indignity which had overtaken the machine, for no boat could carry a boiler large enough to supply steam for it.

So, too, I knew every water-wheel in that part of the county, whether overshot, undershot, breast, or turbine. Everything in the nature of a motor had an especial fascination for me, and for the men in control of such power I entertained a respect which approached awe.

Among all these, my especial reverence was given to the locomotive engineers; in my youthful mind they took on a heroic character. Often during the night watches I thought of them as braving storm and peril, responsible for priceless freights of human lives. Their firm, keen faces come back to me vividly through the mists of sixty years, and to this day I look up to their successors at the throttle with respectful admiration.

After Professor Root's departure the Syracuse Academy greatly declined, Mr. Allen being the only strong man left among its teachers, and, as I was to go to college, I was removed to a "classical school." This school was not at first very successful. Its teacher was a good scholar but careless. Under him I repeated the grammatical forms and rules in Latin and Greek, glibly, term after term, without really understanding their value. His great mistake, which seems to me a not infrequent one, was taking it for granted that repeating rules and forms means understanding them and their application. But a catastrophe came. I had been promoted beyond my deserts from a lower into an upper Latin class, and at a public examination the Rev. Samuel Joseph May, who was present, asked me a question, to which I made an answer revealing utter ignorance of one of the simplest principles of Latin grammar. He was disconcerted at the result, I still more so, and our preceptor most of all. That evening my father very solemnly asked me about it. I was mortified beyond expression, did not sleep at all that night, and of my own accord, began reviewing my Andrews and Stoddard thoroughly and vigorously. But this did not save the preceptor. A successor was called, a man who afterward became an eminent Presbyterian divine and professor in a Southern university, James W. Hoyt, one of the best and truest of men, and his manly, moral influence over his scholars was remarkable. Many of them have reached positions of usefulness, and I think they will agree that his influence upon their lives was most happy. The only drawback was that he was still very young, not yet through his senior year in Union College, and his methods in classical teaching were imperfect. He loved his classics and taught his better students to love them, but he was neither thorough in grammar, nor sure in translation, and this I afterward found to my sorrow. My friend and schoolmate of that time, W. O. S., published a few years since in the "St. Nicholas Magazine," an account of this school. It was somewhat idealized, but we doubtless agree in thinking that the lack of grammatical drill was more than made up by the love of manliness, and the dislike of meanness, which was in those days our very atmosphere. Probably the best thing for my mental training was that Mr. Hoyt interested me in my Virgil, Horace, and Xenophon, and required me to write out my translations in the best English at my command.

But to all his pupils he did not prove so helpful. One of them, though he has since become an energetic man of business on the Pacific Coast, was certainly not helped into his present position by his Latin; for of all the translations I have ever heard or read of, one of his was the worst. Being called to construe the first line of the Æneid, he proceeded as follows: "*Arma,*—arms; *virumque,*—and a man; *cano,*—and a dog." There was a roar, and Mr. Hoyt, though evidently saddened, kept his temper. He did not, like the great and good Arnold of Rugby, under similar provocation, knock the offender down with the text-book.

Still another agency in my development was the debating club, so inevitable in an American village. Its discussions were sometimes pretentious and always crude, but something was gained thereby. I remember that one of the subjects was stated as follows: "Which has done most harm, intemperance or fanaticism?" The debate was without any striking feature until my schoolmate, W. O. S., brought up heavy artillery on the side of the anti-fanatics: namely, a statement of the ruin wrought by Mohammedanism in the East, and, above all, the destruction of the great Alexandrian library by Caliph Omar; and with such eloquence that all the argumentation which any of us had learned in the temperance meetings was paralyzed.

On another occasion we debated the question: "Was the British Government justified in its treatment of Napoleon Bonaparte?" Much historical lore had been brought to bear on the question, when an impassioned young orator wound up a bitter diatribe against the great emperor as follows: "The British Government *was* justified, and if for no other reason, by the Emperor Napoleon's murder of the 'Duck de Engine'" (Duc d'Enghien).

As to education outside of the school very important to me had been the discovery, when I was about ten years old, of "'The Monastery,' by the author of 'Waverley.'" Who the "author of 'Waverley'" was I neither knew nor cared, but read the book three times, end over end, in a sort of fascination. Unfortunately, novels and romances were kept under lock and key, as unfit reading for children, and it was some years before I reveled in Scott's other novels. That they would have been thoroughly good and wholesome reading for me I know, and about my sixteenth year they opened a new world to me and gave healthful play to my imagination. I also read and re-read Bunyan's "Pilgrim's Progress," and, with pleasure even more intense, the earlier works of Dickens, which were then appearing.

My only regret, as regards that time, is that, between the rather trashy "boys' books" on one side and the rather severe books in the family library on the other, I read far less of really good literature than I ought to have done. My reading was absolutely without a guide, hence fitful and scrappy; parts of Rollin's "Ancient History" and Lander's "Travels in Africa" being mixed up with "Robinson Crusoe" and "The Scottish Chiefs." Reflection on my experience has convinced me that some kindly guidance in the reading of a fairly scholarly boy is of the utmost importance, and never more so than now, when books are so many and attractive. I should lay much stress, also, on the hearing of good literature well read, and the interspersing of such reading with some remarks by the reader, pointing out the main beauties of the pieces thus presented.

About my tenth year occurred an event, apparently trivial, but really very important in my mental development during many years afterward. My father brought home one day, as a gift to my mother, a handsome quarto called "The Gallery of British Artists." It contained engravings from pictures by Turner, Stanfield, Cattermole, and others, mainly representing scenes from Shakspere, Scott, Burns, picturesque architecture, and beautiful views in various parts of Europe. Of this book I never tired. It aroused in me an intense desire to know more of the subjects represented, and this desire has led me since to visit and to study every cathedral, church, and town hall of any historical or architectural significance in Europe, outside the Spanish peninsula. But, far more important, it gave an especial zest to nearly all Scott's novels, and especially to the one which I have always thought the most fascinating, "Quentin Durward." This novel led me later, not merely to visit Liège, and Orléans, and Cléry, and Tours, but to devour the chronicles and histories of that period, to become deeply interested in historical studies, and to learn how great principles lie hidden beneath the surface of events. The first of these principles I ever clearly discerned was during my reading of "Quentin Durward" and "Anne of Geierstein," when there was revealed to me the secret of the centralization of power in Europe, and of the triumph of monarchy over feudalism.

In my sixteenth and seventeenth years another element entered into my education. Syracuse, as the central city of the State, was the scene of many conventions and public meetings. That was a time of very deep earnestness in political matters. The last great efforts were making, by the more radical, peaceably to prevent the extension of slavery, and, by the more conservative, peaceably to preserve the Union. The former of these efforts interested me most. There were at Syracuse frequent public debates between the various groups of the anti-slavery party represented by such men as Gerrit Smith, Wendell Phillips, William Lloyd Garrison, John Parker Hale, Samuel Joseph May, and Frederick Douglass. They took strong hold upon me and gave me a higher idea of a man's best work in life. That was the bloom period of the old popular lecture. It was the time when lectures were expected to build character and increase knowledge; the sensation and buffoon business which destroyed the system had not yet come in. I feel to this hour the good influence of lectures then heard, in the old City Hall at Syracuse, from such men as President Mark Hopkins, Bishop Alonzo Potter, Senator Hale of New Hampshire, Emerson, Ware, Whipple, and many others.

As to recreative reading at this period, the author who exercised the strongest influence over me was Charles Kingsley. His novels "Alton Locke" and "Yeast" interested me greatly in efforts for doing away with old abuses in Europe, and his "Two Years After" increased my hatred for negro slavery in America. His "Westward Ho!" extended my knowledge of the Elizabethan period and increased my manliness. Of this period, too, was my reading of Lowell's Poems, many of which I greatly enjoyed. His "Biglow Papers" were a perpetual delight; the dialect was familiar to me since, in the little New England town transplanted into the heart of central New York, in which I was born, the less educated people used it, and the dry and droll Yankee expressions of our "help" and "hired man" were a source of constant amusement in the family.

In my seventeenth year came a trial. My father had taken a leading part in establishing a parish school for St. Paul's church in Syracuse, in accordance with the High Church views of our rector, Dr. Gregory, and there was finally called to the mastership a young candidate for orders, a brilliant scholar and charming man, who has since become an eminent bishop of the Protestant Episcopal Church. To him was intrusted my final preparation for college. I had always intended to enter one of the larger New England universities, but my teacher was naturally in favor of his Alma Mater, and the influence of our bishop, Dr. de Lancey, being also thrown powerfully into the scale, my father insisted on placing me at a small Protestant Episcopal college in western New York. I went most reluctantly. There were in the faculty several excellent men, one of whom afterward became a colleague of my own in Cornell University, and proved of the greatest value to it. Unfortunately, we of the lower college classes could have very little instruction from him; still there was good instruction from others; the tutor in Greek, James Morrison Clarke, was one of the best scholars I have ever known.

It was in the autumn of 1849 that I went into residence at the little college and was assigned a very unprepossessing room in a very ugly barrack. Entering my new quarters I soon discovered about me various cabalistic signs, some of them evidently made by heating large iron keys, and pressing them against the woodwork. On inquiring I found that the room had been occupied some years before by no less a personage than Philip Spencer, a member of the famous Spencer family of Albany, who, having passed some years at this little college, and never having been able to get out of the freshman class, had gone to another institution of about the same grade, had there founded a Greek letter fraternity which is now widely spread among American universities, and then, through the influence of his father, who was Secretary of War, had been placed as a midshipman under Commodore McKenzie on the brig-of-war *Somers*. On the coast of Africa a mutiny was discovered, and as, on examination, young Spencer was found at the head of it, and papers discovered in his cabin revealed the plan of seizing the ship and using it in a career of piracy, the young man, in spite of his connection with a member of the Cabinet, was hanged at the yard-arm with two of his associates.

The most curious relic of him at the college was preserved in the library of the Hermean Society. It was a copy of "The Pirates' Own Book": a glorification of the exploits of "Blackbeard" and other great freebooters, profusely adorned with illustrations of their joys and triumphs. This volume bore on the fly-leaf the words, "Presented to the Hermean Society by Philip Spencer," and was in those days shown as a great curiosity.

The college was at its lowest ebb; of discipline there was none; there were about forty students, the majority of them, sons of wealthy churchmen, showing no inclination to work and much tendency to dissipation. The authorities of the college could not afford to expel or even offend a student, for its endowment was so small that it must have all the instruction fees possible, and must keep on good terms with the wealthy fathers of its scapegrace students. The scapegraces soon found this out, and the result was a little pandemonium. Only about a dozen of our number studied at all; the rest, by translations, promptings, and evasions escaped without labor. I have had to do since, as student, professor, or lecturer, with some half-dozen large universities at home and abroad, and in all of these together have not seen so much carousing and wild dissipation as I then saw in this little "Church college" of which the especial boast was that, owing to the small number of its students, it was "able to exercise a direct Christian influence upon every young man committed to its care."

The evidences of this Christian influence were not clear. The president of the college, Dr. Benjamin Hale, was a clergyman of the highest character; a good scholar, an excellent preacher, and a wise administrator; but his stature was very small, his girth very large, and his hair very yellow. When, then, on the thirteenth day of the month, there was read at chapel from the Psalter the words, "And there was little Benjamin, their ruler," very irreverent demonstrations were often made by the students, presumably engaged in worship; demonstrations so mortifying, indeed, that at last the president frequently substituted for the regular Psalms of the day one of the beautiful "Selections" of Psalms which the American Episcopal Church has so wisely incorporated into its prayerbook.

But this was by no means the worst indignity which these youth "under direct Christian influence" perpetrated upon their reverend instructors. It was my privilege to behold a professor, an excellent clergyman, seeking to quell hideous riot in a student's room, buried under a heap of carpets, mattresses, counterpanes, and blankets; to see another clerical professor forced to retire through the panel of a door under a shower of lexicons, boots, and brushes, and to see even the president himself, on one occasion, obliged to leave his lecture-room by a ladder from a window, and, on another, kept at bay by a shower of beer-bottles.

One favorite occupation was rolling cannon-balls along the corridors at midnight, with frightful din and much damage: a tutor, having one night been successful in catching and confiscating two of these, pounced from his door the next night upon a third; but this having been heated nearly to redness and launched from a shovel, the result was that he wore bandages upon his hands for many days.

Most ingenious were the methods for "training freshmen,"—one of the mildest being the administration of soot and water by a hose-pipe thrust through the broken panel of a door. Among general freaks I remember seeing a horse turned into the chapel, and a stuffed wolf, dressed in a surplice, placed upon the roof of that sacred edifice.

But the most elaborate thing of the kind I ever saw was the breaking up of a "Second Adventist" meeting by a score of student roysterers. An itinerant fanatic had taken an old wooden meeting-house in the lower part of the town, had set up on either side of the pulpit large canvas representations of the man of brass with feet of clay, and other portentous characters of the prophecies, and then challenged the clergy to meet him in public debate. At the appointed time a body of college youth appeared, most sober in habit and demure in manner, having at their head "Bill" Howell of Black Rock and "Tom" Clark of Manlius, the two wildest miscreants in the sophomore class, each over six feet tall, the latter dressed as a respectable farmer, and the former as a country clergyman, wearing a dress-coat, a white cravat, a tall black hat wrapped in crape, leaning on a heavy ivory-knobbed cane, and carrying ostentatiously a Greek Testament. These disguised malefactors, having taken their seats in the gallery directly facing the pulpit, the lecturer expressed his "satisfaction at seeing clergymen present," and began his demonstrations. For about five minutes all went well; then "Bill" Howell solemnly arose and, in a snuffling voice, asked permission to submit a few texts from scripture. Permission being granted, he put on a huge pair of goggles, solemnly opened his Greek Testament, read emphatically the first passage which attracted his attention and impressively asked the lecturer what he had to say to it. At this, the lecturer, greatly puzzled, asked what the reverend gentleman was reading. Upon this Howell read in New Testament Greek another utterly irrelevant passage. In reply the lecturer said, rather roughly, "If you will speak English I will answer you." At this Howell said with the most humble suavity, "Do I understand that the distinguished gentleman does not recognize what I have been reading?" The preacher answered, "I don't understand any such gibberish; speak English." Thereupon Howell threw back his long black hair and launched forth into eloquent denunciation as follows: "Sir, is it possible that you come here to interpret to us the Holy Bible and do not recognize the language in which that blessed book was written? Sir, do you dare to call the very words of the Almighty 'gibberish?'" At this all was let loose; some students put asafetida on the stove; others threw pigeon-shot against the ceiling and windows, making a most appalling din, and one wretch put in deadly work with a syringe thrust through the canvas representation of the man of brass with feet of clay. But, alas, Constable John Dey had recognized Howell and Clark, even amid their disguises. He had dealt with them too often before. The next tableau showed them, with their tall hats crushed over their heads, belaboring John Dey and his myrmidons, and presently, with half a dozen other ingenuous youth, they were haled to the office of justice. The young judge who officiated on this occasion was none other than a personage who will be mentioned with great respect more than once in these reminiscences,—Charles James Folger, —afterward my colleague in the State Senate, Chief Justice of the State and Secretary of the Treasury of the United States. He had met Howell often, for they were members of the same Greek letter fraternity,—the thrice illustrious Sigma Phi,—and, only a few days before, Howell had presented me to him; but there was no fraternal bond visible now; justice was sternly implacable, and good round fines were imposed upon all the culprits caught.

The philosophy of all this waywardness and dissipation was very simple. There was no other outlet for the animal spirits of these youth. Athletics were unknown; there was no gymnasium, no ball-playing, and, though the college was situated on the shore of one of the most beautiful lakes in the world, no boating. As regards my own personal relation to this condition of things I have pictured, it was more that of a good-natured spectator than of an active accomplice. My nearest friends were in the thick of it, but my tastes kept me out of most of it. I was fond of books, and, in the little student's library in my college building I reveled. Moreover, I then began to accumulate for myself the library which has since grown to such large proportions. Still the whole life of the place became more and more unsatisfactory to me, and I determined, at any cost, to escape from it and find some seat of learning where there was less frolic and more study.

YALE AND EUROPE

1850–1857

A T THE CLOSE OF MY YEAR AT THE LITTLE WESTERN
New York College I felt that it was enough time wasted,
and, anxious to try for something better, urged upon my father
my desire to go to one of the larger New England universities.
But to this he would not listen. He was assured by the
authorities of the little college that I had been doing well, and
his churchmanship, as well as his respect for the bishop, led
him to do what was very unusual with him—to refuse my request. Up to this period he had allowed me to take my own
course; but now he was determined that I should take his.
He was one of the kindest of men, but he had stern ideas as to
proper subordination, and these he felt it his duty to maintain.
I was obliged to make a *coup d'état,* and for a time it cost me
dear. Braving the censure of family and friends, in the early
autumn of 1850 I deliberately left the college, and took refuge
with my old instructor P———, who had prepared me for college at Syracuse, and who was now principal of the academy at
Moravia, near the head of Owasco Lake, some fifty miles
distant. To thus defy the wishes of those dearest to me was a
serious matter. My father at first took it deeply to heart. His
letters were very severe. He thought my career wrecked,
avowed that he had lost all interest in it, and declared that he
would rather have received news of my death than of such a

disgrace. But I knew that my dear mother was on my side. Her letters remained as affectionate as ever; and I determined to atone for my disobedience by severe and systematic work. I began to study more earnestly than ever before, reviewed my mathematics and classics vigorously, and began a course of reading which has had great influence on all my life since. Among my books was D'Aubigné's "History of the Reformation." Its deficiencies were not of a sort to harm me, its vigor and enthusiasm gave me a great impulse. I not only read but studied it, and followed it with every other book on the subject that I could find. No reading ever did a man more good. It not only strengthened and deepened my better purposes, but it continued powerfully the impulse given me by the historical novels of Scott, and led directly to my devoting myself to the study and teaching of modern history. Of other books which influenced me about this period, Emerson's "Representative Men" was one; another was Carlyle's "Past and Present," in which the old Abbot of Bury became one of my ideals; still another was Ruskin's "Seven Lamps of Architecture"; and to such a degree that this art has given to my life some of its greatest pleasures. Ruskin was then at his best. He had not yet been swept from his bearings by popular applause, or intoxicated by his own verbosity. In later years he lost all influence over me, for, in spite of his wonderful style, he became trivial, whimsical, peevish, goody-goody;—talking to grown men and women as a dyspeptic Sunday-school teacher might lay down the law to classes of little girls. As regards this later period, Max Nordau is undoubtedly right in speaking of Ruskin's mind as "turbid and fallacious"; but the time of which I speak was his best, and his influence upon me was good. I remember especially that his "Lamp of Power" made a very deep impression upon me. Carlyle, too, was at his best. He was the simple, strong preacher;—with nothing of the spoiled cynic he afterward became.

The stay of three months with my friend—the future bishop —in the little country town, was also good for me physically.

In our hours of recreation we roamed through the neighboring woods, shooting squirrels and pigeons, with excellent effect on my health. Meantime I kept up my correspondence with all the members of the family, save my father;—from him there was no sign. But at last came a piece of good news. He was very fond of music, and on the arrival of Jenny Lind in the United States he went to New York to attend her concerts. During one of these my mother turned suddenly toward him and said: "What a pity that the boy cannot hear this; how he would enjoy it!" My father answered, "Tell him to come home and see us." My mother, of course, was not slow in writing me, and a few days later my father cordially greeted my home-coming, and all difficulties seemed over. Shortly after Christmas he started with me for Yale; but there soon appeared a lion in the path. Our route lay through Hartford, the seat of Trinity College, and to my consternation I found at the last moment that he had letters from our rector and others to the president and professors of that institution. Still more alarming, we had hardly entered the train when my father discovered a Trinity student on board. Of course, the youth spoke in the highest terms of his college and of his faculty, and more and more my father was pleased with the idea of staying a day or two at Hartford, taking a look at Trinity, and presenting our letters of introduction. During a considerably extended career in the diplomatic service I have had various occasions to exercise tact, care, and discretion, but I do not think that my efforts on all these together equaled those which I then put forth to avoid stopping at Hartford. At last my father asked me, rather severely, why I cared so much about going to New Haven, and I framed an answer offhand to meet the case, saying that Yale had an infinitely finer library than Trinity. Thereupon he said, "My boy, if you will go to Trinity College I will give you the best private library in the United States." I said, "No, I am going to New Haven; I started for New Haven, and I will go there." I had never braved him

before. He said not a word. We passed quietly through
Hartford, and a day or two later I was entered at Yale.

It was a happy change. I respected the institution, for its
discipline, though at times harsh, was, on the whole, just, and
thereby came a great gain to my own self-respect. But as to
the education given, never was a man more disappointed at
first. The president and professors were men of high character
and attainments; but to the lower classes the instruction was
given almost entirely by tutors, who took up teaching for
bread-winning while going through the divinity school. Naturally most of the work done under these was perfunctory.
There was too much reciting by rote and too little real intercourse between teacher and taught. The instructor sat in a
box, heard students' translations without indicating anything
better, and their answers to questions with very few suggestions or remarks. The first text-book in Greek was Xenophon's
"Memorabilia," and one of the first men called up was my
classmate Delano Goddard. He made an excellent translation,
—clean, clear, in thoroughly good English; but he elicited no
attention from the instructor, and was then put through sundry
grammatical puzzles, among which he floundered until stopped
by the word, "Sufficient." Soon afterward another was called
up who rattled off glibly a translation without one particle of
literary merit, and was then plied with the usual grammatical
questions. Being asked to "synopsize" the Greek verb, he went
through the various moods and tenses, in all sorts of ways and
in all possible combinations, his tongue rattling like the clapper
of a mill. When he sat down my next neighbor said to me,
"That man will be our valedictorian." This disgusted me. If
that was the style of classical scholarship at Yale, I knew that
there was nothing in it for me. It turned out as my friend
said. That glib reciter did become the valedictorian of the
class, but stepped from the commencement stage into nothing-
ness, and was never heard of more. Goddard became the
editor of one of the most important metropolitan newspapers

of the United States, and, before his early death, distinguished himself as a writer on political and historical topics.

Nor was it any better in Latin. We were reading, during that term the "De Senectute" of Cicero,—a beautiful book; but to our tutor it was neither more nor less than a series of pegs on which to hang Zumpt's rules for the subjunctive mood. The translation was hurried through, as of little account. Then came questions regarding the subjunctives;—questions to which very few members of the class gave any real attention. The best Latin scholar in the class, G. W. S——, since so distinguished as the London correspondent of the "New York Tribune," and, at present, as the New York correspondent of the London "Times," having one day announced to some of us,—with a very round expletive,—that he would answer no more such foolish questions, the tutor soon discovered his recalcitrancy, and thenceforward plied him with such questions and nothing else. S——always answered that he was not prepared on them; with the result that at the Junior Exhibition he received no place on the programme.

In the junior year matters improved somewhat; but, though the professors were most of them really distinguished men, and one at least, James Hadley, a scholar who, at Berlin or Leipsic, would have drawn throngs of students from all Christendom, they were fettered by a system which made everything of gerund-grinding and nothing of literature.

The worst feature of the junior year was the fact that through two terms, during five hours each week, "recitations" were heard by a tutor in "Olmsted's Natural Philosophy." The text-book was simply repeated by rote. Not one student in fifty took the least interest in it; and the man who could give the words of the text most glibly secured the best marks. One exceedingly unfortunate result of this kind of instruction was that it so disgusted the class with the whole subject, that the really excellent lectures of Professor Olmsted, illustrated by probably the best apparatus then possessed by any American university, were voted a bore. Almost as bad was the historical

instruction given by Professor James Hadley. It consisted
simply in hearing the student repeat from memory the dates
from "Pütz's Ancient History." How a man so gifted as Hadley
could have allowed any part of his work to be so worthless, it
is hard to understand. And, worse remained behind. He had
charge of the class in Thucydides; but with every gift for
making it a means of great good to us, he taught it in the
perfunctory way of that period;—calling on each student to
construe a few lines, asking a few grammatical questions, and
then, with hardly ever a note or comment, allowing him to sit
down. Two or three times during a term something would
occur to draw Hadley out, and then it delighted us all to hear
him. I recall, to this hour, with the utmost pleasure, some of
his remarks which threw bright light into the general subject;
but alas! they were few and far between.

The same thing must be said of Professor Thatcher's instruction in Tacitus. It was always the same mechanical sort
of thing, with, occasionally, a few remarks which really aroused
interest.

In the senior year the influence of President Woolsey and
Professor Porter was strong for good. Though the "Yale system" fettered them somewhat, their personality often broke
through it. Yet it amazes me to remember that during a considerable portion of our senior year no less a man than Woolsey
gave instruction in history by hearing men recite the words of
a text-book;—and that text-book the Rev. John Lord's little,
popular treatise on the "Modern History of Europe!" Far
better was Woolsey's instruction in Guizot. That was stimulating. It not only gave some knowledge of history, but
suggested thought upon it. In this he was at his best. He had
not at that time begun his new career as a professor of International Law, and that subject was treated by a kindly old
governor of the State, in a brief course of instruction, which
was, on the whole, rather inadequate. Professor Porter's instruction in philosophy opened our eyes and led us to do some
thinking for ourselves. In political economy, during the senior

year, President Woolsey heard the senior class "recite" from Wayland's small treatise, which was simply an abridged presentation of the Manchester view, the most valuable part of this instruction being the remarks by Woolsey himself, who discussed controverted questions briefly but well. He also delivered, during one term, a course of lectures upon the historical relations between the German States, which had some interest, but, not being connected with our previous instruction, took little hold upon us. As to natural science, we had in chemistry and geology, doubtless, the best courses then offered in the United States. The first was given by Benjamin Silliman, the elder, an American pioneer in science, and a really great character; the second, by James Dwight Dana, and in his lecture-room one felt himself in the hands of a master. I cannot forgive myself for having yielded to the general indifference of the class toward all this instruction. It was listlessly heard, and grievously neglected. The fault was mainly our own;—but it was partly due to "The System," which led students to neglect all studies which did not tell upon "marks" and "standing."

Strange to say, there was not, during my whole course at Yale, a lecture upon any period, subject, or person in literature, ancient or modern:—our only resource, in this field, being the popular lecture courses in the town each winter, which generally contained one or two presentations of literary subjects. Of these, that which made the greatest impression upon me was by Ralph Waldo Emerson. Sundry lectures in my junior year, by Whipple, and at a later period by George William Curtis, also influenced me. It was one of the golden periods of English literature, the climax of the Victorian epoch;—the period of Wordsworth, Tennyson, and the Brownings, of Thackeray and Dickens, of Macaulay and Carlyle on one side of the Atlantic, and of Emerson, Irving, Hawthorne, Bancroft, Prescott, Motley, Lowell, Longfellow, Horace Bushnell, and their compeers on the other. Hence came strong influences; but in dealing with them we were left to ourselves.

Very important in shaping my intellectual development at this time were my fellow-students. The class of 1853 was a very large one for that day, and embraced far more than the usual proportion of active-minded men. Walks and talks with these were of great value to me; thence came some of my best impulses and suggestions to reading and thought.

Especially fortunate was I in my "chum," the friend that stood closest to me. He was the most conservative young man I ever knew, and at the very opposite pole from me on every conceivable subject. But his deeply religious character, his thorough scholarship, and his real devotion to my welfare, were very precious to me. Our very differences were useful, since they obliged me to revise with especial care all my main convictions and trains of thought. He is now, at this present writing, the Bishop of Michigan, and a most noble and affectionate pastor of his flock.

The main subjects of interest to us all had a political bearing. Literature was considered as mainly subsidiary to political discussion. The great themes, in the minds of those who tried to do any thinking, were connected with the tremendous political struggle then drawing toward its climax in civil war. Valuable to me was my membership of sundry student fraternities. They were *vealy*, but there was some nourishment in them; by far the best of all being a senior club which, though it had adopted a hideous emblem, was devoted to offhand discussions of social and political questions;—on the whole, the best club I have ever known.

The studies which interested me most were political and historical; from classical studies the gerund-grinding and reciting by rote had completely weaned me. One of our Latin tutors, having said to me: "If you would try you could become a first-rate classical scholar," I answered: "Mr. B——, I have no ambition to become a classical scholar, as scholarship is understood here."

I devoted myself all the more assiduously to study on my own lines, especially in connection with the subjects taught by President Woolsey in the senior year, and the one thing which encouraged me was that, at the public reading of essays, mine seemed to interest the class. Yet my first trial of strength with my classmates in this respect did not apparently turn out very well. It was at a prize debate, in one of the large open societies, but while I had prepared my speech with care, I had given no thought to its presentation, and, as a result, the judges passed me by. Next day a tutor told me that Professor Porter wished to see me. He had been one of the judges, but it never occurred to me that he could have summoned me for anything save some transgression of college rules. But, on my arrival at his room, he began discussing my speech, said some very kind things of its matter, alluded to some defects in its manner, and all with a kindness which won my heart. Thus began a warm personal friendship which lasted through his professorship and presidency to the end of his life. His kindly criticism was worth everything to me; it did far more for me than any prize could have done. Few professors realize how much a little friendly recognition may do for a student. To this hour I bless Dr. Porter's memory.

Nor did my second effort, a competition in essay-writing, turn out much better. My essay was too labored, too long, too crabbedly written, and it brought me only half a third prize.

This was in the sophomore year. But in the junior year came a far more important competition; that for the Yale Literary Gold Medal, and without any notice of my intention to any person, I determined to try for it. Being open to the entire university, the universal expectation was that it would be awarded to a senior, as had hitherto been the case, and speculations were rife as to what member of the graduating class would take it. When the committee made their award to the essay on "The Greater Distinctions in Statesmanship," opened the sealed envelopes and assigned the prize to me, a junior, there was great surprise. The encouragement came to me just at the right time, and did me great good. Later, there were awarded to me the first Clarke Prize for the discussion of a political subject, and the De Forest Gold Medal, then the most important premium awarded in the university, my subject being, "The Diplomatic History of Modern Times." Some details regarding this latter success may serve to show certain ways in which influence can be exerted powerfully upon a young man. The subject had been suggested to me by hearing Edwin Forrest in Bulwer's drama of "Richelieu." The character of the great cardinal, the greatest statesman that France has produced, made a deep impression upon me, and suggested the subjects in both the Yale Literary and the De Forest competitions, giving me not only the initial impulse, but maintaining that interest to which my success was largely due. Another spur to success was even more effective. Having one day received a telegram from my father, asking me to meet him in New York, I did so, and passed an hour with him, all the time at a loss to know why he had sent for me. But, finally, just as I was leaving the hotel to return to New Haven, he said, "By the way, there is still another prize to be competed for, the largest of all." "Yes," I answered, "the De Forest; but I have little chance for that; for though I shall probably be one of the six Townsend prize men admitted to the competition, there are other speakers so much better, that I have little hope of taking it." He gave me rather a contemptuous look, and said, somewhat scornfully: "If I were one of the first *six* competitors, in a class of over a hundred men, I would try hard to be the first *one*." That was all. He said nothing more, except goodbye. On my way to New Haven I thought much of this, and on arriving, went to a student, who had some reputation as an elocutionist, and engaged him for a course in vocal gymnastics. When he wished me to recite my oration before him, I declined, saying that it must be spoken in my own way, not in his; that his way might be better, but that mine was my own, and I would have no other. He confined himself, therefore, to a course of vocal gymnastics, and the result was a surprise to myself and all my friends. My voice, from being weak and hollow, became round, strong, and flexible. I then went to a student in the class above my own, a natural and forcible speaker, and made an arrangement with him to hear me pronounce my oration, from time to time, and to criticize it in a common-sense way. This he did. At passages where he thought my manner wrong, he raised his finger, gave me an imitation of my manner, then gave the passage in the way he thought best, and allowed me to choose between his and mine. The result was that, at the public competition, I was successful. This experience taught me what I conceive to be the true theory of elocutionary training in our universities—vocal gymnastics, on one side; common-sense criticism, on the other.

As to my physical education: with a constitution far from robust, there was need of special care. Fortunately, I took to boating. In an eight-oared boat, spinning down the harbor or up the river, with G. W. S—— at the stroke—as earnest and determined in the *Undine* then as in the New York office of the London "Times" now, every condition was satisfied for bodily exercise and mental recreation. I cannot refrain from mentioning that our club sent the first challenge to row that ever passed between Yale and Harvard, even though I am obliged to confess that we were soundly beaten; but neither that defeat at Lake Winnipesaukee, nor the many absurdities which have grown out of such competitions since, have prevented my remaining an apostle of college boating from that day to this. If guarded by common-sense rules enforced with firmness by college faculties, it gives the maximum of healthful exercise, with a minimum of danger. The most detestable product of college life is the sickly cynic; and a thorough course in boating, under a good stroke oar, does as much as anything to make him impossible.

At the close of my undergraduate life at Yale I went abroad for nearly three years, and fortunately had, for a time, one of the best of companions, my college mate, Gilman, later president of Johns Hopkins University, and now of the Carnegie Institution, who was then, as he has been ever since, a source of good inspirations to me,—especially in the formation of my ideas regarding education. During the few weeks I then passed in England I saw much which broadened my views in various ways. History was made alive to me by rapid studies of persons and places while traveling, and especially was this the case during a short visit to Oxford, where I received some strong impressions, which will be referred to in another chapter. Dining at Christ Church with Osborne Gordon, an eminent tutor of that period, I was especially interested in his accounts of John Ruskin, who had been his pupil. Then, and afterward, while enjoying the hospitalities of various colleges at Oxford and Cambridge, I saw the excellencies of their tutorial system, but also had my eyes opened to some of their deficiencies.

Going thence to Paris I settled down in the family of a very intelligent French professor, where I remained nearly a year. Not a word of English was spoken in the family; and, with the daily lesson in a French method, and lectures at the Sorbonne and Collège de France, the new language soon became familiar. The lectures then heard strengthened my conception of what a university should be. Among my professors were such men as St. Marc Girardin, Arnould, and, at a later period, Laboulaye. In connection with the lecture-room work, my studies in modern history were continued, especially by reading Guizot, Thierry, Mignet, Thiers, Châteaubriand, and others, besides hearing various masterpieces in French dramatic literature, as given at the Théâtre Français, where Rachel was then in her glory, and at the Odéon, where Mlle. Georges, who had begun her career under the first Napoleon, was ending it under Napoleon III.

My favorite subject of study was the French Revolution, and, in the intervals of reading and lectures, I sought out not only the spots noted in its history, but the men who had taken part in it. At the Hôtel des Invalides I talked with old soldiers, veterans of the Republic and of the Napoleonic period, discussing with them the events through which they had passed; and, at various other places and times, with civilians who had heard

orations at the Jacobin and Cordelier clubs, and had seen the
guillotine at work. The most interesting of my old soldiers at
the Invalides wore upon his breast the cross of the Legion of
Honor, which he had received from Napoleon at Austerlitz.
Still another had made the frightful marches through the
Spanish Peninsula under Soult, and evidently felt very humble
in the presence of those who had taken part in the more famous
campaigns under Napoleon himself. The history of another of
my old soldiers was pathetic. He was led daily into the *cab-
aret*, where my guests were wont to fight their battles o'er
again, his eyes absolutely sightless, and his hair as white as
snow. Getting into conversation with him I learned that he
had gone to Egypt with Bonaparte, had fought at the Battle of
the Pyramids, had been blinded by the glaring sun on the sand
of the desert, and had been an inmate at the Invalides ever
since;—more than half a century. At a later period I heard
from another of my acquaintances how, as a schoolboy, he saw
Napoleon beside his camp-fire at Cannes, just after his landing
from Elba.

There still remained at Paris, in those days, one main connecting link between the second empire and the first, and this
was the most contemptible of all the Bonapartes,—the younger
brother of the great Napoleon,—Jérome, ex-king of Westphalia.
I saw him, from time to time, and was much struck by his re-
semblance to the first emperor. Though taller, he still had
something of that Roman imperial look, so remarkable in the
founder of the family; but in Jérome, it always recalled to me
such Cæsars as Tiberius and Vitellius.

It was well known that the ex-king, as well as his son, Prince
Jérome Napoleon, were thorns in the side of Napoleon III, and
many stories illustrating this were current during my stay in
Paris, the best, perhaps, being an answer made by Napoleon
III to another representative of his family. The question
having been asked, "What is the difference between an accident and a misfortune (*un accident et un malheur*)?" the
emperor answered, "If my cousin, Prince Napoleon, should

fall into the Seine, it would be an *accident;* if anybody were
to pull him out, it would be a *misfortune."* Although this
cousin had some oratorical ability, both he and his father
were most thoroughly despised. The son bore the nickname
of "Plon-Plon," probably with some reference to his reputation for cowardice; the father had won the appellation of
"Le Roi Loustic," and, indeed, had the credit of introducing
into the French language the word "loustic," derived from
the fact that, during his short reign at Cassel, King Jérome
was wont, after the nightly orgies at his palace, to dismiss his
courtiers with the words: "Morgen wieder loustic, Messieurs."

During the summer of 1854 I employed my vacation in
long walks and drives with a college classmate through northern, western, and central France, including Picardy, Nor-
mandy, Brittany, and Touraine, visiting the spots of most
historical and architectural interest. There were, at that
time, few railways in those regions, so we put on blouses and
took to the road, sending our light baggage ahead of us, and
carrying only knapsacks. In every way it proved a most valuable experience. Pleasantly come back to me my walks and
talks with the peasantry, and vividly dwell in my memory the
cathedrals of Beauvais, Amiens, Rouen, Bayeux, Coutances,
Le Mans, Tours, Chartres, and Orléans, the fortress of Mont
St. Michel, the Châteaux of Chenonceaux, Chambord, Nantes,
Amboise, and Angers, the tombs of the Angevine kings at
Fontevrault, and the stone cottage of Louis XI at Cléry. Visiting the grave of Châteaubriand at St. Malo, we met a little
old gentleman, bent with age, but very brisk and chatty. He
was standing with a party of friends on one side of the tomb,
while we stood on the other. Presently, one of the gentlemen
in his company came over and asked our names, saying that
his aged companion was a great admirer of Châteaubriand,
and was anxious to know something of his fellow pilgrims.
To this I made answer, when my interlocutor informed me
that the old gentleman was the Prince de Rohan-Soubise.
Shortly afterward the old gentleman came round to us and

began conversation, and on my making answer in a way which showed that I knew his title, he turned rather sharply on me and said, "How do you know that?" To this I made answer that even in America we had heard the verse:

> "Roi, je ne puis,
> Prince ne daigne,
> Rohan je suis."

At this he seemed greatly pleased, grasped my hand, and launched at once into extended conversation. His great anxiety was to know who was to be the future king of our Republic, and he asked especially whether Washington had left any direct descendants. On my answering in the negative, he insisted that we would have to find some descendant in the collateral line, "for," said he, "you can't escape it; no nation can get along for any considerable time without a monarch."

Returning to Paris I resumed my studies, and, at the request of Mr. Randall, the biographer of Jefferson, made some search in the French archives for correspondence between Jefferson and Robespierre,—search made rather to put an end to calumny than for any other purpose.

At the close of this stay in France, by the kindness of the American minister to Russia, Governor Seymour, of Connecticut, I was invited to St. Petersburg, as an *attaché* of the American Legation, and resided for over six months in his household. It was a most interesting period. The Crimean War was going on, and the death of the Emperor Nicholas, during my stay, enabled me to see how a great change in autocratic administration is accomplished. An important part of my duty was to accompany the minister as an interpreter, not only at court, but in his interviews with Nesselrode, Gortschakoff, and others then in power. This gave me some chance also to make my historical studies more real by close observation of a certain sort of men who have had the making of far too much history; but books interested me none the less.

An epoch in my development, intellectual and moral, was made at this time by my reading large parts of Gibbon, and especially by a very careful study of Guizot's "History of Civilization in France," which greatly deepened and strengthened the impression made by his "History of Civilization in Europe," as read under President Woolsey at Yale. During those seven months in St. Petersburg and Moscow, I read much in modern European history, paying considerable attention to the political development and condition of Russia, and, for the first time, learned the pleasures of investigating the history of our own country. Governor Seymour was especially devoted to the ideas of Thomas Jefferson, and late at night, as we sat before the fire, after returning from festivities or official interviews, we frequently discussed the democratic system, as advocated by Jefferson, and the autocratic system, as we saw it in the capital of the Czar. The result was that my beginning of real study in American history was made by a very close examination of the life and writings of Thomas Jefferson, including his letters, messages, and other papers, and of the diplomatic history revealed in the volumes of correspondence preserved in the Legation. The general result was to strengthen and deepen my democratic creed, and a special result was the preparation of an article on "Jefferson and Slavery," which, having been at a later period refused by the "New Englander," at New Haven, on account of its too pronounced sympathy with democracy against federalism, was published by the "Atlantic Monthly," and led to some acquaintances of value to me afterward.

Returning from St. Petersburg, I was matriculated at the University of Berlin, and entered the family of a very scholarly gymnasial professor, where nothing but German was spoken. During this stay at the Prussian capital, in the years 1855 and 1856, I heard the lectures of Lepsius, on Egyptology; August Boeckh, on the History of Greece; Friedrich von Raumer, on the History of Italy; Hirsch, on Modern History in general; and Carl Ritter, on Physical Geography. The lectures of

Ranke, the most eminent of German historians, I could not follow. He had a habit of becoming so absorbed in his subject, as to slide down in his chair, hold his finger up toward the ceiling, and then, with his eye fastened on the tip of it, to go mumbling through a kind of rhapsody, which most of my German fellow-students confessed they could not understand. It was a comical sight: half a dozen students crowding around his desk, listening as priests might listen to the sibyl on her tripod, the other students being scattered through the room, in various stages of discouragement. My studies at this period were mainly in the direction of history, though with considerable reading on art and literature. Valuable and interesting to me at this time were the representations of the best dramas of Goethe, Schiller, Lessing, and Gutzkow, at the Berlin theaters. Then, too, really began my education in Shakspere, and the representations of his plays (in Schlegel and Tieck's version) were, on the whole, the most satisfactory I have ever known. I thus heard plays of Shakspere which, in English-speaking countries, are never presented, and, even into those better known, wonderful light was at times thrown from this new point of view.

As to music, the Berlin Opera was then at the height of its reputation, the leading singer being the famous Joanna Wagner. But my greatest satisfaction was derived from the "Liebig Classical Concerts." These were, undoubtedly, the best instrumental music then given in Europe, and a small party of us were very assiduous in our attendance. Three afternoons a week we were, as a rule, gathered about our table in the garden where the concerts were given, and, in the midst of us, Alexander Thayer, the biographer of Beethoven, who discussed the music with us during its intervals. Beethoven was, for him, the one personage in human history, and Beethoven's music the only worthy object of human concern. He knew every composition, every note, every variant, and had wrestled for years with their profound meanings. Many of his explanations were fantastic, but some were suggestive and all were interesting. Even more inspiring was another new-found friend, Henry Simmons Frieze; a thorough musician, and a most lovely character. He broached no theories, uttered no comments, but sat rapt by the melody and harmony—transfigured—"his face as it had been the face of an angel." In these Liebig concerts we then heard, for the first time, the music of a new composer,—one *Wagner*,—and agreed that while it was all very strange, there was really something in the overture to "Tannhäuser."

At the close of this stay in Berlin, I went with a party of fellow-students through Austria to Italy. The whole journey was a delight, and the passage by steamer from Trieste to Venice was made noteworthy by a new acquaintance,—James Russell Lowell. As he had already written the "Vision of Sir Launfal," the "Fable for Critics," and the "Biglow Papers," I stood in great awe of him; but this feeling rapidly disappeared in his genial presence. He was a student like the rest of us,—for he had been passing the winter at Dresden, working in German literature, as a preparation for succeeding Longfellow in the professorship at Harvard. He came to our rooms, and there linger delightfully in my memory his humorous accounts of Italian life as he had known it.

During the whole of the journey, it was my exceeding good fortune to be thrown into very close relations with two of our party, both of whom became eminent Latin professors, and one of whom,—already referred to,—Frieze, from his lecture-room in the University of Michigan, afterward did more than any other man within my knowledge to make classical scholarship a means of culture throughout our Western States. My excursions in Rome, under that guidance, I have always looked upon as among the fortunate things of life. The day was given to exploration, the evening to discussion, not merely of archæological theories, but of the weightier matters pertaining to the history of Roman civilization and its influence. Dear Frieze and Fishburne! How vividly come back the days in the tower of the Croce di Malta, at Genoa, in our sky-parlor of the Piazza di Spagna at Rome, and in the old "Capuchin Hotel" at Amalfi, when we held high debate on the analogies between the Roman Empire and the British, and upon various kindred subjects.

An episode, of much importance to me at this time, was my meeting our American minister at Naples, Robert Dale Owen. His talks on the political state of Italy, and his pictures of the monstrous despotism of "King Bomba" took strong hold upon me. Not even the pages of Colletta or of Settembrini have done so much to arouse in me a sense of the moral value of political history.

Then, too, I made the first of my many excursions through the historic towns of Italy. My reading of Sismondi's "Italian Republics" had deeply interested me in their history, and had peopled them again with their old turbulent population. I seemed to see going on before my eyes the old struggle between Guelphs and Ghibellines, and between the demagogues and the city tyrants. In the midst of such scenes my passion for historical reading was strengthened, and the whole subject took on new and deeper meanings.

On my way northward, excursions among the cities of southern France, especially Nismes, Arles, and Orange, gave me a far better conception of Roman imperial power than could be obtained in Italy alone, and Avignon, Bourges, and Toulouse deepened my conceptions of mediæval history.

Having returned to America in the summer of 1856 and met my class, assembled to take the master's degree in course at Yale, I was urged by my old Yale friends, especially by Porter and Gilman, to remain in New Haven. They virtually pledged me a position in the school of art about to be established; but my belief was in the value of historical studies, and I accepted an election to a professorship of history at the University of Michigan. The work there was a joy to me from first to last, and my relations with my students of that period, before I had become distracted from them by the cares of an executive position, were among the most delightful of my life.

Then, perhaps, began the most real part of my education. The historical works of Buckle, Lecky, and Draper, which were then appearing, gave me a new and fruitful impulse; but most stimulating of all was the atmosphere coming from the great thought of Darwin and Herbert Spencer,—an atmosphere in which history became less and less a matter of annals, and more and more a record of the unfolding of humanity. Then, too, was borne in upon me the meaning of the proverb *docendo disces*. I found energetic Western men in my classes ready to discuss historical questions, and discovered that in order to keep up my part of the discussions, as well as to fit myself for my class-room duties, I must work as I had never worked before. The education I then received from my classes at the University of Michigan was perhaps the most effective of all.

LIFE AT THE UNIVERSITY OF MICHIGAN

1857–1864

A S I LOOKED OUT UPON THE WORLD DURING MY CHILD-hood, there loomed up within my little horizon certain personages as ideals. Foremost of these was the surpliced clergyman of the parish. So strong was my admiration for him that my dear mother, during her entire life, never relinquished the hope, and indeed the expectation, that I would adopt the clerical profession.

Another object of my admiration—to whose profession I aspired—was the village carpenter. He "did things," and from that day to this I have most admired the men who "do things."

Yet another of these personages was the principal of Cortland Academy. As I saw him addressing his students, or sitting in the midst of them observing with a telescope the satellites of Jupiter, I was overawed. A sense of my littleness overcame me, and I hardly dared think of aspiring to duties so exalted.

But at the age of seven a new ideal appeared. The family had removed from the little town where I was born to Syracuse, then a rising village of about five thousand inhabitants. The railways, east and west, had just been created,—the beginnings of what is now the New York Central Railroad,—and every day, so far as possible, I went down-town "to see the cars go out." During a large part of the year there was but one passenger-train in each direction, and this was made up of but three or four small compartment-cars drawn by a locomotive which would now be considered ridiculously small, at the rate of twelve to fifteen miles an hour.

Yet I doubt whether the express trains on the New York Central, drawn by hundred-ton locomotives at a speed of sixty miles an hour, produce on the youth of the present generation anything like the impression made by those simple beginnings. The new personage who now attracted my homage was the locomotive-driver. To me his profession transcended all others. As he mounted the locomotive, and especially as he pulled the starting-bar, all other functions seemed insignificant. Every day I contemplated him; often I dreamed of him; saw him in my mind's eye dashing through the dark night, through the rain and hail, through drifting snow, through perils of "washouts" and "snake-heads," and no child in the middle ages ever thought with more awe of a crusading knight leading his troops to the Holy City than did I think of this hero standing at his post in all weathers, conducting his train to its destination beyond the distant hills. It was indeed the day of small things. The traveler passing from New York to Buffalo in those days changed from the steamer at Albany to the train for Schenectady, there changed to the train for Utica, thence took the train for Syracuse, there stayed overnight, then took a train for Auburn, where he found the train for Rochester, and after two more changes arrived in Buffalo after a journey of two days and a night, which is now made in from eight to ten hours.

But the locomotive-driver was none the less a personage, and I must confess that my old feeling of respect for him clings to me still. To this hour I never see him controlling his fiery steed without investing him with some of the attributes which I discerned in him during my childhood. It is evident to me that the next heroes whom poets will exploit will be the drivers of our railway trains and the pilots of our ocean steamers. One poet has, indeed, made a beginning already,—and this poet the Secretary of State of the United States under whom I am now serving, the Hon. John Hay. Still another poet, honored throughout the world, has also found a hero in the engine-driver, and Rudyard Kipling will no doubt be followed by others.

But my dream of becoming a locomotive-driver faded, and while in college I speculated not a little as to what, after all, should be my profession. The idea of becoming a clergyman had long since left my mind. The medical profession had never attracted me. For the legal profession I sought to prepare myself somewhat, but as I saw it practised by the vast majority of lawyers, it seemed a waste of all that was best in human life. Politics were from an early period repulsive to me, and, after my first sight of Washington in its shabby, sleazy, dirty, unkempt condition under the old slave oligarchy, political life became absolutely repugnant to my tastes and desires. At times a longing came over me to settle down in the country, to make an honest living from a farm—a longing which took its origin in a visit which I had made as a child to the farm of an uncle who lived upon the shores of Seneca Lake. He was a man of culture, who, by the aid of a practical farmer and an income from other sources, got along very well. His roomy, old-fashioned house, his pleasant library, his grounds sloping to the lake, his peach-orchard, which at my visit was filled with delicious fruit, and the pleasant paths through the neighboring woods captivated me, and for several years the agricultural profession lingered in my visions as the most attractive of all.

As I now look back to my early manhood, it seems that my natural inclination should have been toward journalism; but although such a career proves attractive to many of our best university-bred men now, it was not so then. In those days men did not prepare for it; they drifted into it. I do not think that at my graduation there was one out of the one hundred and eight members of my class who had the slightest expectation of permanently connecting himself with a newspaper. This seems all the more singular since that class has since produced a large number of prominent journalists, and among these George Washburne Smalley, the most eminent, by far, among American newspaper correspondents of our time; Evarts Greene, a leading editor of Worcester; Delano Goddard, late editor of the "Boston Advertiser"; Kinsley Twining, for a considerable time an editor òf the "Independent"; Isaac Bromley, who for years delighted the Republican party with his contributions to the editorial page of the "Tribune"; Dr. James Morris Whiton, a leading writer for the "Outlook"; and others. Yet in those days probably not one of these ever thought of turning to journalism as a career. There were indeed at that time eminent editors, like Weed, Croswell, Greeley, Raymond, and Webb, but few college-bred men thought of journalism as a profession. Looking back upon all this, I feel certain that, were I to begin life again with my present experience, that would be the career for which I would endeavor to fit myself. It has in it at present many admirable men, but far more who are manifestly unfit. Its capacities for good or evil are enormous, yet the majority of those at present in it seem to me like savages who have found a watch. I can think of no profession in which young men properly fitted— gifted with ideas and inspired by a real wish to do something for their land and time—can more certainly do good work and win distinction. To supplant the present race of journalistic prostitutes, who are making many of our newspapers as foul in morals, as low in tone, and as vile in utterance as even the worst of the French press, might well be the ambition of leading thinkers in any of our universities. There is nothing so greatly needed in our country as an uplifting of the daily press, and there is no work promising better returns.

But during my student life in Paris and Berlin another vista began to open before me. I had never lost that respect for the teaching profession which had been aroused in my childhood by the sight of Principal Woolworth enthroned among the students of Cortland Academy, and this early impression was now greatly deepened by my experience at the Sorbonne, the College of France, and the University of Berlin. My favorite studies at Yale had been history and kindred subjects, but these had been taught mainly from text-books. Lectures were few and dry. Even those of President Woolsey were not inspiring; he seemed paralyzed by the system of which he formed a part. But men like Arnould, St. Marc Girardin, and Laboulaye in France, and Lepsius, Ritter, von Raumer, and Curtius in Germany, lecturing to large bodies of attentive students on the most interesting and instructive periods of human history, aroused in me a new current of ideas. Gradually I began to ask myself the question: Why not help the beginnings of this system in the United States? I had long felt deeply the shortcomings of our American universities, and had tried hard to devise something better; yet my ideas as to what could really be done to improve them had been crude and vague. But now, in these great foreign universities, one means of making a reform became evident, and this was, first of all, the substitution of lectures for recitations, and the creation of an interest in history by treating it as a living subject having relations to present questions. Upon this I reflected much, and day by day the idea grew upon me. So far as I can remember, there was not at that time a professor of history pure and simple in any American university. There had been courses of historical lectures at a few institutions, but they were, as a rule, spasmodic and perfunctory. How history was taught at Yale is shown in another chapter of these reminiscences. The lectures of President Sparks had evidently trained up no school of historical professors at Harvard. There had been a noted professor at William and Mary College, Virginia, —doubtless, in his time, the best historical lecturer in the United States,—Dr. William Dew, the notes of whose lectures, as afterward published, were admirable; but he had left no successor. Francis Lieber, at the University of South Carolina, had taught political philosophy with much depth of thought and wealth of historical illustration; but neither there nor elsewhere did there exist anything like systematic courses in history such as have now been developed in so many of our universities and colleges.

During my stay as resident graduate at Yale after my return from Europe in 1856, I often discussed the subject with my old friend and companion Gilman, now president of the Carnegie Institution, and with my beloved instructor, Professor Porter. Both were kind enough to urge me to remain at New Haven, assuring me that in time a professorship would be established. To promote this I wrote an article on "German Instruction in General History," which was well received when published in the "New Englander," and prepared sundry lectures, which were received by the university people and by the New York press more favorably than I now think they deserved. But there seemed, after all, no chance for a professorship devoted to this line of study. More and more, too, I felt that even if I were called to a historical professorship at Yale, the old-fashioned orthodoxy which then prevailed must fetter me: I could not utter the shibboleths then demanded, and the future seemed dark indeed. Yet my belief in the value of better historical instruction in our universities grew more and more, and a most happy impulse was now given to my thinking by a book which I read and reread—Stanley's "Life of Arnold." It showed me much, but especially two things: first, how effective history might be made in bringing young men into fruitful trains of thought regarding present politics; and, secondly, how real an influence an earnest teacher might thus exercise upon his country.

While in this state of mind I met my class assembled at the Yale commencement of 1856 to take the master's degree in course, after the manner of those days. This was the turning-point with me. I had been for some time more and more uneasy and unhappy because my way did not seem to clear; but at this commencement of 1856, while lounging among my classmates in the college yard, I heard some one say that President Wayland of Brown University was addressing the graduates in the Hall of the Alumni. Going to the door, I looked in, and saw at the high table an old man, strong-featured, heavy-browed, with spectacles resting on the top of his head, and just at that moment he spoke very impressively as follows: "The best field of work for graduates is now in the *West;* our country is shortly to arrive at a switching-off place for good or evil; our Western States are to hold the balance of power in the Union, and to determine whether the country shall become a blessing or a curse in human history."

I had never seen him before; I never saw him afterward. His speech lasted less than ten minutes, but it settled a great question for me. I went home and wrote to sundry friends that I was a candidate for the professorship of history in any Western college where there was a chance to get at students, and as a result received two calls—one to a Southern university, which I could not accept on account of my anti-slavery opinions; the other to the University of Michigan, which I accepted. My old college friends were kind enough to tender me later the professorship in the new School of Art at Yale, but my belief was firm in the value of historical studies. The words of Wayland rang in my ears, and I went gladly into the new field.

On arriving at the University of Michigan in October, 1857, although I had much to do with other students, I took especial charge of the sophomore class. It included many young men of ability and force, but had the reputation of being the most unmanageable body which had been known there in years. Thus far it had been under the charge of tutors, and it had made life a burden to them. Its preparation for the work I sought to do was wretchedly imperfect. Among my duties was the examination of entrance classes in modern geography as a preliminary to their admission to my course in history, and I soon discovered a serious weakness in the public-school system. In her preparatory schools the State of Michigan took especial pride, but certainly at that time they were far below their reputation. If any subject was supposed to be thoroughly taught in them it was geography, but I soon found that in the great majority of my students there was not a trace of real knowledge of physical geography and very little of political. With this state of things I at once grappled, and immediately "conditioned" in these studies about nine tenths of the entering class. At first there were many protests; but I said to my ingenuous youths that no pedantic study was needed, that all I required was a preparation such as would enable any one of them to read intelligently his morning newspaper, and to this end I advised each one of them to accept his conditions, to abjure all learning by rote from textbooks, to take up simply any convenient atlas which came to hand, studying first the map of our own country, with its main divisions, physical and political, its water communications, trend of coasts, spurring of mountains, positions of leading cities, etc., and then to do the same thing with each of the leading countries of Europe, and finally with the other main divisions of the world. To stimulate their interest and show them what was meant, I gave a short course of lectures on physical geography, showing some of its more striking effects on history; then another course on political geography, with a similar purpose; and finally notified my young men that they were admitted to my classes in history only under condition that, six weeks later, they should pass an examination in geography, full, satisfactory, and final. The young fellows now took their conditions very kindly, for they clearly saw the justice of them. One young man said to me: "Professor, you are entirely right in conditioning me, but I was never so surprised in my life; if there was anything which I supposed I knew well it was geography; why, I have taught it, and very successfully, in a large public school." On my asking him how he taught a subject in which he was so deficient, he answered that he had taught his pupils to "sing" it. I replied that if he would sing the answers to my questions, I would admit him at once; but this he declined, saying that he much preferred to accept the conditions. In about six weeks I held the final examinations, and their success amazed us all. Not a man failed, and some really distinguished themselves. They had all gone at the work cordially and heartily, arranging themselves in squads and clubs for mutual study and examination on each physical and political map; and it is certain that by this simple, common-sense method they learned more in six weeks than they had previously learned in years of plodding along by rote, day after day, through text-books.

Nor was this mere "cram." Their geographical knowledge lasted and was increased, as was proved at my historical examinations afterward.

I soon became intensely interested in my work, and looked forward to it every day with pleasure. The first part of it was instruction in modern history as a basis for my lectures which were to follow, and for this purpose I used with the sophomores two text-books. The first of these was Robertson's "Philosophical View of the Middle Ages," which forms the introduction to his "Life of Charles the Fifth." Although superseded in many of its parts by modern investigation, very defective in several important matters, and in some things— as, for example, in its appreciation of medieval literature— entirely mistaken, it was, when written one hundred years ago, recognized as a classic, and it remains so to this day. It was a work of genius. Supplemented by elucidations and extensions, it served an admirable purpose in introducing my students to the things really worth knowing in modern history, without confusing them with masses of pedantic detail.

The next text-book which I took up was Dr. John Lord's "Modern History," the same which President Woolsey had used with my class during its senior year at Yale. It was imperfect in every respect, with no end of gaps and errors, but it had one real merit—it interested its readers. It was, as every such work ought to be, largely biographic. There was enthusiasm, a sort of "go," in Dr. Lord, and this quality he had communicated to his book, so that, with all its faults, it formed the best basis then obtainable for further instruction. Its omissions and errors I sought to rectify—as Woolsey, I am sorry to say, had never done to any extent—by offhand talks and by pointing out supplementary reading, such as sundry chapters of Gibbon and Hallam, essays by Macaulay, extracts from Lingard, Ranke, Prescott, Motley, and others. Once a fortnight through the winter, the class assembled at my house "socially," the more attractive young women of the little city being invited to meet them; but the social part was always preceded by an hour and a half's reading of short passages from eminent historians or travelers, bearing on our classroom work during the previous fortnight. These passages were read by students whom I selected for the purpose, and they proved useful from the historical, literary, and social point of view.

For the class next above, the juniors, I took for text-book preparation Guizot's "History of Civilization in Europe"—a book tinged with the doctrinairism of its author, but a work of genius; a *great* work, stimulating new trains of thought, and opening new vistas of knowledge. This, with sundry supplementary talks, and with short readings from Gibbon, Thierry, Guizot's "History of Civilization in France," and Sir James Stephen's "Lectures on French History," served an excellent purpose.

Nor was the use of Guizot's book entirely confined to historical purposes. Calling attention to the Abbé Bautain's little book on extemporaneous speaking, as the best treatise on the subject I had ever seen, I reminded my students that these famous lectures of Guizot, which had opened a new epoch in modern historical investigation and instruction, were given, as regards phrasing, extemporaneously, but that, as regards matter, they were carefully prepared beforehand, having what Bautain calls a "self-developing order"; and I stated that I would allow any member of my class who might volunteer for the purpose to give, in his own phrasing, the substance of an entire lecture. For a young man thus to stand up and virtually deliver one of Guizot's lectures required great concentration of thought and considerable facility in expression, but several students availed themselves of the permission, and acquitted themselves admirably. This seemed to me an excellent training for effective public speaking, and several of my old students, who have since distinguished themselves in public life, have confessed to me that they found it so.

My next and highest duty was giving lectures to the senior class and students from the law school. Into this I threw myself heartily, and soon had the satisfaction of seeing my large lecture-room constantly full. The first of these courses was on the "Development of Civilization during the Middle Ages"; and, as I followed the logical rather than the chronological order,—taking up the subject, not by a recital of events, but by a discussion of epochs and subjects,—I thought it best to lecture without manuscript or even notes. This was, for me, a bold venture. I had never before attempted anything in the way of extended extemporaneous speaking; and, as I entered the old chapel of the university for my first lecture, and saw it full of students of all classes, I avowed my trepidation to President Tappan, who, having come to introduce me, was seated by my side. He was an admirable extemporaneous speaker in the best sense, and he then and there gave me a bit of advice which proved of real value. He said: "Let me, as an old hand, tell you one thing: never stop dead; keep saying something." This course of lectures was followed by others on modern history, one of these being on "German History from the Revival of Learning and the Reformation to Modern Times," another on "French History from the Consolidation of the Monarchy to the French Revolution," and still another on the "French Revolution." To this latter course I gave special attention, the foundation having been laid for it in France, where I had visited various interesting places and talked with interesting men who recalled events and people of the Revolutionary and Napoleonic periods. For a text-book foundation I read with my lower classes Mignet's "History of the Revolution," which still remained what Carlyle pronounced it—the best short summary of that great period.

To further the work of my students in the lecture-room, I published an interleaved syllabus of each course, and was, I think, the first person in our country who ever did this in connection with historical lectures. It is a matter of wonder to me that so few professors in these days resort to this simple means of strengthening their instruction. It ought to be required by university statutes. It seems to me indispensable to anything like thorough work. A syllabus, properly interleaved, furnishes to a student by far the best means of taking notes on each lecture, as well as of reviewing the whole course afterward, and to a professor the best means of testing the faithfulness of his students. As regards myself personally, there came to me from my syllabus an especial advantage; for, as I have shown in my political experiences, it gained for me the friendship of Charles Sumner.

I have stated elsewhere that my zeal in teaching history was by no means the result of a mere liking for that field of thought. Great as was my love for historical studies, there was something I prized far more—and that was the opportunity to promote a better training in thought regarding our great national problems then rapidly approaching solution, the greatest of all being the question between the supporters and opponents of slavery.

In order that my work might be fairly well based, I had, during my college days and my first stay abroad, begun collecting the private library which has added certainly to the pleasures, and probably to the usefulness, of my life. Books which are now costly rarities could then be bought in the European capitals for petty sums. There is hardly any old European city which has not been, at some time, one of my happy hunting-grounds in the chase for rare books bearing upon history; even now, when my collection, of which the greater part has been transferred to Cornell University, numbers not far short of forty thousand volumes, the old passion still flames up at times; and during the inditing of this chapter I have secured two series of manuscripts of very great value in illustrating the evolution of modern civilization. My reason for securing such original material was not the desire to possess rarities and curiosities. I found that passages actually read from important originals during my lectures gave a reality and vividness to my instruction which were otherwise unattainable. A citation of the *ipsissima verba* of Erasmus, or Luther, or Melanchthon, or Peter Canisius, or Louis XIV, or Robespierre, or Marat, interested my students far more than any quotation at second hand could do. No rhetoric could impress on a class the real spirit and strength of the middle ages as could one of my illuminated psalters or missals; no declamation upon the boldness of Luther could impress thinking young men as did citations from his "Erfurt Sermon," which, by weakening his safe-conduct, put him virtually at the mercy of his enemies at the Diet of Worms; no statements as to the fatuity of Robespierre could equal citations from an original copy of his "Report on the Moral and Religious Considerations which Ought to Govern the Republic"; all specifications of the folly of Marat paled before the ravings in the original copies of his newspaper, "L'Ami du Peuple"; no statistics regarding the paper-money craze in France could so impress its actuality on students as did the seeing and handling of French revolutionary assignats and mandats, many of them with registration numbers clearly showing the enormous quantities of this currency then issued; no illustration, at second hand, of the methods of the French generals during the Revolutionary period could produce the impression given by a simple exhibition of the broadsides issued by the proconsuls of that period; no description of the collapse of the triumvirate and the Reign of Terror could equal a half-hour's reading from the "Moniteur"; and all accounts of the Empire were dim compared to grandiose statements read from the original bulletins of Napoleon.

In this way alone can history be made real to students. Both at my lectures and in the social gatherings at my house, I laid out for my classes the most important originals bearing upon their current work; and it was no small pleasure to point out the relations of these to the events which had formed the subject of our studies together. I say "our studies together," because no one of my students studied more hours than myself. They stimulated me greatly. Most of them were very near my own age; several were older. As a rule, they were bright, inquiring, zealous, and among them were some of the best minds I have ever known. From among them have since come senators, members of Congress, judges, professors, lawyers, heads of great business enterprises, and foreign ministers. One of them became my successor in the professorship in the University of Michigan and the presidency of Cornell, and, in one field, the leading American historian of his time. Another became my predecessor in the embassy to Germany. Though I had what might be fairly called "a good start" of these men, it was necessary to work hard to maintain my position; but such labor was then pleasure.

Nor was my work confined to historical teaching. After the fashion of that time, I was called upon to hear the essays and discussions of certain divisions of the upper classes. This demanded two evenings a week through two terms in each year, and on these evenings I joyfully went to my lecture-room, not infrequently through drifts of snow, and, having myself kindled the fire and lighted the lamps, awaited the discussion. This subsidiary work, which in these degenerate days is done by janitors, is mentioned here as showing the simplicity of a bygone period. The discussions thus held were of a higher range than any I had known at Yale, and some were decidedly original. One deserves especial mention. A controversy having arisen in Massachusetts and spread throughout the country regarding the erection of a statue of Daniel Webster in front of the State House at Boston, and bitter opposition having been aroused by his seventh-of-March speech, two groups of my student-disputants agreed to take up this subject and model their speeches upon those of Demosthenes and Æschines on the crown, which they were then reading in the original. It was a happy thought, and well carried out.

UNIVERSITY LIFE IN THE WEST

1857–1864

I T MUST BE CONFESSED THAT ALL WAS NOT PLAIN SAILING in my new position. One difficulty arose from my very youthful, not to say boyish, appearance. I was, indeed, the youngest member of the faculty; but at twenty-four years one has the right to be taken for a man, and it was vexatious to be taken for a youth of seventeen. At my first arrival in the university town I noticed, as the train drew up to the station, a number of students, evidently awaiting the coming of such freshmen as might be eligible to the various fraternities; and, on landing, I was at once approached by a sophomore, who asked if I was about to enter the university. For an instant I was grievously abashed, but pulling myself together, answered in a sort of affirmative way; and at this he became exceedingly courteous, taking pains to pilot me to a hotel, giving me much excellent advice, and even insisting on carrying a considerable amount of my baggage. Other members of fraternities joined us, all most courteous and kind, and the dénouement came only at the registration of my name in the hotel book, when they recognized in me "the new professor." I must say to their credit that, although they were for a time laughed at throughout the university, they remained my warm personal friends.

But after I had discharged the duties of my professorship

for a considerable period, this same difficulty existed. On a shooting excursion, an old friend and myself came, during the middle of the afternoon, upon a farm-house, and, being very hungry, asked for bread and milk. My companion being delayed outside, cleaning the guns, the farmer's wife left me and went out to talk with him. I continued eating my bread and milk voraciously, and shortly afterward they entered, he laughing heartily and she looking rather shamefaced. On my asking the cause, he declined for a time to state it, but at length said that she had come out to warn him that if he did not come in pretty soon "that boy would eat up all the bread and milk in the house." This story leaked out, and even appeared in a local paper, but never, I think, did me any harm.

Another occurrence, shortly afterward, seemed likely for a time to be more serious. The sophomore class, exuberant and inventive as ever, were evidently determined to "try it on" their young professor—in fact, to treat me as they had treated their tutors. Any mistake made by a student at a quiz elicited from sundry benches expressions of regret much too plaintive, or ejaculations of contempt much too explosive; and from these and various similar demonstrations which grew every day among a certain set in my class-room, it was easy to see that a trial of strength must soon come, and it seemed to me best to force the fighting. Looking over these obstreperous youths I noticed one tall, black-bearded man with a keen twinkle in his eye, who was evidently the leader. There was nothing in him especially demonstrative. He would occasionally nod in this direction, or wink in that, or smile in the other; but he was solemn when others were hilarious, unconcerned when others applauded. It was soon clear to me that in him lay the key to the situation, and one day, at the close of the examination, I asked him to remain. When we were alone I said to him, in an easy-going way, "So, F——, I see that either you or I must leave the university." He at once bristled up, feigned indignation, and said that he could not understand me. This I pooh-poohed, saying that we understood each other perfectly; that I had been only recently a student myself; that, if the growing trouble in the class continued, either he or I must give it up, and added, "I believe the trustees will prefer your departure to mine." At this he protested that he had made no demonstrations, to which I answered that if I put him on his honor he would not deny that he was the real center of the difficulty; that the others were, comparatively, men of small account; and that, with him gone, the backbone of the whole difficulty would be broken. He seemed impressed by this view—possibly he was not wholly displeased at the importance it gave him; and finally he acknowledged that perhaps he had been rather foolish, and suggested that we try to live together a little longer. I answered cordially, we shook hands at parting, and there was never any trouble afterward. I soon found what sort of questions interested him most, took especial pains to adapt points in my lectures to his needs, and soon had no stronger friend in the university.

But his activity finally found a less fortunate outcome. A year or two afterward came news of a terrible affair in the university town. A student was lying dead at the coroner's rooms, and on inquiry it was found that his death was the result of a carousal in which my friend F—— was a leading spirit. Eight men were concerned, of whom four were expelled—F—— being one—and four suspended. On leaving, he came to me and thanked me most heartily for what I had done for him, said that the action of the faculty was perfectly just, that no other course was open to us, but that he hoped yet to show us all that he could make a man of himself. He succeeded. Five years later he fell as a general at the head of his brigade at Gettysburg.

In addition to my regular work at the university, I lectured frequently in various cities throughout Michigan and the neighboring States. It was the culminating period of the popular-lecture system, and through the winter months my Friday and Saturday evenings were generally given to this sort of duty. It was, after its fashion, what in these days is called "university extension"; indeed, the main purpose of those members of the faculty thus invited to lecture was to spread the influence of the university. But I received from the system more than I gave to it; for it gave me not only many valuable acquaintances throughout the West, but it brought to Ann Arbor the best men then in the field, among them such as Emerson, Curtis, Whipple, Wendell Phillips, Carl Schurz, Moncure Conway, Bayard Taylor, and others noted then, but, alas, how few of them remembered now! To have them by my fireside and at my table was one of the greatest pleasures of a professorial life. It was at the beginning of my housekeeping; and under my roof on the university grounds we felt it a privilege to welcome these wise men from the East, and to bring the faculty and students into closer relations with them.

As regards the popular-lecture pulpit, my main wish was to set people thinking on various subjects, and especially regarding slavery and "protection." This presently brought a storm upon me. Some years before there had settled in the university town a thin, vociferous lawyer, past his prime, but not without ideas and force. He had for many years been a department subordinate at Washington; but, having accumulated some money, he had donned what was then known as senatorial costume—namely, a blue swallow-tailed coat, and a buff vest, with brass buttons—and coming to this little Michigan town, he had established a Whig paper, which afterward became Republican. He was generally credited, no doubt justly, with a determination to push himself into the United States Senate; but this determination was so obvious that people made light of it, and he never received the honor of a nomination to that or any other position. The main burden of his editorials was the greatness of Henry Clay, and the beauties of a protective tariff, his material being largely drawn from a book he had published some years before; and, on account of the usual form of his arguments, he was generally referred to, in the offhand Western way, as "Old Statistics."

In a public lecture based upon my Russian experiences, I had incidentally attacked paternal government, and especially such developments of it as tariffs for protection. The immediate result was a broadside from this gentleman's paper, and this I answered in an article which was extensively copied throughout the State. At this he evidently determined to crush this intruder upon his domain. That an "upstart"—a "mere school-teacher"—should presume to reply to man like himself, who had sat at the feet of Henry Clay, and was old enough to be my father, was monstrous presumption; but that a professor in the State university of a commonwealth largely Republican should avow free-trade opinions was akin to treason, and through twelve successive issues of his paper he lashed me in all the moods and tenses. As these attacks soon became scurrilous, I made no reply to any after the first; but his wrath was increased when he saw my reply quoted by the press throughout the State and his own diatribes neglected. Among his more serious charges I remember but one, and this was that I had evidently come into the State as a secret emissary of Van Burenism. But I recalled the remark of my enemy's idol, Henry Clay, to the effect that no one should ever reply to an attack by an editor, a priest, or a woman, since each of them is sure to have the last word. This feeling was soon succeeded by indifference; for my lecture-rooms, both at the university and throughout the State, were more and more frequented, and it became clear that my opponent's attacks simply advertised me. The following year I had my revenge. From time to time debates on current topics were held at the city hall, the participants being generally young professional men; but, the subject of a tariff for protection having been announced, my old enemy declared, several weeks beforehand, his intention of taking part in the discussion. Among my students that winter was one of the most gifted young scholars and speakers I have ever known. Not long after his graduation he was sent to the United States

Senate from one of the more important Western States, and nothing but his early death prevented his attaining a national reputation. He was a man of convictions, strong and skilful in impressing them upon his hearers, of fine personal appearance, with a pleasing voice, and in every way fitted to captivate an audience. Him I selected as the David who was to punish the protectionist Goliath. He had been himself a protectionist, having read Greeley's arguments in the "New York Tribune," but he had become a convert to my views, and day after day and week after week I kept him in training on the best expositions of free trade, and, above all, on Bastiat's "Sophisms of Protection." On the appointed evening the city hall was crowded, and my young David having modestly taken a back seat, the great Goliath appeared at the front in full senatorial costume, furbished up for the occasion, with an enormous collection of books and documents; and, the subject being announced, he arose, assumed his most imposing senatorial attitude, and began a dry, statistical oration. His manner was harsh, his matter wearisome; but he plodded on through an hour—and then my David arose. He was at his best. In five minutes he had the audience fully with him. Every point told. From time to time the house shook with applause; and at the close of the debate, a vote of the meeting being taken after the usual fashion in such assemblies, my old enemy was left in a ridiculous minority. Not only free-traders, but even protectionists voted against him. As he took himself very seriously, he was intensely mortified, and all the more so when he learned from one of my students that I now considered that we were "even." [1]

The more I threw myself into the work of the university the more I came to believe in the ideas on which it was founded, and to see that it was a reality embodying many things of which I had previously only dreamed. Up to that time the highest institutions of learning in the United States were al-

---

[1] The causes of my change of views on the question of "protection" are given in my political reminiscences.

most entirely under sectarian control. Even the University of Virginia, which Thomas Jefferson had founded as a center of liberal thought, had fallen under the direction of sectarians, and among the great majority of the Northern colleges an unwritten law seemed to require that a university president should be a clergyman. The instruction in the best of these institutions was, as I have shown elsewhere, narrow, their methods outworn, and the students, as a rule, confined to one simple, single, cast-iron course, in which the great majority of them took no interest. The University of Michigan had made a beginning of something better. The president was Dr. Henry Philip Tappan, formerly a Presbyterian clergyman, a writer of repute on philosophical subjects, a strong thinker, an impressive orator, and a born leader of men, who, during a visit to Europe, had been greatly impressed by the large and liberal system of the German universities, and had devoted himself to urging a similar system in our own country. On the Eastern institutions—save, possibly, Brown—he made no impression. Each of them was as stagnant as a Spanish convent, and as self-satisfied as a Bourbon duchy; but in the West he attracted supporters, and soon his ideas began to show themselves effective in the State university over which he had been called to preside.

The men he summoned about him were, in the main, admirably fitted to aid him. Dearest of all to me, though several years my senior, was Henry Simmons Frieze, professor of Latin. I had first met him at the University of Berlin, had then traveled with him through Germany and Italy, and had found him one of the most charming men I had ever met—simple, modest, retiring to a fault, yet a delightful companion and a most inspiring teacher. There was in him a combination which at first seemed singular; but experience has since shown me that it is by no means unnatural, for he was not only an ideal professor of Latin, but a gifted musician. The first revelation of this latter quality was made to me in a manner which showed his modesty. One evening during our student days at Berlin, at a reception given by the American minister of that period,—Governor Vroom of New Jersey,—I heard the sound of music coming from one of the more distant apartments. It was a sonata of Beethoven, wonderfully interpreted, showing not only skill but deep feeling. On my asking my neighbors who the performer might be, no one seemed to know, until, at last, some one suggested that it might be Professor Frieze. I made my way through the crowd toward the room from which the sounds came, but before arriving there the music had ended; and when I met the professor shortly afterward, and asked him if he had been the musician, his reply was so modest and evasive that I thought the whole thing a mistake and said nothing more about it. On our way to Italy some months later, I observed that, as we were passing through Bohemia, he jotted down in his note-book the quaint songs of the peasants and soldiers, and a few weeks later still he gave an exhibition of his genius. Sitting down one evening at the piano on the little coasting steamer between Genoa and Città Vecchia, he began playing, and though it has been my good fortune to hear all the leading pianists of my time, I have never heard one who seemed to interpret the masterpieces of music more worthily. At Ann Arbor I now came to know him intimately. Once or twice a week he came to my house, and, as mine was the only grand piano in the town, he enjoyed playing upon it. His extemporizations were flights of genius. At these gatherings he was inspired by two other admirable musicians, one being my dear wife, and the other Professor Brunnow, the astronomer. Nothing could be more delightful than their interpretations together of the main works of Beethoven, Handel, Mozart, Haydn, Weber, and other masters. On one of these evenings, when I happened to speak of the impression made upon me at my first hearing of a choral in a German church, Frieze began playing Luther's hymn, "Ein' feste Burg ist unser Gott," throwing it into all forms and keys, until we listened to his improvisations in a sort of daze which continued until nearly midnight. Next day, at St. Andrew's Church, he, as usual, had charge of the organ. Into his opening voluntary he wove the music of the preceding evening, the "Feste Burg"; it ran through all the chants of the morning service; it pervaded the accompaniment to the hymns; it formed the undertone of all the interludes; it was not relinquished until the close of the postlude. And the same was true of the afternoon service. I have always insisted that, had he lived in Germany, he would have been a second Beethoven. This will seem a grossly exaggerated tribute, but I do not hesitate to maintain it. So passionately was he devoted to music that at times he sent his piano away from his house in order to shun temptation to abridge his professorial work, and especially was this the case when he was preparing his edition of Vergil. A more lovely spirit never abode in mortal frame. No man was ever more generally beloved in a community; none, more lamented at his death. The splendid organ erected as a memorial to him in the great auditorium of the university; the noble monument which his students have placed over his grave; his portrait, which hangs in one of the principal rooms; the society which commemorates his name—all combine to show how deeply he was respected and beloved.

Entwined also with my happiest recollections is Brunnow, professor of astronomy and director of the observatory. His eminence in his department was widely recognized, as was shown when he was afterward made director of the Dudley Observatory at Albany, N. Y., and, finally, astronomer royal of Ireland. His musical abilities, in connection with those of Frieze, aided to give a delightful side to this period of my life. There was in him a quiet simplicity which led those who knew him best to love him most, but it occasionally provoked much fun among the students. On one occasion, President Tappan, being suddenly called out of town, requested Brunnow, who had married his daughter and was an inmate of his family, to find some member of the faculty to take his place at morning prayers next day. Thereupon Brunnow visited several professors, his first question to each of them being, with his German use of the consonants, "Professor, can you *bray?*" and henceforward this was added to the many standing jokes upon him in the student world.

I also found at the university other admirable men, and among those to whom I became specially attached was Thomas M. Cooley. When he had become chief justice of the State, and the most eminent writer of his time on the Constitution of the United States, he was still the same man, gentle, simple, and kindly. Besides these were such well-known professors as Fasquelle in modern literature; Williams, Douglass, and Winchell in science; Boise in Greek; Palmer, Sager, and Gunn in medicine and surgery; Campbell and Walker in law. Of these Judge Campbell was to me one of the main attractions of the place—a profound lawyer, yet with a kindly humor which lighted up all about him. He was especially interested in the early French history of the State, to which he had been drawn by his study of the titles to landed property in Detroit and its neighborhood, and some of his discoveries were curious. One of these had reference to an island in the straits near Detroit known as "Skillagalee," which had puzzled him a long time. The name seemed to be Irish, and the question was how an Irish name could have been thus applied. Finally he found on an old map an earlier name. It was Île aux Galets, or Pebble Island, which, in the mouths of Yankee sailors, had taken this apparently Celtic form. Another case was that of a river in Canada emptying into the straits not far from Detroit. It was known as "Yellow Dog River"; but, on rummaging through the older maps, he discovered that the earlier name was River St. John. To account for the transformation was at first difficult, but the mystery was finally unraveled: the Rivière St. Jean became, in the Canadian patois, Rivière Saan Jawne, and gradually Rivière Chien Jaune; recent geographers had simply translated it into English.

The features which mainly distinguished the University of

Michigan from the leading institutions of the East were that it was utterly unsectarian, that various courses of instruction were established, and that options were allowed between them. On these accounts that university holds a most important place in the history of American higher education; for it stands practically at the beginning of the transition from the old sectarian college to the modern university, and from the simple, single, cast-iron course to the form which we now know, in which various courses are presented, with free choice between them. The number of students was about five hundred, and the faculty corresponded to these in numbers. Now that the university includes over four thousand students, with a faculty in proportion, those seem the days of small things; but to me at that period it was all very grand. It seemed marvelous that there were then very nearly as many students at the University of Michigan as at Yale; and, as a rule, they were students worth teaching—hardy, vigorous, shrewd, broad, with faith in the greatness of the country and enthusiasm regarding the nation's future. It may be granted that there was, in many of them, a lack of elegance, but there was neither languor nor cynicism. One seemed, among them, to breathe a purer, stronger air. Over the whole institution Dr. Tappan presided, and his influence, both upon faculty and students, was, in the main, excellent. He sympathized heartily with the work of every professor, allowed to each great liberty, yet conducted the whole toward the one great end of developing a university more and more worthy of our country. His main qualities were of the best. Nothing could be better than his discussions of great questions of public policy and of education. One of the noblest orations I have ever heard was an offhand speech of his on receiving for the university museum a cast of the Laocoön from the senior class; yet this speech was made without preparation, and in the midst of engrossing labor. He often showed, not only the higher qualities required in a position like his, but a remarkable shrewdness and tact in dealing with lesser questions. Typical was one example, which taught me much when, in after years, I was called to similar duties at Cornell. The present tower and chime of the University of Michigan did not then exist; between the two main buildings on the university grounds there was simply a wooden column, bearing a bell of moderate size, which was rung at every lecture-hour by the principal janitor. One cold winter night those of us living in the immediate neighborhood heard the sound of axe-strokes. Presently there came a crash, and all was still. Next morning, at the hour for chapel, no bell was rung; it was found that the column had been cut down and the bell carried off. A president of less shrewdness would have declaimed to the students on the enormity of such a procedure, and have accentuated his eloquence with threats. Not so Dr. Tappan. At the close of the morning prayers he addressed the students humorously. There was a great attendance, for all wished to know how he would deal with the affair. Nothing could be better than his matter and manner. He spoke somewhat on this wise: "Gentlemen, there has doubtless been a mistake in the theory of some of you regarding the college bell. It would seem that some have believed that if the bell were destroyed, time would cease, and university exercises would be suspended. But, my friends, time goes on as ever, without the bell as with it; lectures and exercises of every sort continue, of course, as usual. The only thing which has occurred is that some of you have thought it best to dispense with the aid in keeping time which the regents of the university have so kindly given you. Knowing that large numbers of you were not yet provided with watches, the regents very thoughtfully provided the bell, and a man to ring it for you at the proper hours; and they will doubtless be pleased to learn that you at last feel able to dispense with it, and save them the expense of maintaining it. You are trying an interesting experiment. In most of the leading European universities, students get along perfectly without a bell; why should we not? In the interests of the finances of the university, I am glad to see you trying this experiment, and will only suggest that it be tried thoroughly. Of course the rolls will be called in the lecture-rooms promptly, as usual, and you will, of course, be present. If the experiment succeeds, it will enable us to dispense with a university bell forever; but if, after a suitable time, you decide that it is better to have the bell back again to remind you of the hours, and if you will make a proper request to the regents through me, I trust that they will allow you to restore it to its former position.'"

The students were greatly amused to see the matter taken in this way. They laughingly acknowledged themselves outwitted, and greeted the doctor's speech with applause. All of the faculty entered into the spirit of the matter; rolls were called perhaps rather more promptly than formerly, and students not present were marked rather more mercilessly than of old. There was evidently much reluctance on their part to ask for excuses, in view of the fact that they had themselves abolished the bell which had enabled them to keep the time; and one morning, about a month or six weeks later, after chapel, a big jolly student rose and asked permission to make a motion. This motion was that the president of the university be requested to allow the students to restore the bell to its former position. The proposal was graciously received by the doctor, put by him after the usual parliamentary manner, carried unanimously, and, a few mornings later, the bell was found in its old place on a new column, was rung as usual, and matters went on after the old fashion.

Every winter Dr. Tappan went before the legislature to plead the cause of the university, and to ask for appropriations. He was always heard with pleasure, since he was an excellent speaker; but certain things militated against him. First of all, he had much to say of the excellent models furnished by the great German universities, and especially by those of Prussia. This gave demagogues in the legislature, anxious to make a reputation in buncombe, a great chance. They orated to the effect that we wanted an American and not a Prussian system. Moreover, some unfortunate legends were developed. Mrs. Tappan, a noble and lovely woman belonging to the Livingston family, had been brought up in New York and New England, and could hardly suppress her natural preference for her old home and friends. A story grew that in an assembly of Michigan ladies she once remarked that the doctor and herself considered themselves as "missionaries to the West." This legend spread far and wide. It was resented, and undoubtedly cost the doctor dear.

The worst difficulty by far which he had to meet was the steady opposition of the small sectarian colleges scattered throughout the State. Each, in its own petty interest, dreaded the growth of any institution better than itself; each stirred the members of the legislature from its locality to oppose all aid to the State university; each, in its religious assemblages, its synods, conferences, and the like, sought to stir prejudice against the State institution as "godless." The result was that the doctor, in spite of his eloquent speeches, became the butt of various wretched demagogues in the legislature, and he very rarely secured anything in the way of effective appropriations. The university had been founded by a grant of public lands from the United States to Michigan; and one of his arguments was based on the fact that an immensely valuable tract, on which a considerable part of the city of Toledo now stands, had been taken away from the university without any suitable remuneration. But even this availed little, and it became quite a pastime among demagogues at the State Capitol to bait the doctor. On one of these occasions he was inspired to make a prophecy. Disgusted at the poor, cheap blackguardism, he shook the dust of the legislature off his feet, and said: "The day will come when my students will take your places, and then something will be done." That prophecy was fulfilled. In a decade the leading men in the legislature began to be the graduates of the State university; and now these graduates are largely in control, and they have dealt nobly with their alma mater. The State has justly become proud of it, and has wisely developed it.

Dr. Tappan's work was great, indeed. He stood not only at the beginning of the institution at Ann Arbor, but really at the beginning of the other universities of the Western States, from which the country is gaining so much at present, and is sure to gain vastly more in the future. The day will come when his statue will commemorate his services.

But there was another feature in his administration to which I refer with extreme reluctance. He had certain "defects of his qualities." Big, hearty, frank, and generous, he easily became the prey of those who wrought upon his feelings; and, in an evil hour, he was drawn into a quarrel not his own, between two scientific professors. This quarrel became exceedingly virulent; at times it almost paralyzed the university, and finally it convulsed the State. It became the main object of the doctor's thoughts. The men who had drawn him into it quietly retired under cover, and left him to fight their battle in the open. He did this powerfully, but his victories were no less calamitous than his defeats; for one of the professors, when overcome, fell back upon the church to which he belonged, and its conference was led to pass resolutions warning Christian people against the university. The forces of those hostile to the institution were marshaled to the sound of the sectarian drum. The quarrel at last became political; and when the doctor unwisely entered the political field in hopes of defeating the candidates put forward by his opponents, he was beaten at the polls, and his resignation followed. A small number of us, including Judge Cooley and Professors Frieze, Fasquelle, Boise, and myself, simply maintained an "armed neutrality," standing by the university, and refusing to be drawn into this whirlpool of intrigue and objurgation. Personally, we loved the doctor. Every one of us besought him to give up the quarrel, but in vain. He would not; he could not. It went on till the crash came. He was virtually driven from the State, retired to Europe, and never returned.

Years afterward, the citizens of Michigan in all parts of the State sought to make amends to him. The great body of the graduates, who loved and respected him, with leading men throughout the commonwealth, joined in a letter inviting him to return as a public guest; but he declined, and never again saw his native land. His first main place of residence was Basel, where, at the university, he superintended the education of his grandson, who, at a later period, became a professor at Heidelberg. Finally, he retired to a beautiful villa on the shores of Lake Leman, and there, with his family about him, peacefully followed his chosen studies. At his death he was buried amid the vineyards and orchards of Vevey.

Though I absolutely refused to be drawn into any of his quarrels, my relations with the doctor remained kindly, and not a single feeling was left which marred my visit to him in after years at Basel, or my later pilgrimage to his grave on the shores of Lake Leman. To no man is any success I may have afterward had in the administration of Cornell University so greatly due as to him.

In this summary I have hardly touched upon the most important part of my duty,—namely, the purpose of my lecture-courses, with their relations to that period in the history of our country, and to the questions which thinking men, and especially thinking young men, were then endeavoring to solve, —since all this has been given in my political reminiscences.

So much for my main work at the University of Michigan. But I had one recreation which was not without its uses. The little city of Ann Arbor is a beautiful place on the Huron River, and from the outset interested me. Even its origin had a peculiar charm. About a quarter of a century before my arrival, three families came from the East to take up the land which they had bought of the United States; and, as their three holdings touched each other at one corner, they brought boughs of trees to that spot and erected a sort of hut, or arbor, in which to live until their log houses were finished. On coming together in this arbor they discovered that the Christian name of each of the three wives was Ann: hence the name of the place; and this fact gave a poetic coloring to it which was a permanent pleasure to me. It was an unending satisfaction to reflect that no misguided patriot had been allowed to inflict upon that charming university town the name of "Athens," or "Oxford," or "Socratopolis," or "Anacreonsburg," or "Platoville," or "Emporium," or "Eudaimonia." What, but for those three good women, the name might have been, may be judged from the fact that one of the founders of the university did his best to have it called a "Katholoëpistemiad"!

But there was one drawback. The "campus," on which stood the four buildings then devoted to instruction, greatly disappointed me. It was a flat, square inclosure of forty acres, unkempt and wretched. Throughout its whole space there were not more than a score of trees outside the building sites allotted to professors; unsightly plank walks connected the buildings, and in every direction were meandering paths, which in dry weather were dusty and in wet weather muddy. Coming, as I did, from the glorious elms of Yale, all this distressed me, and one of my first questions was why no trees had been planted. The answer was that the soil was so hard and dry that none would grow. But on examining the territory in the neighborhood, especially the little inclosures about the pretty cottages of the town, I found fine large trees, and among them elms. At this, without permission from any one, I began planting trees within the university inclosure; established, on my own account, several avenues; and set out elms to overshadow them. Choosing my trees with care, carefully protecting and watering them during the first two years, and gradually adding to them a considerable number of evergreens, I preached practically the doctrine of adorning the campus. Gradually some of my students joined me; one class after another aided in securing trees and in planting them, others became interested, until, finally, the university authorities made me "superintendent of the grounds," and appropriated to my work the munificent sum of seventy-five dollars a year. So began the splendid growth which now surrounds those buildings. These trees became to me as my own children. Whenever I revisit Ann Arbor my first care'is to go among them, to see how they prosper, and especially how certain peculiar examples are flourishing; and at my recent visit, forty-six years after their planting, I found one of the most beautiful academic groves to be seen in any part of the world.

The most saddening thing during my connection with the university I have touched upon in my political reminiscences. Three years after my arrival the Civil War broke out, and there came a great exodus of students into the armies, the vast majority taking up arms for the Union, and a few for the Confederate States. The very noblest of them thus went forth —many of them, alas! never to return, and among them not a few whom I loved as brothers and even as my own children. Of all the experiences of my life, this was among the most saddening.

My immediate connection with the University of Michigan as resident professor of history lasted about six years; and then, on account partly of business interests which resulted from the death of my father, partly of my election to the New York State Senate, and partly of my election to the presidency of Cornell University, I resided in central New York, but retained a lectureship at the Western institution. I left the work and the friends who had become so dear to me with the greatest reluctance, and as long as possible I continued to revisit the old scenes, and to give courses of lectures. But at last my duties at Cornell absolutely forbade this, and so ended a connection which was to me one of the most fruitful in useful experiences and pregnant thoughts that I have ever known.

~~~~~~

5.

EVOLUTION OF "THE CORNELL IDEA"

1850–1865

TO TRINITY HALL AT HOBART COLLEGE MAY BE AS-
signed whatever honor that shadowy personage, the future historian, shall think due the place where was conceived
and quickened the germ idea of Cornell University. In that
little stone barrack on the shore of Seneca Lake, rude in its
architecture but lovely in its surroundings, a room was assigned me during my first year at college; and in a neighboring
apartment, with charming views over the lake and distant
hills, was the library of the Hermean Society. It was the
largest collection of books I had ever seen,—four thousand
volumes,—embracing a mass of literature from "The Pirates'
Own Book" to the works of Lord Bacon. In this paradise I
reveled, browsing through it at my will. This privilege was
of questionable value, since it drew me somewhat from closer
study; but it was not without its uses. One day I discovered
in it Huber and Newman's book on the English universities.
What a new world it opened! My mind was sensitive to any
impression it might make, on two accounts: first, because, on
the intellectual side, I was woefully disappointed at the
inadequacy of the little college as regarded its teaching force
and equipment; and next, because, on the esthetic side, I
lamented the absence of everything like beauty or fitness in
its architecture.

As I read in this new-found book of the colleges at Oxford and Cambridge, and pored over the engraved views of quadrangles, halls, libraries, chapels,—of all the noble and dignified belongings of a great seat of learning,—my heart sank within me. Every feature of the little American college seemed all the more sordid. But gradually I began consoling myself by building air-castles. These took the form of structures suited to a great university:—with distinguished professors in every field, with libraries as rich as the Bodleian, halls as lordly as that of Christ Church or of Trinity, chapels as inspiring as that of King's, towers as dignified as those of Magdalen and Merton, quadrangles as beautiful as those of Jesus and St. John's. In the midst of all other occupations I was constantly rearing these structures on that queenly site above the finest of the New York lakes, and dreaming of a university worthy of the commonwealth and of the nation. This dream became a sort of obsession. It came upon me during my working hours, in the class-rooms, in rambles along the lake shore, in the evenings, when I paced up and down the walks in front of the college buildings, and saw rising in their place and extending to the pretty knoll behind them, the worthy home of a great university. But this university, though beautiful and dignified, like those at Oxford and Cambridge, was in two important respects very unlike them. First, I made provision for other studies beside classics and mathematics. There should be professors in the great modern literatures—above all, in our own; there should also be a professor of modern history and a lecturer on architecture. And next, my university should be under control of no single religious organization; it should be free from all sectarian or party trammels; in electing its trustees and professors no questions should be asked as to their belief or their attachment to this or that sect or party. So far, at least, I went in those days along the road toward the founding of Cornell.

The academic year of 1849–1850 having been passed at this little college in western New York, I entered Yale. This was nearer my ideal; for its professors were more distinguished, its equipment more adequate, its students more numerous, its general scope more extended. But it was still far below my dreams. Its single course in classics and mathematics, through which all students were forced alike, regardless of their tastes, powers, or aims; its substitution of gerund-grinding for ancient literature; its want of all instruction in modern literature; its substitution of recitals from text-books for instruction in history —all this was far short of my ideal. Moreover, Yale was then far more under denominational control than at present—its president, of necessity, as was then supposed, a Congregational minister; its professors, as a rule, members of the same sect; and its tutors, to whom our instruction during the first two years was almost entirely confined, students in the Congregational Divinity School.

Then, too, its outward representation was sordid and poor. The long line of brick barracks, the cheapest which could be built for money, repelled me. What a contrast to Oxford and Cambridge, and, above all, to my air-castles! There were, indeed, two architectural consolations: one, the library building, which had been built just before my arrival; and the other, the Alumni Hall, begun shortly afterward. These were of stone, and I snatched an especial joy from the grotesque Gothic heads in the cornices of the library towers and from the little latticed windows at the rear of the Alumni Hall. Both seemed to me features worthy of "colleges and halls of ancient days."

The redeeming feature of the whole was its setting, the "green," with superb avenues overarched by elms; and a further charm was added by East and West Rock, and by the views over New Haven Harbor into Long Island Sound. Among these scenes I erected new air-castles. First of all, a great quadrangle, not unlike that which is now developing at Yale, and, as a leading feature, a gate-tower like that since erected in memory of William Walter Phelps, but, unlike that, adorned with statues in niches and on corbels, like those on the entrance tower of Trinity at Cambridge—statues of old Yalensian worthies, such as Elihu Yale in his costume of the Georgian period, Bishop Berkeley in his robes, President Dwight in his Geneva gown, and Nathan Hale in fetters. There was also in my dream another special feature, which no one has as yet attempted to realize—a lofty campanile, which I placed sometimes at the intersection of College and Chapel, and sometimes at the intersection of College and Elm streets—a clock-tower looking proudly down the slope, over the traffic of the town, and bearing a deep-toned peal of bells.

My general ideas on the subject were further developd by Charles Astor Bristed's book, "Five Years in an English University," and by sundry publications regarding student life in Germany. Still, my opinions regarding education were wretchedly imperfect, as may be judged from one circumstance. The newly established Sheffield Scientific School had just begun its career in the old president's house in front of the former Divinity Hall on the college green; and, one day in my senior year, looking toward it from my window in North College, I saw a student examining a colored liquid in a test-tube. A feeling of wonder came over me! What could it all be about? Probably not a man of us in the whole senior class had any idea of a chemical laboratory save as a sort of small kitchen back of a lecture-desk, like that in which an assistant and a colored servant prepared oxygen, hydrogen, and carbonic acid for the lectures of Professor Silliman. I was told that this new laboratory was intended for experiment, and my wonder was succeeded by disgust that any human being should give his time to pursuits so futile.

The next period in the formation of my ideas regarding a university began, after my graduation at Yale, during my first visit to Oxford. Then and at later visits, both to Oxford and Cambridge, I not only reveled in the architectural glories of those great seats of learning, but learned the advantages of college life in common—of the "halls," and the general social life which they promote; of the "commons" and "combination rooms," which give a still closer relation between those most directly concerned in university work; of the quadrangles, which give a sense of scholarly seclusion, even in the midst of crowded cities; and of all the surroundings which give a dignity befitting these vast establishments. Still more marked progress in my ideas was made during my attendance at the Sorbonne and the Collège de France. In those institutions, during the years 1853–1854, I became acquainted with the French university-lecture system, with its clearness, breadth, wealth of illustration, and its hold upon large audiences of students; and I was seized with the desire to transfer something like it to our own country. My castles in the air were now reared more loftily and broadly; for they began to include laboratories, museums, and even galleries of art.

Even St. Petersburg, during my attachéship in 1854–1855, contributed to these airy structures. In my diary for that period, I find it jotted down that I observed and studied at various times the Michael Palace in that city as a very suitable structure for a university. Twenty years afterward, when I visited, as minister of the United States, the Grand Duchess Catherine, the aunt of the Emperor Alexander III, in that same palace, and mentioned to her my old admiration for it, she gave me a most interesting account of the building of it, and of the laying out of the beautiful park about it by her father, the old Grand Duke Michael, and agreed with me that it would be a noble home for an institution of learning.

My student life at Berlin, during the year following, further intensified my desire to do something for university education in the United States. There I saw my ideal of a university not only realized, but extended and glorified—with renowned professors, with ample lecture-halls, with everything possible in the way of illustrative materials, with laboratories, museums, and a concourse of youth from all parts of the world.

I have already spoken, in the chapter on my professorship at the University of Michigan, regarding the influence on my ideas of its president, Henry Philip Tappan, and of the whole work in that institution. Though many good things may be justly said for the University of Virginia, the real beginning of a university in the United States, in the modern sense, was made by Dr. Tappan and his colleagues at Ann Arbor. Its only defects seemed to me that it included no technical side, and did not yet admit women. As to the first of these defects, the State had separated the agricultural college from the university, placing it in what, at that period, was a remote swamp near the State Capitol, and had as yet done nothing toward providing for other technical branches. As to the second, though a few of us favored the admission of women, President Tappan opposed it; and, probably, in view of the condition of the university and of public opinion at that time, his opposition was wise.

Recalled to Syracuse after five years in Michigan, my old desire to see a university rising in the State of New York was stronger than ever. Michigan had shown me some of my ideals made real; why might not our own much greater commonwealth be similarly blessed?

The first thing was to devise a plan for a suitable faculty. As I felt that this must not demand too large an outlay, I drew up a scheme providing for a few resident teachers supported by endowments, and for a body of nonresident professors or lecturers supported by fees. These lecturers were to be chosen from the most eminent professors in the existing colleges and from the best men then in the public-lecture field; and my confidant in the matter was George William Curtis, who entered into it heartily, and who afterward, in his speech at my inauguration as president of Cornell, referred to it in a way which touched me deeply.[1]

The next thing was to decide upon a site. It must naturally be in the central part of the State; and, rather curiously, that which I then most coveted, frequently visited, walked about, and inspected was the rising ground southeast of Syracuse

---

[1] See Mr. Curtis's speech, September 8, 1868, published by the university.

since selected by the Methodists for their institution which takes its name from that city.

My next effort was to make a beginning of an endowment, and for this purpose I sought to convert Gerrit Smith. He was, for those days, enormously wealthy. His property, which was estimated at from two to three millions of dollars, he used munificently; and his dear friend and mine, Samuel Joseph May, had told me that it was not too much to hope that Mr. Smith might do something for the improvement of higher instruction. To him, therefore, I wrote, proposing that if he would contribute an equal sum to a university at Syracuse, I would give to it one half of my own property. In his answer he gave reasons why he could not join in the plan, and my scheme seemed no nearer reality than my former air-castles. It seemed, indeed, to have faded away like

"The baseless fabric of a vision"

and to have left

"Not a wrack behind"—

when all its main features were made real in a way and by means utterly unexpected; for now began the train of events which led to my acquaintance, friendship, and close alliance with the man through whom my plans became a reality, larger and better than any ever seen in my dreams—Ezra Cornell.

6.

EZRA CORNELL

1864–1874

O N THE FIRST DAY OF THE YEAR 1864, TAKING MY SEAT for the first time in the State Senate at Albany, I found among my associates a tall, spare man, apparently very reserved and austere, and soon learned his name—Ezra Cornell.

Though his chair was near mine, there was at first little intercourse between us, and there seemed small chance of more. He was steadily occupied, and seemed to have no desire for new acquaintances. He was, perhaps, the oldest man in the Senate; I, the youngest: he was a man of business; I was fresh from a university professorship: and, upon the announcement of committees, our paths seemed separated entirely; for he was made chairman of the committee on agriculture, while to me fell the chairmanship of the committee on education.

Yet it was this last difference which drew us together; for among the first things referred to my committee was a bill to incorporate a public library which he proposed to found in Ithaca.

On reading this bill I was struck, not merely by his gift of one hundred thousand dollars to his townsmen, but even more by a certain breadth and largeness in his way of making it. The most striking sign of this was his mode of forming a board of trustees; for, instead of the usual effort to tie up the organization forever in some sect, party, or clique, he had named the best men of his town—his political opponents as well as his friends; and had added to them the pastors of all the principal churches, Catholic and Protestant. This breadth of mind, even more than his munificence, drew me to him. We met several times, discussed his bill, and finally I reported it substantially as introduced, and supported it until it became a law.

Our next relations were not, at first, so pleasant. The great Land Grant of 1862, from the General Government to the State, for industrial and technical education, had been turned over, at a previous session of the legislature, to an institution called the People's College, in Schuyler County; but the Agricultural College, twenty miles distant from it, was seeking to take away from it a portion of this endowment; and among the trustees of this Agricultural College was Mr. Cornell, who now introduced a bill to divide the fund between the two institutions.

On this I at once took ground against him, declaring that the fund ought to be kept together at some one institution; that on no account should it be divided; that the policy for higher education in the State of New York should be concentration; that we had already suffered sufficiently from scattering our resources; that there were already over twenty colleges in the State, and not one of them doing anything which could justly be called university work.

Mr. Cornell's first effort was to have his bill referred, not to my committee, but to his; here I resisted him, and, as a solution of the difficulty, it was finally referred to a joint committee made up of both. On this double-headed committee I deliberately thwarted his purpose throughout the entire session, delaying action and preventing any report upon his bill.

Most men would have been vexed by this; but he took my course calmly, and even kindly. He never expostulated, and always listened attentively to my arguments against his view;

meanwhile I omitted no opportunity to make these arguments as strong as possible, and especially to impress upon him the importance of keeping the fund together.

After the close of the session, during the following summer, as it had become evident that the trustees of the People's College had no intention of raising the additional endowment and providing the equipment required by the act which gave them the land grant, there was great danger that the whole fund might be lost to the State by the lapsing of the time allowed in the congressional act for its acceptance. Just at this period Mr. Cornell invited me to attend a meeting of the State Agricultural Society, of which he was the president, at Rochester; and, when the meeting had assembled, he quietly proposed to remove the difficulty I had raised, by drawing a new bill giving the State Agricultural College half of the fund, and by inserting a clause requiring the college to provide an additional sum of three hundred thousand dollars. This sum he pledged himself to give, and, as the comptroller of the State had estimated the value of the land grant at six hundred thousand dollars, Mr. Cornell supposed that this would obviate my objection, since the fund of the Agricultural College would thus be made equal to the whole original land-grant fund as estimated, which would be equivalent to keeping the whole fund together.

The entire audience applauded, as well they might: it was a noble proposal. But, much to the disgust of the meeting, I persisted in my refusal to sanction any bill dividing the fund, declared myself now more opposed to such a division than ever; but promised that if Mr. Cornell and his friends would ask for the *whole* grant—keeping it together, and adding his three hundred thousand dollars, as proposed—I would support such a bill with all my might.

I was led to make this proposal by a course of circumstances which might, perhaps, be called "providential." For some years I had been dreaming of a university; had looked into the questions involved, at home and abroad; had approached sundry wealthy and influential men on the subject; but had obtained no encouragement, until this strange and unexpected combination of circumstances—a great land grant, the use of which was to be determined largely by the committee of which I was chairman, and this noble pledge by Mr. Cornell.

Yet for some months nothing seemed to come of our conference. At the assembling of the legislature in the following year, it was more evident than ever that the trustees of the People's College intended to do nothing. During the previous session they had promised through their agents to supply the endowment required by their charter; but, though this charter obliged them, as a condition of taking the grant, to have an estate of two hundred acres, buildings for the accommodation of two hundred students, and a faculty of not less than six professors, with a sufficient library and other apparatus, yet our committee, on again taking up the subject, found hardly the faintest pretense of complying with these conditions. Moreover, their charter required that their property should be free from all encumbrance; and yet the so-called donor of it, Mr. Charles Cook, could not be induced to cancel a small mortgage which he held upon it. Still worse, before the legislature had been in session many days, it was found that his agent had introduced a bill to relieve the People's College of all conditions, and to give it, without any pledge whatever, the whole land grant, amounting to very nearly a million of acres.

But even worse than this was another difficulty. In addition to the strong lobby sent by Mr. Cook to Albany in behalf of the People's College, there came representatives of nearly all the smaller denominational colleges in the State, men eminent and influential, clamoring for a division of the fund among their various institutions, though the fragment which would have fallen to each would not have sufficed to endow even a single professorship.

While all this was uncertain, and the fund seemed likely to be utterly frittered away, I was one day going down from the State Capitol, when Mr. Cornell joined me and began conversation. He was, as usual, austere and reserved in appearance; but I had already found that below this appearance there was a warm heart and noble purpose. No observant associate could fail to notice that the only measures in the legislature which he cared for were those proposing some substantial good to the State or nation, and that he despised all political wrangling and partizan jugglery.

On this occasion, after some little general talk, he quietly said, "I have about half a million dollars more than my family will need: what is the best thing I can do with it for the State?" I answered: "Mr. Cornell, the two things most worthy of aid in any country are charity and education; but, in our country, the charities appeal to everybody. Any one can understand the importance of them, and the worthy poor or unfortunate are sure to be taken care of. As to education, the lower grades will always be cared for in the public schools by the State; but the institutions of the highest grade, without which the lower can never be thoroughly good, can be appreciated by only a few. The policy of our State is to leave this part of the system to individuals; it seems to me, then, that if you have half a million to give, the best thing you can do with it is to establish or strengthen some institution for higher instruction." I then went on to show him the need of a larger institution for such instruction than the State then had; that such a college or university worthy of the State would require far more in the way of faculty and equipment than most men supposed; that the time had come when scientific and technical education must be provided for in such an institution; and that education in history and literature should be the bloom of the whole growth.

He listened attentively, but said little. The matter seemed to end there; but not long afterward he came to me and said: "I agree with you that the land-grant fund ought to be kept together, and that there should be a new institution fitted to the present needs of the State and the country. I am ready to pledge to such an institution a site and five hundred thousand dollars as an addition to the land-grant endowment, instead of three hundred thousand, as I proposed at Rochester."

As may well be imagined, I hailed this proposal joyfully, and soon sketched out a bill embodying his purpose so far as education was concerned. But here I wish to say that, while Mr. Cornell urged Ithaca as the site of the proposed institution, he never showed any wish to give his own name to it. The suggestion to that effect was mine. He at first doubted the policy of it; but, on my insisting that it was in accordance with time-honored American usage, as shown by the names of Harvard, Yale, Dartmouth, Amherst, Bowdoin, Brown, Williams, and the like, he yielded.

We now held frequent conferences as to the leading features of the institution to be created. In these I was more and more impressed by his sagacity and largeness of view; and, when the sketch of the bill was fully developed,—its financial features by him, and its educational features by me,—it was put into shape by Charles J. Folger of Geneva, then chairman of the judiciary committee of the Senate, afterward chief judge of the Court of Appeals, and finally Secretary of the Treasury of the United States. The provision forbidding any sectarian or partizan predominance in the board of trustees or faculty was proposed by me, heartily acquiesced in by Mr. Cornell, and put into shape by Judge Folger. The State-scholarship feature and the system of alumni representation on the board of trustees were also accepted by Mr. Cornell at my suggestion.

I refer to these things especially because they show one striking characteristic of the man—namely, his readiness to be advised largely by others in matters which he felt to be outside his own province, and his willingness to give the largest measure of confidence when he gave any confidence at all.

On the other hand, the whole provision for the endowment, the part relating to the land grant, and, above all, the supplementary legislation allowing him to make a contract with the

State for "locating" the lands, were thought out entirely by himself; and in all these matters he showed, not only a public spirit far beyond that displayed by any other benefactor of education in his time, but a foresight which seemed to me then, and seems to me now, almost miraculous. He alone, of all men in the United States, was able to foresee what might be done by an individual to develop the land-grant fund, and he alone was willing to make the great personal sacrifice thereby required.

But, while he thus left the general educational features to me, he uttered, during one of our conversations, words which showed that he had arrived at the true conception of a university. He expressed the hope that in the proposed institution every student might find instruction in whatever study interested him. Hence came the legend now surrounding his medallion portrait upon the university seal: "I would found an institution where any person can find instruction in any study."

The introduction of this new bill into the legislature was a signal for war. Nearly all the denominational colleges girded themselves for the fray, and sent their agents to fight us at Albany; they also stirred up the secular press, without distinction of party, in the regions where they were situated, and the religious organs of their various sects in the great cities.

At the center of the movement against us was the People's College; it had rallied in force and won over the chairman of the educational committee in the Assembly, so that under various pretexts he delayed considering the bill. Worst of all, there appeared against us, late in the session, a professor from the Genesee College—a man of high character and great ability; and he did his work most vigorously. He brought the whole force of his sect to bear upon the legislature, and insisted that every other college in the State had received something from the public funds, while his had received none.

As a first result came a proposal from some of his associates that twenty-five thousand dollars of the land-grant fund be paid to Genesee College; but this the friends of the Cornell bill resisted, on the ground that, if the fund were broken into in one case, it would be in others.

It was next proposed that Mr. Cornell should agree to give twenty-five thousand dollars to Genesee College on the passage of the bill. This Mr. Cornell utterly refused, saying that not for the passage of any bill would he make any private offer or have any private understanding; that every condition must be put into the bill, where all men could see it; and that he would then accept or reject it as he might think best. The result was that our opponents forced into the bill a clause requiring him to give twenty-five thousand dollars to Genesee College, before he could be allowed to give five hundred thousand dollars to the proposed university; and the friends of the bill, not feeling strong enough to resist this clause, and not being willing to see the enterprise wrecked for the want of it, allowed it to go unopposed. The whole matter was vexatious to the last degree. A man of less firmness and earnestness, thus treated, would have thrown up his munificent purpose in disgust; but Mr. Cornell quietly persevered.

Yet the troubles of the proposed university had only begun. Mr. Charles Cook, who, during his senatorship, had secured the United States land grant of 1862 for the People's College, was a man of great force, a born leader of men, anxious to build up his part of the State, and especially the town from which he came, though he had no special desire to put any considerable part of his own wealth into a public institution. He had seen the opportunities afforded by the land grant, had captured it, and was now determined to fight for it. The struggle became bitter. His emissaries, including the members of the Senate and Assembly from his part of the State, made common cause with the sectarian colleges, and with various corporations and persons who, having bills of their own in the legislature, were ready to exchange services and votes.

The coalition of all these forces against the Cornell University bill soon became very formidable, and the committee

on education in the Assembly, to which the bill had been
referred, seemed more and more controlled by them. Our
only hope now was to enlighten the great body of the senators
and assemblymen. To this end Mr. Cornell invited them by
squads, sometimes to his rooms at Congress Hall, sometimes
to mine at the Delavan House. There he laid before them
his general proposal and the financial side of the plan, while
I dwelt upon the need of a university in the true sense of the
word; upon the opportunity now offered by this great fund;
upon the necessity of keeping it together; upon the need of
large means to carry out any scheme of technical and general
education such as was contemplated by the congressional act
of 1862; showed the proofs that the People's College would
and could do nothing to meet this want; that division of the
fund among the existing colleges was simply the annihilation
of it; and, in general, did my best to enlighten the reason and
arouse the patriotism of the members on the subject of a
worthy university in our State. These points and others were
finally embodied in my speech before the Senate, and this
having been published in the "Albany Journal," Mr. Cornell
provided for its circulation broadcast over the State and thus
aroused public opinion.

In this way we won to our support several strong friends in
both Houses, among them some men of great natural force
of character who had never enjoyed the privilege of much
early education, but who were none the less anxious that those
who came after them should have the best opportunities. Of
these I may name especially Senators Cook of Saratoga and
Ames of Oswego. Men of high education and culture also
aided us, especially Mr. Andrews, Mr. Havens, and, finally,
Judge Folger in the Senate, with Mr. Lord and Mr. Weaver
in the Assembly.

While we were thus laboring with the legislature as a
whole, serious work had to be done with the Assembly committee; and Mr. Cornell employed a very eminent lawyer to
present his case, while Mr. Cook employed one no less noted

to take the opposite side. The session of the committee was held in the Assembly chamber, and there was a large attendance of spectators; but, unfortunately, the lawyer employed by Mr. Cornell having taken little pains with the case, his speech was cold, labored, perfunctory, and fell flat. The speech on the other side was much more effective; it was thin and demagogical, but the speaker knew well the best tricks for catching the average man. He indulged in eloquent tirades against the Cornell bill as a "monopoly," a "wild project," a "selfish scheme," a "job," a "grab," and the like; denounced Mr. Cornell as "seeking to erect a monument to himself"; hinted that he was "planning to rob the State"; and, before he had finished, had pictured Mr. Cornell as a swindler and the rest of us as dupes or knaves.

I can never forget the quiet dignity with which Mr. Cornell took this abuse. Mrs. Cornell sat at his right, I at his left. In one of the worst tirades against him, he turned to me and said quietly, and without the slightest anger or excitement: "If I could think of any other way in which half a million of dollars would do as much good to the State, I would give the legislature no more trouble." Shortly afterward, when the invective was again especially bitter, he turned to me and said: "I am not sure but that it would be a good thing for me to give the half a million to old Harvard College in Massachusetts, to educate the descendants of the men who hanged my forefathers."

There was more than his usual quaint humor in this—there was that deep reverence which he always bore toward his Quaker ancestry, and which seemed to have become part of him. I admired Mr. Cornell on many occasions, but never more than during that hour when he sat, without the slightest anger, mildly taking the abuse of that prostituted pettifogger, the indifference of the committee, and the laughter of the audience. It was a scene for a painter, and I trust that some day it will be fitly perpetuated for the university.

This struggle being ended, the Assembly committee could

not be induced to report the bill. It was easy, after such a speech, for its members to pose as protectors of the State against a swindler and a monopoly; the chairman, who, shortly after the close of the session, was mysteriously given a position in the New York custom-house, made pretext after pretext without reporting, until it became evident that we must have a struggle in the Assembly and drag the bill out of the committee in spite of him. To do this required a two-thirds vote. All our friends were set to work, and some pains taken to scare the corporations which had allied themselves with the enemy, in regard to the fate of their own bills, by making them understand that, unless they stopped their interested opposition to the university bill in the House, a feeling would be created in the Senate very unfortunate for them. In this way their clutch upon sundry members of the Assembly was somewhat relaxed, and these were allowed to vote according to their consciences.

The Cornell bill was advocated most earnestly in the House by Mr. Henry B. Lord: in his unpretentious way he marshaled the university forces, and moved that the bill be taken from the committee and referred to the Committee of the Whole. Now came a struggle. Most of the best men in the Assembly stood by us; but the waverers—men who feared local pressure, sectarian hostility, or the opposition of Mr. Cook to measures of their own—attempted, if not to oppose the Cornell bill, at least to evade a vote upon it. In order to give them a little tone and strength, Mr. Cornell went with me to various leading editors in the city of New York, and we explained the whole matter to them, securing editorial articles favorable to the university, the most prominent among these gentlemen being Horace Greeley of the "Tribune," Erastus Brooks of the "Express," and Manton Marble of the "World." This did much for us, yet when the vote was taken the old cowardice was again shown; but several of us stood in the cloak-room and fairly shamed the waverers back into their places. As a result, to the surprise and disgust of the chairman of the Assembly

committee, the bill was taken out of his control, and referred
to the Committee of the Whole House.

Another long struggle now ensued, but the bill was finally
passed in the Assembly and came back to the Senate. There
the struggle was renewed, all kinds of delaying tactics were
resorted to, but the bill was finally carried, and received the
signature of Governor Fenton.

Now came a new danger. During their struggle against the
bill, our enemies had been strong enough to force into it a
clause enabling the People's College to retain the land fund,
provided that institution should be shown, within six months
of the passage of the bill, to be in possession of a sum such
as the Board of Regents should declare would enable it to
comply with the conditions on which it had originally received
the grant. The Board of Regents now reported that the possession of one hundred and fifty thousand dollars would be
sufficient for such a compliance, and would insure the fund
to the People's College. Naturally we watched, in much
uneasy suspense, during those six months, to see whether Mr.
Cook and the People's College authorities would raise this
sum of money, so small in comparison with that which Mr.
Cornell was willing to give, in order to secure the grant.
But our fears were baseless; and on the fifth day of September,
1865, the trustees of Cornell University were assembled for
the first time at Ithaca.

Then came to them a revelation of a quality in Mr. Cornell
unknown to most of them before. In one of the petitions
forwarded from Ithaca to the legislature by his fellow-citizens
it had been stated that "he never did less than he promised,
but generally more." So it was found in this case. He turned
over to the trustees, not only the securities for the five hundred
thousand dollars required by the charter, but also gave two
hundred acres of land as a site. Thus came into being Cornell
University.

Yet the services of Mr. Cornell had only begun: he at once
submitted to us a plan for doing what no other citizen had done

for any other State. In the other commonwealths which had received the land grant, the authorities had taken the scrip representing the land, sold it at the market price, and, as the market was thus glutted, had realized but a small sum; but Mr. Cornell, with that foresight which was his most striking characteristic, saw clearly what could be done by using the scrip to take up land for the institution. To do this he sought aid in various ways; but no one dared join him, and at last he determined to bear the whole burden himself. Scrip representing over seven hundred thousand acres still remained in the hands of the comptroller. The trustees received Mr. Cornell's plan for dealing with the scrip somewhat doubtfully, but the enabling act was passed, by which he was permitted to "locate" this land for the benefit of the university. So earnest was he in this matter that he was anxious to take up the entire amount, but here his near friends interposed: we saw too well what a crushing load the taxes and other expenses on such a vast tract of land would become before it could be sold to advantage. Finally he yielded somewhat: it was agreed that he should take up five hundred thousand acres, and he now gave himself day and night to this great part of the enterprise, which was to provide a proper financial basis for a university such as we hoped to found.

Meanwhile, at Mr. Cornell's suggestion, I devoted myself to a more careful plan of the new institution; and, at the next meeting of the board, presented a "plan of organization," which sketched out the purpose and constitution of such a university as seemed needed in a great commonwealth like ours. Mr. Cornell studied it carefully, gave it his approval, and a copy of it with marginal notes in his own hand is still preserved.

I had supposed that this was to end my relations with Mr. Cornell, so far as the university was concerned. A multitude of matters seemed to forbid my taking any further care for it, and a call to another position very attractive to me drew me away from all thought of connection with it, save, perhaps,

such as was involved in meeting the trustees once or twice a
year.

Mr. Cornell had asked me, from time to time, whether I
could suggest any person for the presidency of the university.
I mentioned various persons, and presented the arguments in
their favor. One day he said to me quietly that he also had a
candidate; I asked him who it was, and he said that he preferred to keep the màtter to himself until the next meeting of
the trustees. Nothing more passed between us on that subject. I had no inkling of his purpose, but thought it most
likely that his candidate was a Western gentleman whose claims
had been strongly pressed upon him. When the trustees came
together, and the subject was brought up, I presented the
merits of various gentlemen, especially of one already at the
head of an important college in the State, who, I thought,
would give us success. Upon this, Mr. Cornell rose, and, in a
very simple but earnest speech, presented my name. It was
entirely unexpected by me, and I endeavored to show the
trustees that it was impossible for me to take the place in view
of other duties; that it needed a man of more robust health,
of greater age, and of wider reputation in the State. But Mr.
Cornell quietly persisted, our colleagues declared themselves
unanimously of his opinion, and, with many misgivings, I gave
a provisional acceptance.

The relation thus begun ended only with Mr. Cornell's life,
and from first to last it grew more and more interesting to me.
We were thrown much together at Albany, at Ithaca, and on
various journeys undertaken for the university; and, the more
I saw of him, the deeper became my respect for him. There
were, indeed, toward the end of his life, some things trying to
one of my temperament, and among these things I may mention
his exceeding reticence, and his willingness not only to labor
but to wait; but these stood not at all in the way of my respect
and affection for him.

His liberality was unstinted. While using his fortune in

taking up the lands, he was constantly doing generous things for the university and those connected with it. One of the first of these was his gift of the library in classical literature collected by Dr. Charles Anthon of Columbia College. Nothing could apparently be more outside his sympathy than the department needing these seven thousand volumes; but he recognized its importance in the general plan of the new institution, bought the library for over twelve thousand dollars, and gave it to the university.

Then came the Jewett collection in geology, which he gave at a cost of ten thousand dollars; the Ward collection of casts, at a cost of three thousand; the Newcomb collection in conchology, at a cost of sixteen thousand; an addition to the university grounds, valued at many thousands more; and it was only the claims of a multitude of minor university matters upon his purse which prevented his carrying out a favorite plan of giving a great telescope, at a cost of fifty thousand dollars. At a later period, to extinguish the university debt, to increase the equipment, and eventually to provide free scholarships and fellowships, he made an additional gift of about eighty thousand dollars.

While doing these things, he was constantly advancing large sums in locating the university lands, and in paying university salaries, for which our funds were not yet available; while from time to time he made many gifts which, though smaller, were no less striking evidences of the largeness of his view. I may mention a few among these as typical.

Having found, in the catalogue of a London bookseller, a set of Piranesi's great work on the "Antiquities of Rome,"—a superb copy, the gift of a pope to a royal duke,—I showed it to him, when he at once ordered it for our library at a cost of about a thousand dollars. At another time, seeing the need of some costly works to illustrate agriculture, he gave them to us at a somewhat greater cost; and, having heard Professor Tyndall's lectures in New York, he bought additional physical apparatus to enable our resident professor to repeat the lectures at Ithaca, and this cost him fifteen hundred dollars.

Characteristic of him, too, was another piece of quiet munificence. When the clause forced into the university charter, requiring him to give twenty-five thousand dollars to another institution before he could be allowed to give half a million to his own, was noised abroad through the State, there was a general feeling of disgust; and at the next session of the legislature a bill was brought in to refund the twenty-five thousand dollars to him. Upon this, he remarked that what he once gave he never took back, but that if the university trustees would accept it he had no objection. The bill was modified to this effect, and thus the wrong was righted.

During my stay in Europe, through the summer of 1868, under instructions to study various institutions for technical education, to make large purchases of books, and to secure one or two men greatly needed in special departments not then much cultivated in this country, his generosity was unfailing. Large as were the purchases which I was authorized to make, the number of desirable things outside this limit steadly grew larger; but my letters to him invariably brought back the commission to secure this additional material.

During this occupation of mine in Europe, he was quite as busy in the woods of the upper Mississippi and on the plains of Kansas, selecting university lands. No fatigue or expenditure deterred him.

At various periods I passed much time with Mr. Cornell on his home farm. He lived generously, in a kind of patriarchal simplicity, and many of his conversations interested me intensely. His reticence gradually yielded, and he gave me much information regarding his earlier years: they had been full of toil and struggle, but through the whole there was clear evidence of a noble purpose. Whatever worthy work his hand had found to do, he had done it with his might: the steamers of Cayuga Lake; the tunnel which carries the waters of Fall

Creek to the mills below; the mills themselves; the dams against that turbulent stream, which he built after others had failed, and which stand firmly to this day; the calendar clocks for which Ithaca has become famous, and of which he furnished the original hint—all these he touched upon, though so modestly that I never found out his full agency in them until a later period, when I had made the acquaintance of many of his townsmen.

Especially interesting were his references to the beginnings of American telegraphic enterprise, with which he had so much to do.

His connection with it began in a curious way. Traveling in northern New England to dispose of a plow which he had invented, he entered the office of a gentleman who had taken the contract for laying the first telegraphic wires underground between Washington and Baltimore, and found him in much doubt and trouble: the difficulty was to lay the leaden pipe containing the two insulated wires at a cost within the terms of the contract. Hearing this, Mr. Cornell said: "I will build you a machine which will dig the trench, lay the pipe and wires, and cover them with earth rapidly and cheaply."

This proposal was at first derided; but, as Mr. Cornell insisted upon it, he was at last allowed to show what he could do. The machine having been constructed, he exhibited it to a committee; but when the long line of horses attached to it were started, it was so thrown about by the inequalities of the surface that the committee declared it a failure. Presently Mr. Cornell took them to the ground over which the machine had just passed, and, showing them a line of newly turned earth, asked them to dig in it. Having done this, they found the pipe incasing the wires, acknowledged his triumph, and immediately gave him and his machine permanent employment.

But before long he became convinced that this was not the best way. Having studied all the books on electricity that he could find in the Congressional Library, he had satisfied himself that it would be far better and cheaper to string the wires through the open air between poles. This idea the men controlling the scheme for a time resisted. Some of them regarded such interference in a scientific matter by one whom they considered a plain working-man as altogether too presuming. But one day Professor Morse came out to decide the matter. Finding Mr. Cornell at his machine, the professor explained the difficulties in the case, especially the danger of shaking the confidence of Congress, and so losing the necessary appropriation, should any change in plan be adopted, and then asked him if he could see any way out of the difficulty. Mr. Cornell answered that he could, whereupon Professor Morse expressed a wish that it might be taken. At this Mr. Cornell gave the word to his men, started up the long line of horses dragging the ponderous machine, guided it with his own hands into a boulder lying near, and thus deranged the whole machinery.

As a natural result it was announced by various journals at the national capital that the machinery for laying the wires had been broken by the carelessness of an employee, but that it would doubtless soon be repaired and the work resumed. Thanks to this stratagem, the necessary time was gained without shaking the confidence of Congress, and Mr. Cornell at once began stringing the wires upon poles: the insulation was found far better than in the underground system, and there was no more trouble.

The confidence of the promoters of the enterprise being thus gained, Mr. Cornell was employed to do their work in all parts of the country; and his sturdy honesty, energy, and persistence justified their confidence and laid the foundations of his fortune.

Very striking were the accounts of his troubles and trials during the prosecution of this telegraphic work—troubles from men of pretended science, from selfish men, from stupid men— all chronicled by him without the slightest bitterness against any human being, yet with a quaint humor which made the story very enjoyable.

Through his personal history, as I then began to learn it, ran a thread, or rather a strong cord, of stoicism. He had clung with such desperate tenacity to his faith in the future of the telegraphic system, that, sooner than part with his interest in it, even when its stock was utterly discredited, he suffered from poverty, and almost from want. While pressing on his telegraphic construction, he had been terribly wounded in a Western railroad accident, but had extricated himself from the dead and dying, and, as I learned from others, had borne his sufferings without a murmur. At another time, overtaken by ship-fever at Montreal, and thought to be beyond help, he had quietly made up his mind that, if he could reach a certain hydropathic establishment in New York, he would recover; and had dragged himself through that long journey, desperately ill as he was, in railway cars, steamers, and stages, until he reached his desired haven; and there he finally recovered, though nearly every other person attacked by the disease at his Montreal hotel had died.

Pursuing his telegraphic enterprise, he had been obliged at times to fight many strong men and great combinations of capital; but this same stoicism carried him through: he used to say laughingly that his way was to "tire them out."

When, at last, fortune had begun to smile upon him, his public spirit began to show itself in more striking forms, though not in forms more real, than in his earlier days. Evidences of this met the eye of his visitors at once, and among these were the fine cattle, sheep, fruit-trees, and the like, which he had brought back from the London Exposition of 1851. His observations of the agricultural experiments of Lawes and Gilbert at Rothamstead in England, and his visits to various agricultural exhibitions, led him to attempt similar work at home. Everything that could improve the community in which he lived was matter of concern to him. He took the lead in establishing "Cascadilla Place," in order to give a very gifted woman an opportunity to show her abilities in administering hydropathic treatment to disease; his public library, when I first visited Ithaca, was just completed.

He never showed the slightest approach to display or vanity regarding any of these things, and most of them I heard of first, at a later period, from others.

Although his religious ideas were very far from those generally considered orthodox, he had a deep sympathy with every good effort for religion and morality, no matter by whom made; and he contributed freely to churches of every name and to good purposes of every sort. He had quaint ways at times in making such gifts, and from the many stories showing these I select one as characteristic. During the Civil War, the young women of the village held large sewing-circles, doing work for the soldiers. When Mr. Cornell was asked to contribute to their funds, he declined, to the great surprise of those who asked him, and said dryly: "Of course these women don't really come together to sew for the soldiers; they come together to gossip." This was said, no doubt, with that peculiar twinkle of the eye which his old friends can well remember; but, on the young ladies protesting that he did them injustice, he answered: "If you can prove that I am wrong, I will gladly contribute; if you will only sew together all one afternoon, and no one of you speak a word, I will give you a hundred dollars." The society met, and complete silence reigned. The young men of the community, hearing of this, and seeing an admirable chance to tease their fair friends, came in large numbers to the sewing-circle, and tried to engage them in conversation. At first their attempts were in vain; but, finally, to a question skilfully put, one of the young ladies made a reply. This broke the spell. Of course, the whole assembly were very unhappy; but, when all was told to Mr. Cornell, he said: "They shall have their hundred dollars, for they have done better than any other women ever did."

But I ought to say here that this little episode would be grossly misunderstood were it supposed to indicate any tendency in his heart or mind toward a cynical view of womankind. Nothing could be more manly and noble than his reference to her who had stood at his side courageously, hopefully, and cheerily during his years of struggle and want of appreciation. Well might he speak of her, as he did once in my hearing, as "the best woman that ever lived." And his gentle courtliness and thoughtful kindness were also deeply appreciated in other households. His earnestness, too, in behalf of the higher education of women, and of their fair treatment in various professions and occupations, showed something far deeper than conventional politeness.

From the time when I began to know him best, his main thought was concentrated upon the university. His own business interests were freely sacrificed; his time, wealth, and effort were all yielded to his work in taking up its lands, to say nothing of supplementary work which became in many ways a heavy burden to him.

During the summer preceding the opening of the university, this labor and care began to wear upon him, and he was attacked by an old malady which gave him great pain; yet his stoicism asserted itself. Through night after night, as I lay in the room next his at his farm-house, I could hear him groan, and to my natural sympathy was added a fear lest he might not live through this most critical period in the history of the new institution; but, invariably, when I met him next morning and asked how he felt, his answer was, "All right," or "Very well." I cannot remember ever hearing him make any complaint of his sufferings or even any reference to them.

Nor did pain diminish his steady serenity or generosity. I remember that on one hot afternoon of that summer, when he had come into the house thoroughly weary, a young man called upon him to ask for aid in securing school-books. Mr. Cornell questioned him closely, and then rose, walked with him down the hill into the town, and bought the books which were needed.

As the day approached for the formal opening of the university, he was obliged to remain in bed. Care and toil had prostrated me also; and both of us, a sorry couple indeed, had to be taken from our beds to be carried to the opening exercises.

A great crowd had assembled from all parts of the State:—many enthusiastic, more doubtful, and some decidedly inclined to scoff.

Some who were expected were not present. The Governor of the State, though he had been in Ithaca the day before, quietly left town on the eve of the opening exercises. His Excellency was a very wise man in his generation, and evidently felt that it was not best for him to have too much to do with an institution which the sectarian press had so generally condemned. I shall not soon forget the way in which Mr. Cornell broke the news to me, and the accent of calm contempt in his voice. Fortunately there remained with us the lieutenant-governor, General Stewart Lyndon Woodford. He came to the front nobly, and stood by us firmly and munificently ever afterward.

Mr. Cornell's speech on that occasion was very simple and noble; his whole position, to one who knew what he had gone through in the way of obloquy, hard work, and self-sacrifice, was touching. Worn down by illness, he was unable to stand, and he therefore read his address in a low tone from his chair. It was very impressive, almost incapacitating me from speaking after him, and I saw tears in the eyes of many in the audience. Nothing could be more simple than this speech of his; it was mainly devoted to a plain assertion of the true university theory in its most elementary form, and to a plea that women should have equal privileges with men in advanced education. In the midst of it came a touch of his quaint shrewdness; for, in replying to a recent charge that everything at the university was unfinished, he remarked in substance, "We have not invited you to see a university finished, but to see one begun."

The opening day seemed a success, but this very success stirred up the enemy. A bitter letter from Ithaca to a leading denominational organ in New York gave the signal, and soon the whole sectarian press was in full cry, steadily pressing upon Mr. Cornell and those who stood near him. Very many of the secular presses also thought it wise to join in the attack, and it was quickly extended from his ideas to his honor, and even to his honesty. It seemed beyond the conception of many of these gentlemen that a Hicksite Quaker, who, if he gave any thought at all to this or that creed, or this or that "plan of salvation," passed it all by as utterly irrelevant and inadequate, could be a religious man; and a far greater number seemed to find it just as difficult to believe that a man could sacrifice his comfort and risk his fortune in managing so great a landed property for the public interest without any concealed scheme of plunder.

But he bore all this with his usual stoicism. It seemed to increase his devotion to the institution, rather than to diminish it. When the receipts from the endowment fell short or were delayed, he continued to advance money freely to meet the salaries of the professors; and for apparatus, books, and equipment of every sort his purse was constantly opened.

Yet, in those days of toil and care and obloquy, there were some things which encouraged him much. At that period all patriotic Americans felt deep gratitude to Goldwin Smith for his courage and eloquence in standing by our country during the Civil War, and great admiration for his profound and brilliant historical lectures at Oxford. Naturally, on arriving in London, I sought to engage him for the new university, and was authorized by Mr. Cornell to make him large pecuniary offers. Professor Smith entered at once into our plans heartily; wrote to encourage us; came to us; lived with us amid what, to him, must have been great privations; lectured for us year after year as brilliantly as he had ever lectured at Oxford; gave his library to the university, with a large sum for its increase; lent his aid very quietly, but none the less effectually, to needy and meritorious students; and steadily refused then, as he has ever since done, and now does, to accept a dollar of compensation. Nothing ever gave Mr. Cornell more encouragement than this. For "Goldwin," as he called him in his Quaker way, there was always a very warm corner in his heart.

He also found especial pleasure in many of the lecture-courses established at the opening of the university. For Professor Agassiz he formed a warm friendship; and their discussions regarding geological questions were very interesting, eliciting from Agassiz a striking tribute to Mr. Cornell's closeness of observation and sagacity in reasoning. The lectures on history by Goldwin Smith, and on literature by James Russell Lowell, George William Curtis, and Bayard Taylor, he also enjoyed greatly.

The scientific collections and apparatus of various sorts gave him constant pleasure. I had sent from England, France, and Germany a large number of charts, models, and pieces of philosophical apparatus, and regarding some of them had thought it best to make careful explanations to him, in order to justify so large an expenditure; but I soon found this unnecessary. His shrewd mind enabled him to understand any piece of apparatus quickly, and to appreciate it fully. I have never had to deal with any man whose instinct in such matters was more true. If a book or scientific specimen or piece of apparatus was necessary to the proper work of a department, he could easily be made to see it; and then it *must* come to us, no matter at what cost. Like the great prince of navigators in the fifteenth century, he was a man "who had the taste for great things"—"*qui tenia gusto en cosas grandes.*" He felt that the university was to be great, and he took his measures accordingly. His colleagues generally thought him over-sanguine; and when he declared that the university should yet have an endowment of three millions, most of them regarded him as a dreamer.

I have never known a man more entirely unselfish. I have seen him, when his wealth was counted in millions, devote it so generously to university objects that he felt it necessary to stint himself in some matters of personal comfort. When urged to sell a portion of the university land at a sacrifice, in order to better our foundations, he answered in substance, "Don't let us do that yet; I will wear my old hat and coat a little longer, and let you have a little more money from my own pocket."

This feeling seemed never diminished, even under the worst opposition. He "kept the faith," no matter who opposed him.

An eminent and justly respected president of one of the oldest Eastern universities published a treatise, which was widely circulated, to prove that the main ideas on which the new university was based were utterly impracticable; and especially that the presentation of various courses of instruction suited to young men of various aims and tastes, with liberty of choice between them, was preposterous. It is interesting to note that this same eminent gentleman was afterward led to adopt this same "impracticable" policy at his own university. Others of almost equal eminence insisted that to give advanced scientific and technical instruction in the same institution with classical instruction was folly; and these gentlemen were probably not converted until the plan was adopted at English Cambridge. Others still insisted that an institution not belonging to any one religious sect must be "godless," would not be patronized, and could not succeed. Their eyes were opened later by the sight of men and women of different Christian denominations pressing forward at Cornell University to contribute sums which, in the aggregate, amounted to much more than the original endowment.

He earned the blessing of those who, not having seen, have yet believed. Though he did not live long enough to see the fundamental principles of the university thus force their way to recognition and adoption by those who had most strongly opposed them, his faith remained undiminished to the end of his life.

But the opposition to his work developed into worse shapes; many leading journals in the State, when not openly hostile to him, were cold and indifferent, and some of them were steadily abusive. This led to a rather wide-spread feeling that "where there is smoke, there must be fire"; and we who knew the purity of his purpose, his unselfishness, his sturdy honesty, labored long against this feeling.

I regret to say that some eminent men connected with important universities in the country showed far too much readiness to acquiesce in this unfavorable view of our founder. From very few of our sister institutions came any word of cheer; and from some of them came most bitter attacks, not only upon the system adopted in the new university, but upon Mr. Cornell himself. But his friends were more afflicted, by far, than he; all this opposition only served to strengthen his faith. As to this effect upon him, I recall one or two quaint examples. At the darkest period in the history of the university, I mentioned to him that a fine collection of mathematical books was offered us for five thousand dollars. Under ordinary circumstances he would have bought it for us at once; but at that moment, when any addition to his burdens would not have been advised by any of his friends, he quietly said, "Somewhere there is a man walking about who wants to give us that five thousand dollars." I am glad to say that his faith was soon justified; such a man appeared,—a man who was glad to give the required sum as a testimony to his belief in Mr. Cornell's integrity: William Kelly of Rhinebeck.

Another example may be given as typical. Near the close of the first celebration of Founder's Day at one of the college buildings, a pleasant social dance sprang up among the younger people—students from the university and young ladies from the village. This brought a very severe protest from sundry clergymen of the place, declaring dancing to be "destructive of vital godliness." Though this was solemnly laid before the faculty, no answer was ever made to it; but we noticed that, at every social gathering on Founder's Day afterward, as long as Mr. Cornell lived, he had arrangements made for dancing. I never knew a man more open to right reason, and never one less influenced by cant or dogmatism.

To most attacks upon him in the newspapers he neither made nor suggested any reply; but one or two which were especially misleading he answered simply and conclusively. This had no effect, of course, in stopping the attacks; but it had one effect, at which the friends of the university rejoiced: it bound his old associates to him all the more closely, and led them to support him all the more vigorously. When a paper in one of the largest cities in western New York had been especially abusive, one of Mr. Cornell's old friends living in that city wrote: "I know that the charges recently published are utterly untrue; but I am not skilled in newspaper controversy, so I will simply add to what I have already given to the university a special gift of thirty thousand dollars, which will testify to my townsmen here, and perhaps to the public at large, my confidence in Mr. Cornell."

Such was the way of Hiram Sibley. Upon another attack, especially violent, from the organ of one of the denominational colleges, another old friend of Mr. Cornell in the eastern part of the State, a prominent member of the religious body which this paper represented, sent his check for several thousand dollars, to be used for the purchase of books for the library, and to show confidence in Mr. Cornell by deeds as well as words.

Vile as these attacks were, worse remained behind. A local politician, who had been sent to the legislature from the district where the "People's College" had lived its short life, prepared, with pettifogging ability, a long speech to show that the foundation of Cornell University, Mr. Cornell's endowment of it, and his contract to locate the lands for it were parts of a great cheat and swindle. This thesis, developed in all the moods and tenses of abuse before the legislature, was next day published at length in the leading journals of the metropolis, and echoed throughout the Union. The time for these attacks was skilfully chosen; the Crédit Mobilier and other schemes had been revealed at Washington, and everybody was only too ready to believe any charge against anybody. That Mr. Cornell had been known for forty years as an honest man seemed to go for nothing.

The enemies of the university were prompt to support the

charges, and they found some echoes even among those who were benefited by his generosity—even among the students themselves. At this I felt it my duty to call the whole student body together, and, in a careful speech, to explain Mr. Cornell's transactions, answering the charges fully. This speech, though spread through the State, could evidently do but little toward righting the wrong; but it brought to me what I shall always feel a great honor—a share in the abuse showered mainly on him.

Very characteristic was Mr. Cornell's conduct under this outrage. That same faith in justice, that same patience under wrong, which he always showed, was more evident than ever.

On the morning after the attack in the legislature had been blazoned in all the leading newspapers—in the early hours, and after a sleepless night—I heard the rattle of gravel against my window-panes. On rising, I found Mr. Cornell standing below. He was serene and cheerful, and had evidently taken the long walk up the hill to quiet my irritation. His first words were a jocose prelude. The bells of the university, which were then chimed at six o'clock, were ringing merrily, and he called out, "Come down here and listen to the chimes; I have found a spot where you can hear them directly with one ear, and their echo with the other."

When I had come down, we first investigated the echo of the chime, which had really aroused his interest; then he said seriously: "Don't make yourself unhappy over this matter; it will turn out to be a good thing for the university. I have long foreseen that this attack must come, but have feared that it would come after my death, when the facts would be forgotten, and the transactions little understood. I am glad that the charges are made now, while I am here to answer them." We then discussed the matter, and it was agreed that he should telegraph and write Governor Dix, asking him to appoint an investigating committee, of which the majority should be from the political party opposed to his own. This was done. The committee was composed of Horatio Seymour, formerly governor of the State and Democratic candidate for the Presidency of the United States; William A. Wheeler, Vice-President of the United States; and John D. Van Buren, all three men of the highest standing, and two of them politically opposed to Mr. Cornell.

During the long investigation which ensued in New York and at Ithaca, he never lost his patience, though at times sorely tried. Various disappointed schemers, among these one person who had not been allowed to make an undue profit out of the university lands, and another who had been allowed to depart from a professorship on account of hopeless incompetency, were the main witnesses. The onslaught was led by the person who made the attack in the legislature, and he had raked together a mass of half-truths and surmises; but the evidence on Mr. Cornell's side consisted of a complete exhibition of all the facts and documents. The unanimous report of the committee was all that his warmest friends could desire; and its recommendations regarding the management of the fund were such as Mr. Cornell had long wished, but which he had hardly dared ask. The result was a complete triumph for him.

Yet the attacks continued. The same paper which had been so prominent in sounding them through the western part of the State continued them as before, and, almost to the very day of his death, assailed him periodically as a "land jobber," "land grabber," and "land thief." But he took these foul attacks by tricky declaimers and his vindication by three of his most eminent fellow-citizens with the same serenity. That there was in him a profound contempt for the wretched creatures who assailed him and imputed to him motives as vile as their own can hardly be doubted; yet, though I was with him constantly during this period, I never heard him speak harshly of them; nor could I ever see that this injustice diminished his good will toward his fellow-men and his desire to benefit them.

At the very time when these attacks were at their worst, he was giving especial thought to the problem of bringing education at the university within reach of young men of good ability and small means. I am quite within bounds in saying that he gave an hour to thought upon this for every minute he gave to thought upon the attacks of his enemies.

It was during this period that he began building his beautiful house near the university, and in this he showed some of his peculiarities. He took much pains to secure a tasteful plan, and some of the ideas embodied in it evidently resulted from his study of beautiful country-houses in England. Characteristic of him also was his way of carrying on the work. Having visited several quarries in various parts of the State, in order to choose the best possible building-stone, he employed some German stone-carvers who had recently left work upon the Cathedral of Cologne, brought them to Ithaca, and allowed them to work on with no interference save from the architect. If they gave a month or more to the carving of a single capital or corbel, he made no remonstrance. When he had thus secured the best stone-work, he selected the best seasoned oak and walnut and called skilful carpenters from England.

In thus going abroad for artisans there was no want of loyalty to his countrymen, nor was there any alloy of vanity in his motives. His purpose evidently was to erect a house which should be as perfect a specimen of the builder's art as he could make it, and therefore useful, as an example of thoroughly good work, to the local workmen.

In connection with this, another incident throws light upon his characteristics. Above the front entrance of the house was a scroll, or ribbon, in stone, evidently intended for a name or motto. The words carved there were, "True and Firm." It is a curious evidence of the petty criticism which beset him in those days, that this motto was at times cited as a proof of his vainglory. It gives me pleasure to relieve any mind sensitive on this point, and to vindicate the truth of history, by saying that it was I who placed the motto there. Calling his attention one day to the scroll and to the need of an inscription, I suggested a translation of the old German motto, *"Treu und Fest"*; and, as he made no objection, I wrote it out for the stonecutters, but told Mr. Cornell that there were people, perhaps, who might translate the last word "obstinate."

The point of this lay in the fact, which Mr. Cornell knew very well, that he was frequently charged with obstinacy. Yet an obstinate man, in the evil sense of that word, he was not. For several years it fell to my lot to discuss a multitude of questions with him, and reasonableness was one of his most striking characteristics. He was one of those very rare strong men who recognize adequately their own limitations. True, when he had finally made up his mind in a matter fully within his own province, he remained firm; but I have known very few men, wealthy, strong, successful, as he was, so free from the fault of thinking that, because they are good judges of one class of questions, they are equally good in all others. One mark of an obstinate man is the announcement of opinions upon subjects regarding which his experience and previous training give him little or no means of judging. This was not at all the case with Mr. Cornell. When questions arose regarding internal university management, or courses of study, or the choice of professors, or plans for their accommodation, he was never quick in announcing or tenacious in holding an opinion. There was no purse pride about him. He evidently did not believe that his success in building up a fortune had made him an expert or judge in questions to which he had never paid special attention.

During the last year or two of his life, I saw not so much of him as during several previous years. He had become greatly interested in various railway projects having as their purpose the connection of Ithaca, as a university town, with the State at large; and he threw himself into these plans with great energy. His course in this was prompted by a public spirit as large and pure as that which had led him to found the university. When, at the suggestion of sundry friends, I ventured to remonstrate with him against going so largely into these railway enterprises at his time of life, he said: "I shall live twenty years longer, and make a million of dollars more

for the university endowment." Alas! within six months from
that day he lay dead in the midst of many broken hopes. His
plans, which, under other circumstances, would have been
judged wise, seemed for a time wrecked by the financial crisis
which had just come upon the country.

In his last hours I visited him frequently. His mind remained clear, and he showed his old freedom from any fault-
finding spirit, though evidently oppressed by business cares and
bodily suffering. His serenity was especially evident as I sat
with him the night before his death, and I can never forget the
placidity of his countenance, both then and on the next morning, when all was ended.

Something should be said regarding Mr. Cornell's political
ideas. In the legislature he was a firm Republican, but as free
as possible from anything like partizan bigotry. Party ties in
local matters sat lightly upon him. He spoke in public very
little, and took far greater interest in public improvement than
in party advantage. With many of his political opponents his
relations were most friendly. For such Democrats as Hiram
Sibley, Erastus Brooks, and William Kelly he had the deepest
respect and admiration. He cared little for popular clamor
on any subject, braving it more than once by his votes in the
legislature. He was evidently willing to take any risk involved in waiting for the sober second thought of the people.
He was as free from ordinary ambition as from selfishness:
when there was a call from several parts of the State for his
nomination as governor, he said quietly, "I prefer work for
which I am better fitted."

There was in his ordinary bearing a certain austerity and in
his conversation an abruptness which interfered somewhat
with his popularity. A student once said to me, "If Mr. Cornell
would simply stand upon his pedestal as our 'Honored
Founder,' and let us hurrah for him, that would please us
mightily; but when he comes into the laboratory and asks us
gruffly, 'What are you wasting your time at now?' we don't
like him so well." The fact on which this remark was based

was that Mr. Cornell liked greatly to walk quietly through the laboratories and drafting-rooms, to note the work. Now and then, when he saw a student doing something which especially interested him, he was evidently anxious, as he was wont to say, "to see what the fellow is made of," and he would frequently put some provoking question, liking nothing better than to receive a pithy answer. Of his kind feelings toward students I could say much. He was not inclined to coddle them, but was ever ready to help any who were deserving.

Despite his apparent austerity, he was singularly free from harshness in his judgments. There were times when he would have been justified in outbursts of bitterness against those who attacked him in ways so foul and maligned him in ways so vile; but I never heard any bitter reply from him. In his politics there was never a drop of bitterness. Only once or twice did I hear him allude to any conduct which displeased him, and then his comments were rather playful than otherwise. On one occasion, when he had written to a gentleman of great wealth and deserved repute as a philanthropist, asking him to join in carrying the burden of the land locations, and had received an unfavorable answer, he made a remark which seemed to me rather harsh. To this I replied: "Mr. Cornell, Mr.—— is not at all in fault; he does not understand the question as you do; everybody knows that he is a very liberal man." "Oh," said Mr. Cornell, "it's easy enough to be liberal; the only hard part is drawing the check."

Of his intellectual characteristics, foresight was the most remarkable. Of all men in the country who had to do with the college land grant of 1862, he alone discerned the possibilities involved and had courage to make them actual.

Clearness of thought on all matters to which he gave his attention was another striking characteristic; hence, whenever he put anything on paper, it was lucid and cogent. There seems at times in his writings some of the clear, quaint shrewdness so well known in Abraham Lincoln. Very striking examples of this are to be found in his legislative speeches, in his address at the opening of the university, and in his letters.

Among his moral characteristics, his truthfulness, persistence, courage, and fortitude were most strongly marked. These qualities made him a man of peace. He regarded life as too short to be wasted in quarrels; his steady rule was never to begin a lawsuit or have anything to do with one, if it could be avoided. The joy in litigation and squabble, which has been the weakness of so many men claiming to be strong, and the especial curse of so many American churches, colleges, universities, and other public organizations, had no place in his strong, tolerant nature. He never sought to publish the sins of any one in the courts or to win the repute of an uncompromising fighter. In this peaceable disposition he was prompted not only by his greatest moral quality:—his charity toward his fellow-men, but by his greatest intellectual quality:—his foresight; for he knew well "the glorious uncertainty of the law." He was a builder, not a gladiator.

There resulted from these qualities an equanimity which I have never seen equaled. When his eldest son had been elected to the highest office in the gift of the State Assembly, and had been placed, evidently, on the way to the governor's chair,—afterward attained,—though it must have gratified such a father, he never made any reference to it in my hearing; and when the body of his favorite grandson, a most winning and promising boy, killed instantly by a terrible accident, was brought into his presence, though his heart must have bled, his calmness seemed almost superhuman.

His religious ideas were such as many excellent people would hardly approve. He had been born into the Society of Friends; and their quietness, simplicity, freedom from noisy activity, and devotion to the public good attached him to them. But his was not a bigoted attachment; he went freely to various churches, aiding them without distinction of sect, though finally he settled into a steady attendance at the Unitarian Church in Ithaca, for the pastor of which he conceived a great respect and liking. He was never inclined to say much about religion; but, in our talks, he was wont to quote with approval from Pope's "Universal Prayer"—and especially the lines:

> "Teach me to feel another's woe,
>   To hide the fault I see;
> The mercy I to others show,
>   That mercy show to me."

On the mere letter of Scripture he dwelt little; and, while he never obtruded opinions that might shock any person, and was far removed from scoffing or irreverence, he did not hesitate to discriminate between parts of our Sacred Books which he considered as simply legendary and parts which were to him pregnant with eternal truth.

His religion seemed to take shape in a deeply reverent feeling toward his Creator, and in a constant desire to improve the condition of his fellow-creatures. He was never surprised or troubled by anything which any other human being believed or did not believe; of intolerance he was utterly incapable. He sought no reputation as a philanthropist, cared little for approval, and nothing for applause; but I can say of him, without reserve, that, during all the years I knew him, "he went about doing good."

7.

ORGANIZATION OF CORNELL UNIVERSITY

1865–1868

A LTHOUGH MY FORMAL ELECTION TO THE UNIVERSITY
presidency did not take place until 1867, the duties im-
plied by that office had already been discharged by me during
two years.

While Mr. Cornell devoted himself to the financial questions
arising from the new foundation, he intrusted all other questions to me. Indeed, my duties may be said to have begun
when, as chairman of the Committee on Education in the
State Senate, I resisted all efforts to divide the land-grant fund
between the People's College and the State Agricultural College; to have been continued when I opposed the frittering
away of the entire grant among more than twenty small
sectarian colleges; and to have taken a more direct form when
I drafted the educational clauses of the university charter and
advocated it before the legislature and in the press. This
advocacy was by no means a light task. The influential men
who flocked to Albany, seeking to divide the fund among
various sects and localities, used arguments often plausible and
sometimes forcible. These I dealt with on various occasions,
but especially in a speech before the State Senate in 1865, in
which was shown the character of the interested opposition,
the farcical equipment of the People's College, the failure of

the State Agricultural College, the inadequacy of the sectarian colleges, even though they called themselves universities; and I did all in my power to communicate to my colleagues something of my own enthusiasm for a university suitably endowed, free from sectarian trammels, centrally situated, and organized to meet fully the wants of the State as regarded advanced education, general and technical.

Three points I endeavored especially to impress upon them in this speech. First, that while, as regards primary education, the policy of the State should be diffusion of resources, it should be, as regards university education, concentration of resources. Secondly, that sectarian colleges could not do the work required. Thirdly, that any institution for higher education in the State must form an integral part of the whole system of public instruction; that the university should not be isolated from the school system, as were the existing colleges, but that it should have a living connection with the system, should push its roots down into it and through it, drawing life from it and sending life back into it. Mr. Cornell accepted this view at once. Mr. Horace Greeley, who, up to that time, had supported the People's College, was favorably impressed by it, and, more than anything else, it won for us his support. To insure this vital connection of the proposed university with the school system, I provided in the charter for four "State scholarships" in each of the one hundred and twenty-eight Assembly districts. These scholarships were to be awarded to the best scholars in the public schools of each district, after due examination, one each year; each scholarship entitling the holder to free instruction in the university for four years. Thus the university and the schools were bound closely together by the constant and living tie of five hundred and twelve students. As the number of Assembly districts under the new constitution was made, some years later, one hundred and fifty, the number of these competitive free scholarships is now six hundred. They have served their purpose well. Thirty years of this connection have greatly uplifted the whole school system of the State, and made the university a life-giving power in it; while this uplifting of the school system has enabled the university steadily to raise and improve its own standard of instruction.

But during the earlier period of our plans there was one serious obstacle—Charles James Folger. He was the most powerful member of the Senate, its president, and chairman of the Judiciary Committee. He had already won wide respect as a county judge, had been longer in the Senate than any other member, and had already given ample evidence of the qualities which later in life raised him to some of the highest positions, State and National. His instincts would have brought him to our side; for he was broad-minded, enlightened, and earnestly in favor of all good legislation. He was also my personal friend, and when I privately presented my views to him he acquiesced in them. But there were two difficulties. First, he had in his own city a denominational college, his own alma mater, which, though small, was influential. Still worse for us, he had in his district the State Agricultural College, which the founding of Cornell University must necessarily wipe out of existence. He might rise above the first of these difficulties, but the second seemed insurmountable. No matter how much in sympathy with our main aim, he could not sacrifice a possession so dear to his constituency as the State College of Agriculture. He felt that he had no right to do so; he knew also that to do so would be to sacrifice his political future, and we felt, as he did, that he had no right to do this.

But here came in to help us the culmination of a series of events as unexpected as that which had placed the land-grant fund at our disposal just at the time when Mr. Cornell and myself met in the State Senate. For years a considerable body of thoughtful men throughout the State, more especially of the medical profession, had sought to remedy a great evil in the treatment of the insane. As far back as the middle of the century, Senator Bradford of Cortland had taken the lead in an investigation of the system then existing, and his report was a frightful exposure. Throughout the State, lunatics whose families were unable to support them at the State or private asylums were huddled together in the poorhouses of the various counties. Their condition was heartrending. They were constantly exposed to neglect, frequently to extremes of cold and hunger, and sometimes to brutality: thus mild lunacy often became raving madness. For some years before my election to the Senate the need of a reform had been urged upon the legislative committees by a physician—Dr. Willard of Albany. He had taken this evil condition of things much to heart, and year after year had come before the legislature urging the creation of a new institution, which he wished named after an eminent physician of Albany who had in his day done what was possible to remedy the evil—Dr. Beck. But year after year Dr. Willard's efforts, like those of Dr. Beck before him, had been in vain. Session after session the "Bill to establish the Beck Asylum for the Chronic Insane" was rejected,—the legislature shrinking from the cost of it. But one day, as we were sitting in the Senate, appalling news came from the Assembly: Dr. Willard, while making one more passionate appeal for the asylum, had fallen dead in the presence of the committee. The result was a deep and wide-spread feeling of compunction, and while we were under the influence of this I sought Judge Folger and showed him his opportunity to do two great things. I said: "It rests with you to remedy this cruel evil which has now cost Dr. Willard his life, and at the same time to join us in carrying the Cornell University Bill. Let the legislature create a new asylum for the chronic insane of the State. Now is the time of all times. Instead of calling it the Beck Asylum, give it the name of Willard—the man who died in advocating it. Place it upon the Agricultural College property on the shores of Seneca Lake in your district. Your constituents are sure to prefer a living State asylum to a dying Agricultural College, and will thoroughly support you in both the proposed measures." This suggestion Judge Folger received with favor. The Willard Asylum was created, and he became one of our strongest supporters.

Both Mr. Cornell's financial plans and my educational plans in the new university charter were wrought into final shape by him. As chairman of the Judiciary Committee he reported our bill to the Senate, and at various critical periods gave us his earnest support. Quite likely doctrinaires will stigmatize our conduct in this matter as "log-rolling"; the men who always criticize but never construct may even call it a "bargain." There was no "bargain" and no "log-rolling," but they may call it what they like; I believe that we were both of us thoroughly in the right. For our coming together in this way gave to the State the Willard Asylum and the Cornell University, and without our thus coming together neither of these would have been created.

But in spite of this happy compromise, the struggle for our university charter, as has already been seen, was long and severe. The opposition of over twenty sectarian colleges, and of active politicians from every quarter of the State where these colleges had been established, made our work difficult; but at last it was accomplished. Preparations for the new institution were now earnestly pressed on, and for a year I gave up very much of my time to them, keeping in constant communication with Mr. Cornell, frequently visiting Ithaca, and corresponding with trustees in various parts of the State and with all others at home or abroad who seemed able to throw light on any of the problems we had to solve.

The question now arose as to the presidency of the institution; and, as time passed on and duties increased, this became more and more pressing. In the previous chapter I have given some account of the circumstances attending my election and of Mr. Cornell's relation to it; but this is perhaps the place for stating one of the difficulties which stood in the way of my acceptance, and which, indeed, greatly increased my cares during all the first years of my presidency. The death of my

father and uncle, who had for many years carried on a large
and wide-spread business, threw upon me new responsibilities. It was during the Civil War, when panic after panic ran
through the American business world, making the interests
now devolving upon me all the more burdensome. I had no
education for business and no liking for it, but, under the
pressure of necessity, decided to do the best I could, yet de-
termining that just as soon as these business affairs could be
turned over to others it should be done. Several years elapsed,
and those the busiest so far as the university was concerned,
before such a release became possible. So it happened that
during the first and most trying years of the new institution
of Ithaca, I was obliged to do duty as senator of the State of
New York, president of Cornell University, lecturer at the
University of Michigan, president of the National Bank of
Syracuse and director in two other banks,—one being at Oswego,—director in the New York Central and Lake Shore railways, director in the Albemarle and Chesapeake Canal,—to
say nothing of positions on boards of various similar corporations and the executorship of two widely extended estates.
It was a trying time for me. There was, however, some advantage; for this epoch in my life put me in relations with some
of the foremost business men in the United States, among them
Cornelius Vanderbilt, William H. Vanderbilt, Dean Richmond,
Daniel Drew, and various other men accustomed to prompt
and decisive dealing with large business affairs. I recognized
the value of such associations and endeavored to learn something from them, but was determined, none the less, to end
this sort of general activity as early as it could be done con-
sistently with justice to my family. Several years were required, and those the very years in which university cares were
most pressing. But finally my intention was fully carried out.
The bank over which my father had presided so many years I
was able to wind up in a way satisfactory to all concerned,
not only repaying the shareholders, but giving them a large
surplus. From the other corporations also I gradually escaped,

turning my duties over to those better fitted for them. Still many outside cares remained, and in one way or another I was obliged to take part in affairs which I would have gladly shunned. Yet there was consolation in the idea that, as my main danger was that of drifting into a hermit life among professors and books, anything that took me out of this for a limited length of time was not without compensating advantages.

Just previously to my election to the university presidency I had presented a "plan of organization," which, having been accepted and printed by the trustees, formed the mold for the main features of the new institution; and early among my duties came the selection and nomination of professors. In these days one is able to choose from a large body of young men holding fellowships in the various larger universities of the United States; but then, with the possible exception of two or three at Harvard, there was not a fellowship, so far as I can remember, in the whole country. The choosing of professors was immeasurably more difficult than at present. With reference to this point, a very eminent graduate of Harvard then volunteered to me some advice, which at first sight looked sound, but which I soon found to be inapplicable. He said: "You must secure at any cost the foremost men in the United States in every department. In this way alone can a real university be created." Trying the Socratic method upon him, I asked, in reply, "How are we to get such men? The foremost man in American science is undoubtedly Agassiz, but he has refused all offers of high position at Paris made him by the French Emperor. The main objects of his life are the creation of his great museum at Harvard and his investigations and instruction in connection with it; he has declared that he has 'no time to waste in making money!' What sum or what inducement of any sort can transfer him from Harvard to a new institution on the distant hills of central New York? So, too, with the most eminent men at the other universities. What sum will draw them to us from Harvard, Yale, Columbia, the

University of Virginia, and the University of Michigan? An endowment twice as large as ours would be unavailing." Therefore it was that I broached, as a practical measure, in my "plan of organization," the system which I had discussed tentatively with George William Curtis several years before, and to which he referred afterward in his speech at the opening of the university at Ithaca. This was to take into our confidence the leading professors in the more important institutions of learning, and to secure from them, not the ordinary, conventional paper testimonials, but confidential information as to their young men likely to do the best work in various fields, to call these young men to our resident professorships, and then to call the most eminent men we could obtain for non-resident professorships or lectureships. This idea was carried out to the letter. The most eminent men in various universities gave us confidential advice; and thus it was that I was enabled to secure a number of bright, active, energetic young men as our resident professors, mingling with them two or three older men, whose experience and developed judgment seemed necessary in the ordinary conduct of our affairs.

As to the other part of the plan, I secured Agassiz, Lowell, Curtis, Bayard Taylor, Goldwin Smith, Theodore Dwight, George W. Greene, John Stanton Gould, and at a later period Froude, Freeman, and others, as non-resident professors and lecturers. Of the final working of this system I shall speak later.

The question of buildings also arose; but, alas! I could not reproduce my air-castles. For our charter required us to have the university in operation in October, 1868, and there was no time for careful architectural preparation. Moreover, the means failed us. All that we could then do was to accept a fairly good plan for our main structures; to make them simple, substantial, and dignified; to build them of stone from our own quarries; and so to dispose them that future architects might so combine other buildings with them as to form an impressive quadrangle on the upper part of the university property. To this plan Mr. Cornell gave his hearty assent. It was then arranged, with his full sanction, that the university buildings should ultimately consist of two great groups: the first or upper group to be a quadrangle of stone, and the second or lower group to be made up of buildings of brick more freely disposed, according to our future needs and means. Although this plan has unfortunately been departed from in some minor respects, it has in general turned out well.

Having called a number of professors and seen foundations laid for "Morrill Hall," I sailed in April of 1868 for Europe, in order to study technical institutions, to purchase needed equipment, and to secure certain professors such as could not then be found in our own country. Thus far my knowledge of higher education in Europe had been confined almost entirely to the universities; but now I went carefully through various technical institutions, among them the English Agricultural College at Cirencester, the Agricultural Experiment Station at Rothamstead, the French Agricultural College at Grignon, the Conservatoire des Arts et Métiers at Paris, the Veterinary School at Alfort, the German Agricultural College at Hohenheim, the Technical School and Veterinary College at Berlin, and others. As to equipment, wherever I found valuable material I bought it. Thus were brought together for our library a very large collection of books in all the principal departments; physical and chemical apparatus from London, Paris, Heidelberg, and Berlin; chemicals from Berlin and Erfurt; the only duplicate of the royal collection of cereals and grasses and the great collection of British patent-office publications from the British imperial authorities; the Rau models of plows from Hohenheim; the Brendel plant models from Breslau; the models of machine movements from London, Darmstadt, and Berlin; the plastic models of Auzoux from Paris; and other apparatus and instruments from all parts of Europe, with diagrams and drawings from every institution where I could find them. During three months, from funds furnished by the university, by Mr. Cornell personally, and, I may be allowed to add, from my own personal resources, I expended for these purposes over sixty thousand dollars, a sum which in those days represented much more than in these.

As to non-resident professors, I secured in London Goldwin Smith, who had recently distinguished himself by his works as a historian and as regius professor of history at Oxford; and I was successful in calling Dr. James Law, who, though a young man, had already made himself a name in veterinary science. It seemed to many a comical juxtaposition, and various witticisms were made at my expense over the statement that I had "brought back an Oxford professor and a Scotch horse-doctor." But never were selections more fortunate. Goldwin Smith, by his high character, his broad and deep scholarship, his devotion not only to his professorship but to the general university work, his self-denial in behalf of the university and its students, rendered priceless services. He bore all privations cheerfully and braved all discouragements manfully. Never were there better historical lectures than his. They inspired us all, and the impulse then given is still felt. So, too, Dr. Law, in his field, was invaluable, and this was soon felt throughout the State. Of him I shall speak later.

~~~~~~

8.

THE FIRST YEARS OF CORNELL UNIVERSITY

1868–1870

───

O N THE 7TH OF OCTOBER, 1868, CAME THE FORMAL OPEN-
ing of the university. The struggle for its charter had
attracted much attention in all parts of the State, and a large
body of spectators, with about four hundred students, assembled at the Cornell Library Hall in Ithaca. Though the
charter had required us to begin in October, there had seemed
for some time very little chance of it. Mr. Cornell had been
absent in the woods of the upper Mississippi and on the
plains of Kansas, selecting university lands; I had been absent
for some months in Europe, securing plans and equipment;
and as, during our absence, the contractor for the first main
building, Morrill Hall, had failed, the work was wretchedly
behindhand. The direct roads to the university site were as
yet impracticable, for the Cascadilla ravine and the smaller
one north of it were still unbridged. The grounds were unkempt, with heaps of earth and piles of material in all di-
rections. The great quantities of furniture, apparatus, and
books which I had sent from Europe had been deposited
wherever storage could be found. Typical was the case of the
large Holtz electrical machine from Germany. It was in those
days a novelty, and many were anxious to see it; but it could
not be found, and it was only discovered several weeks later,

when the last pots and pans were pulled out of the kitchen store-room in the cellar of the great stone barrack known as Cascadilla House. All sorts of greatly needed material had been delayed in steamships and on railways, or was stuck fast in custom-houses and warehouses from Berlin and Paris to Ithaca. Our friends had toiled heroically during our absence, but the little town—then much less energetic than now —had been unable to furnish the work required in so short a time. The heating apparatus and even the doors for the students' rooms were not in place until weeks after winter weather had set in. To complicate matters still more, students began to come at a period much earlier and in numbers far greater than we had expected; and the first result of this was that, in getting ready for the opening, Mr. Cornell and myself were worn out. For two or three days before my inauguration both of us were in the hands of physicians and in bed, and on the morning of the day appointed we were taken in carriages to the hall where the ceremony was to take place. To Mr. Cornell's brief speech I have alluded elsewhere; my own presented my ideas more at length. They were grouped in four divisions. The first of these related to "Foundation Ideas," which were announced as follows: First, the close union of liberal and practical instruction; second, unsectarian control; third, a living union between the university and the whole school system of the State; fourth, concentration of revenues for advanced education. The second division was that of "Formative Ideas"; and under these—First, equality between different courses of study. In this I especially developed ideas which had occurred to me as far back as my observations after graduation at Yale, where the classical students belonging to the "college proper" were given a sort of supremacy, and scientific students relegated to a separate institution at considerable distance, and therefore deprived of much general, and even special, culture which would have greatly benefited them. Indeed, they seemed not considered as having any souls to be saved, since no provision was made for them at the college chapel. Second, increased development of scientific studies. The third main division was that of "Governmental Ideas"; and under these—First, "the regular and frequent infusion of new life into the governing board." Here a system at that time entirely new in the United States was proposed. Instead of the usual life tenure of trustees, their term was made five years and they were to be chosen by ballot. Secondly, it was required that as soon as the graduates of the university numbered fifty they should select one trustee each year, thus giving the alumni one third of the whole number elected. Third, there was to be a system of self-government administered by the students themselves. As to this third point, I must frankly confess that my ideas were vague, unformed, and finally changed by the logic of events. As the fourth and final main division, I presented "Permeating Ideas"; and of these—First, the development of the individual man in all his nature, in all his powers, as a being intellectual, moral, and religious. Secondly, bringing the powers of the man thus developed to bear usefully upon society.

In conclusion, I alluded to two groups of "Eliminated Ideas," the first of these being the "Ideas of the Pedants," and the second the "Ideas of the Philistines." As to the former, I took pains to guard the institution from those who, in the higher education, substitute dates for history, gerund-grinding for literature, and formulas for science; as to the latter, I sought to guard it from the men to whom "Gain is God, and Gunnybags his Prophet."

At the close, referring to Mr. Cornell, who had been too weak to stand while delivering his speech, and who was at that moment sitting near me, I alluded to his noble plans and to the opposition, misrepresentation, and obloquy he had met thus far, and in doing so turned toward him. The sight of him, as he thus sat, looking so weak, so weary, so broken, for a few moments utterly incapacitated me. I was myself, at the time, in but little better condition than he; and as there rushed into my mind memories of the previous ten days at his house, when I had heard him groaning in pain through almost every night, it flashed upon me how utterly hopeless was the university without his support. My voice faltered; I could for a moment say nothing; then came a revulsion. I asked myself, "What will this great audience think of us?" How will our enemies, some of whom I see scattered about the audience, exult over this faltering at the outset! A feeling of shame came over me; but just at that moment I saw two or three strong men from different parts of the State, among them my old friend Mr. Sedgwick of Syracuse, in the audience, and Mr. Sage and Mr. McGraw among the trustees, evidently affected by my allusion to the obloquy and injustice which Mr. Cornell had met thus far. This roused me. But I could no longer read; I laid my manuscript aside and gave the ending in words which occurred to me as I stood then and there. They were faltering and inadequate; but I felt that the vast majority in that audience, representing all parts of our commonwealth, were with us, and I asked nothing more.

In the afternoon came exercises at the university grounds. The chime of nine bells which Miss Jenny McGraw had presented to us had been temporarily hung in a wooden tower placed very near the spot where now stands the porch of the library; and, before the bells were rung for the first time, a presentation address was delivered by Mr. Francis Miles Finch, since justice of the Court of Appeals of the State and dean of the University Law School; and this was followed by addresses from the superintendent of public instruction, and from our non-resident professors Agassiz and George William Curtis.

Having again been taken out of bed and wrapped up carefully, I was carried up the hill to hear them. All the speeches were fine; but, just at the close, Curtis burst into a peroration which, in my weak physical condition, utterly unmanned me. He compared the new university to a newly launched ship—"all its sails set, its rigging full and complete from stem to stern, its crew embarked, its passengers on board; and," he added, "even while I speak to you, even while this autumn sun sets in the west, the ship begins to glide over the waves, it goes forth rejoicing, every stitch of canvas spread, all its colors flying, its bells ringing, its heart-strings beating with hope and joy; and I say, God bless the ship, God bless the builder, God bless the chosen captain, God bless the crew, and, gentlemen undergraduates, may God bless all the passengers!"

The audience applauded; the chimes burst merrily forth; but my heart sank within me. A feeling of "goneness" came over me.· Curtis's simile was so perfect that I felt myself indeed on the deck of the ship, but not so much in the character of its "chosen captain" as of a seasick passenger. There was indeed reason for qualmish feelings. Had I drawn a picture of the ship at that moment, it would have been very different from that presented by Curtis. My mind was pervaded by our discouragements—by a realization of Mr. Cornell's condition and my own, the demands of our thoughtless friends, the attacks of our fanatical enemies, the inadequacy of our resources. The sense of all these things burst upon me, and the view about us was not reassuring. Not only were the university buildings unready and the grounds unkempt, but all that part of our domain which is now devoted to the beautiful lawns about the university chapel, Barnes Hall, Sage College, and other stately edifices, was then a ragged corn-field surrounded by rail fences. No one knew better than I the great difficulties which were sure to beset us. Probably no ship was ever launched in a condition so unfit to brave the storms. Even our lesser difficulties, though they may appear comical now, were by no means comical then. As a rule, Mr. Cornell had consulted me before making communications to the public; but during my absence in Europe he had written a letter to the "New York Tribune," announcing that students could support themselves, while pursuing their studies one half of each day in the university, by laboring the other half. In this he showed that sympathy with needy and meritorious young men which was one of his marked qualities, but his proclamation cost us dear. He measured the earnestness and endurance and self-sacrifice of others by his own; he did not realize that not one man in a thousand was, in these respects, his equal. As a result of this "Tribune" letter, a multitude of eager young men pressed forward at the opening of the university and insisted on receiving self-supporting work. Nearly all of those who could offer skilled labor of any sort we were able to employ; and many graduates of whom Cornell University is now proud supported themselves then by working as carpenters, masons, printers, accountants, and shorthand-writers. But besides these were many who had never done any manual labor, and still more who had never done any labor requiring skill. An attempt was made to employ these in grading roads, laying out paths, helping on the farm, doing janitors' work, and the like. Some of them were successful; most were not. It was found that it would be cheaper to support many of the applicants at a hotel and to employ day-laborers in their places. Much of their work had to be done over again at a cost greater than the original outlay should have been. Typical was the husking of Indian corn upon the university farm by student labor: it was found to cost more than the resultant corn could be sold for in the market. The expectations of these youth were none the less exuberant. One of them, who had never done any sort of manual labor, asked whether, while learning to build machinery and supporting himself and his family, he could not lay up something against contingencies. Another, a teamster from a Western State, came to offer his services, and, on being asked what he wished to study, said that he wished to learn to read; on being told that the public school in his own district was the place for that, he was very indignant, and quoted Mr. Cornell's words, "I would found an institution where any person can find instruction in any study." Others, fairly good scholars, but of delicate build, having applied for self-supporting employment, were assigned the lightest possible tasks upon the university grounds; but, finding even this work too severe, wrote bitterly to leading metropolitan journals denouncing Mr. Cornell's

bad faith.   One came all the way from Russia, being able to
make the last stages of his journey only by charity, and on
arriving was found to be utterly incapable of sustained effort,
physical or mental.   The most definite part of his aims, as he
announced them, was to convert the United States to the Russo-
Greek Church.

Added to these were dreamers and schemers of more mature
age.   The mails were burdened with their letters and our
offices with their presence.   Some had plans for the regenera-
tion of humanity by inventing machines which they wished us
to build, some by devising philosophies which they wished us
to teach, some by writing books which they wished us to print;
most by taking professorships which they wished us to endow.
The inevitable politician also appeared; and at the first meeting of the trustees two notorious party hacks came all the way
from New York to tell us "what the people expected,"—which
was the nomination of sundry friends of theirs to positions in
the new institution.   A severe strain was brought upon Mr.
Cornell and myself in showing civility to these gentlemen;
yet, as we were obliged to deny them, no suavity on our part
could stay the inevitable result—their hostility.   The attacks of
the denominational and local presses in the interests of institutions which had failed to tear the fund in pieces and to
secure scraps of it were thus largely reinforced.   Ever and
anon came onslaughts upon us personally and upon every
feature of the institution, whether actual, probable, possible, or
conceivable.   One eminent editorial personage, having vainly
sought to "unload" a member of his staff into one of our professorships, howled in a long article at the turpitude of Mr.
Cornell in land matters, screamed for legislative investigation,
and for years afterward never neglected an opportunity to
strike a blow at the new institution.

Some difficulties also showed themselves in the first working of our university machinery.   In my "plan of organization,"
as well as in various addresses and reports, I had insisted that
the university should present various courses of instruction,

general and special, and that students should be allowed much liberty of choice between these. This at first caused serious friction. It has disappeared, now that the public schools of the State have adjusted themselves to the proper preparation of students for the various courses; but at that time these difficulties were in full force and vigor. One of the most troublesome signs of this was the changing and shifting by students from course to course, which both injured them and embarrassed their instructors. To meet this tendency I not only addressed the students to show that good, substantial, continuous work on any one course which any one of them was likely to choose was far better than indecision and shifting about between various courses, but also reprinted for their use John Foster's famous "Essay on Decision of Character." This tractate had done me much good in my student days and at various times since, when I had allowed myself to linger too long between different courses of action; and I now distributed it freely, the result being that students generally made their election between courses with increased care, and when they had made it stood by it.

Yet for these difficulties in getting the student body under way there were compensations, and best of these was the character and bearing of the students. There were, of course, sundry exhibitions of boyishness, but the spirit of the whole body was better than that of any similar collection of young men I had ever seen. One reason was that we were happily spared any large proportion of rich men's sons, but the main reason was clearly the permission of choice between various courses of study in accordance with individual aims and tastes. In this way a far larger number were interested than had ever been under the old system of forcing all alike through one simple, single course, regardless of aims and tastes; and thus it came that, even from the first, the tone at Cornell was given, not by men who affected to despise study, but by men who devoted themselves to study. It evidently became disreputable for any student not to be really at work in some one of the many courses presented. There were few cases really calling for discipline. I prized this fact all the more because it justified a theory of mine. I had long felt that the greatest cause of student turbulence and dissipation was the absence of interest in study consequent upon the fact that only one course was provided, and I had arrived at the conclusion that providing various courses, suited to various aims and tastes, would diminish this evil.

As regards student discipline in the university, I had dwelt in my "plan of organization" upon the advisability of a departure from the system inherited from the English colleges, which was still widely prevailing. It had been developed in America probably beyond anything known in Great Britain and Germany, and was far less satisfactory than in these latter countries, for the simple reason that in them the university authorities have some legal power to secure testimony and administer punishment, while in America they have virtually none. The result had been most unfortunate, as I have shown in other parts of these chapters referring to various student escapades in the older American universities, some of them having cost human life. I had therefore taken the ground that, so far as possible, students should be treated as responsible citizens; that, as citizens, they should be left to be dealt with by the constituted authorities; and that members of the faculty should no longer be considered as policemen. I had, during my college life, known sundry college tutors seriously injured while thus doing police duty; I have seen a professor driven out of a room, through the panel of a door, with books, boots, and bootjacks hurled at his head; and even the respected president of a college, a doctor of divinity, while patrolling buildings with the janitors, subjected to outrageous indignity.

Fortunately the causes already named, to which may be added athletic sports, especially boating, so greatly diminished student mischief at Cornell, that cases of discipline were reduced to a minimum—so much so, in fact, that there were hardly ever any of a serious character. I felt that then and there was the time to reiterate the doctrine laid down in my "plan of organization," that a professor should not be called upon to be a policeman, and that if the grounds were to be policed, proper men should be employed for that purpose. This doctrine was reasonable and it prevailed. The Cornell grounds and buildings, under the care of a patrol appointed for that purpose, have been carefully guarded, and never has a member of the faculty been called upon to perform police duty.

There were indeed some cases requiring discipline by the faculty, and one of these will provoke a smile on the part of all who took part in it as long as they shall live. There had come to us a stalwart, sturdy New Englander, somewhat above the usual student age, and showing considerable aptitude for studies in engineering. Various complaints were made against him; but finally he was summoned before the faculty for a very singular breach of good taste, if not of honesty. The entire instructing body of that day being gathered about the long table in the faculty room, and I being at the head of the table, the culprit was summoned, entered, and stood solemnly before us. Various questions were asked him, which he parried with great ingenuity. At last one was asked of a very peculiar sort, as follows: "Mr. ———, did you, last month, in the village of Dundee, Yates County, pass yourself off as Professor ——— of this university, announcing a lecture and delivering it in his name?" He answered blandly, "Sir, I did go to Dundee in Yates County; I did deliver a lecture there; I did *not* announce myself as Professor ——— of Cornell University; what others may have done I do not know; all I know is that at the close of my lecture several leading men of the town came forward and said that they had heard a good many lectures given by college professors from all parts of the State, and that they had never had one as good as mine." I think, of all the strains upon my risible faculties during my life, this answer provoked the greatest, and the remainder of the faculty were clearly in the same condition. I dismissed the youth at once, and hardly was he outside the door when a burst of titanic laughter shook the court and the youth was troubled no more.

Far more serious was another case. The usual good-natured bickering between classes had gone on, and as a consequence certain sophomores determined to pay off some old scores against members of the junior class, at a junior exhibition. To do this they prepared a "mock programme," which, had it been merely comic, as some others had been, would have provoked no ill feeling. Unfortunately, some miscreant succeeded in introducing into it allusions of a decidedly Rabelaisian character. The evening arrived, a large audience of ladies and gentlemen were assembled, and this programme was freely distributed. The proceeding was felt to be an outrage; and I served notice on the class that the real offender or offenders, if they wished to prevent serious consequences to all concerned, must submit themselves to the faculty and take due punishment. Unfortunately, they were not manly enough to do this. Thereupon, to my own deep regret and in obedience to my sense of justice, I suspended indefinitely from the university the four officers of the class, its president, vice-president, secretary, and treasurer. They were among the very best men in the class, all of them friends of my own; and I knew to a certainty that they had had nothing directly to do with the articles concerned, that the utmost which could be said against them was that they had been careless as to what appeared in the programme, for which they were responsible. Most bitter feeling arose, and I summoned a meeting of the entire student body. As I entered the room hisses were heard; the time had evidently come for a grapple with the whole body. I stated the case as it was: that the four officers would be suspended and must leave the university town until their return was allowed by the faculty; that such an offense against decency could not be condoned; that I had understood that the entire class proposed to make common cause with their officers and leave the university with them; that to this we interposed no objection; that it simply meant less work for the faculty during the remainder of the year; that it was far more important for the university to maintain a character for decency and good discipline than to have a large body of students; and that, if necessary to maintain such a character, we would certainly allow the whole student body in all the classes to go home and would begin anew. I then drew a picture. I sketched a member of the class who had left the university on account of this discipline entering the paternal door, encountering a question as to the cause of his unexpected home-coming, and replying that the cause was the outrageous tyranny of the president and faculty. I pictured, then, the father and mother of the home-coming student asking what the cause or pretext of this "tyranny" was, and I then said: "I defy any one of you to show your father and mother the 'mock programme' which has caused the trouble. There is not one of you here who dares do it; there is not one of you who would not be turned out of his father's door if he were thus to insult his mother." At this there came a round of applause. I then expressed my personal regret that the penalty must fall upon four men whom I greatly respected; but fall it must unless the offenders were manly enough to give themselves up. The result was that at the close I was greeted with a round of applause; and immediately afterward the four officers came to me, acknowledged the justice of the discipline, and expressed the hope that their suspension might not go beyond that term. It did not: at the close of the term they were allowed to return; and from that day "mock programmes" of the sort concerned, which in many American colleges had been a chronic evil, never reappeared at Cornell. The result of this action encouraged me greatly as to the reliance to be placed on the sense of justice in the great body of our students when directly and properly appealed to.

Still another thing which I sought to promote was a reasonable devotion to athletics. My own experience as a member of a boating-club at Yale had shown me what could be done, and I think one of the best investments I ever made was in giving a racing-boat to the Cornell crew on Cayuga Lake. The fact that there were so many students trained sturdily in rural homes in the bracing air of western New York, who on every working-day of college life tramped up the University Hill, and on other days explored the neighboring hills and vales, gave us a body of men sure to do well as athletes. At their first contest with the other universities on the Connecticut River at Springfield they were beaten, but they took their defeat manfully. Some time after this, General Grant, then President of the United States, on his visit to the university, remarked to me that he saw the race at Springfield; that our young men ought to have won it; and that, in his opinion, they would have won it if they had not been unfortunately placed in shallow water, where there were eddies making against them. This remark struck me forcibly, coming as it did from one who had so keen a judgment in every sort of contest. I bore it in mind, and was not surprised when, a year or two later (1875), the Cornell crews, having met at Saratoga Lake the crews from Harvard, Yale, and other leading universities, won both the freshman and university races. It was humorously charged against me that when the news of this reached Ithaca I rang the university bells. This was not the fact. The simple truth was that, being in the midst of a body of students when the news came, and seeing them rush toward the bell-tower, I went with them to prevent injury to the bells by careless ringing; the ringing was done by them. I will not deny that the victory pleased me, as many others since gained by the Cornell crews have done; but far more to me than the victory itself was a letter written me by a prominent graduate of Princeton who was at Saratoga during the contest. He wrote me, as he said, not merely to congratulate me on the victory, but on the fine way in which our students took it, and the manly qualities which they showed in the hour of triumph and during their whole stay at Saratoga. This gave me courage. From that day I have never felt any fears as to the character of the student body. One leading cause of the success of Cornell University, in the midst of all its trials and struggles, has been the character of its students: working as they do under a system which gives them an interest in the studies they are pursuing, they have used the large liberty granted them in a way worthy of all praise.

Nor is this happy change seen at Cornell alone. The same causes,—mainly the increase in the range of studies and freedom of choice between them, have produced similar results in all the leading institutions. Recalling the student brawl at the Harvard commons which cost the historian Prescott his sight, and the riot at the Harvard commencement which blocked the way of President Everett and the British minister; recalling the fatal wounding of Tutor Dwight, the maiming of Tutor Goodrich, and the killing of two town rioters by students at Yale; and recalling the monstrous indignities to the president and faculty at Hobart of which I was myself witness, as well as the state of things at various other colleges in my own college days, I can testify, as can so many others, to the vast improvement in the conduct and aims of American students during the latter half of the nineteenth century.

9.

DIFFICULTIES AND DANGERS AT CORNELL

1868–1872

T HE FIRST BUSINESS AFTER FORMALLY OPENING THE UNI-
versity was to put in operation the various courses of
instruction, and vitally connected with these were the lectures
of our non-resident professors. From these I had hoped much
and was not disappointed. It had long seemed to me that
a great lack in our American universities was just that sort of
impulse which non-resident professors or lecturers of a high
order could give. At Yale there had been, in my time, very
few lectures of any sort to undergraduates; the work in the
various classes was carried on, as a rule, without the slightest
enthusiasm, and was considered by the great body of students
a bore to be abridged or avoided as far as possible. Hence
such pranks as cutting out the tongue of the college bell, of
which two or three tongues still preserved in university club-
rooms are reminders; hence, also, the effort made by members of my own class to fill the college bell with cement, which
would set in a short time, and make any call to morning prayers
and recitations for a day or two impossible—a performance
which caused a long suspension of several of the best young
fellows that ever lived, some of them good scholars, and all
of them men who would have walked miles to attend a really
inspiring lecture.

And yet, one or two experiences showed me what might be done by arousing an interest in regular class work. Professor Thacher, the head of the department of Latin, who conducted my class through the "Germania" and "Agricola" of Tacitus, was an excellent professor; but he yielded to the system then dominant at Yale, and the whole thing was but weary plodding. Hardly ever was there anything in the shape of explanation or comment; but at the end of his work with us he laid down the book, and gave us admirably the reasons why the study of Tacitus was of value, and why we might well recur to it in after years. Then came painfully into my mind the thought, "What a pity that he had not said this at the beginning of his instruction rather than at the end!"

Still worse was it with some of the tutors, who took us through various classical works, but never with a particle of appreciation for them as literature or philosophy. I have told elsewhere how my classmate Smalley fought it out with one of these. No instruction from outside lectures was provided; but in my senior year there came to New Haven John Lord and George William Curtis, the former giving a course on modern history, the latter one upon recent literature, and both arousing my earnest interest in their subjects. It was in view of these experiences that in my "plan of organization" I dwelt especially upon the value of non-resident professors in bringing to us fresh life from the outside, and in thus preventing a certain provincialism and woodenness which come when there are only resident professors, and these selected mainly from graduates of the institution itself.

The result of the work done by our non-resident professors more than answered my expectations. The twenty lectures of Agassiz drew large numbers of our brightest young men, gave them higher insight into various problems of natural science, and stimulated among many a zeal for special investigation. Thus resulted an enthusiasm which developed out of our student body several scholars in natural science who have since taken rank among the foremost teachers and investigators in the United States. So, too, the lectures of Lowell on early literature and of Curtis on later literature aroused great interest among students of a more literary turn; while those of Theodore Dwight on the Constitution of the United States and of Bayard Taylor upon German literature awakened a large number of active minds to the beauties of these fields. The coming of Goldwin Smith was an especial help to us. He remained longer than the others; in fact, he became for two or three years a resident professor, exercising, both in his lecture-room and out of it, a great influence upon the whole life of the university. At a later period, the coming of George W. Greene as lecturer on American history, of Edward A. Freeman, regius professor at Oxford, as a lecturer on European history, and of James Anthony Froude in the same field, aroused new interest. Some of our experiences with the two gentlemen last named were curious. Freeman was a rough diamond—in his fits of gout very rough indeed. At some of his lectures he appeared clad in a shooting-jacket and spoke sitting, his foot swathed to mitigate his sufferings. From New Haven came a characteristic story of him. He had been invited to attend an evening gathering, after one of his lectures, at the house of one of the professors, perhaps the finest residence in the town. With the exception of himself, the gentlemen all arrived in evening dress; he appeared in a shooting-jacket. Presently two professors arrived; and one of them, glancing through the rooms, and seeing Freeman thus attired, asked the other, "What sort of a costume do you call that?" The answer came instantly, "I don't know, unless it is the costume of a Saxon swineherd before the Conquest." In view of Freeman's studies on the Saxon and Norman periods and the famous toast of the dean of Wells, "In honor of Professor Freeman, who has done so much to reveal to us the rude manners of our ancestors," the Yale professor's answer seemed much to the point.

The lectures of Froude were exceedingly interesting; but every day he began them with the words "Ladies and gentlemen," in the most comical falsetto imaginable,—a sort of Lord Dundreary manner,—so that, sitting beside him, I always noticed a ripple of laughter running over the whole audience, which instantly disappeared as he settled into his work. He had a way of giving color to his lectures by citing bits of humorous history. Thus it was that he threw a vivid light on the horrors of civil war in Ireland during the sixteenth and seventeenth centuries, when he gave the plea of an Irish chieftain on trial for high treason, one of the charges against him being that he had burned the Cathedral of Cashel. His plea was: "Me lords, I niver would have burned the cathaydral but that I supposed that his grace the lord archbishop was inside."

Speaking of the strength of the clan spirit, he told me a story of the late Duke of Argyll, as follows: At a banquet of the great clan of which the duke was chief, a splendid snuff-box belonging to one of the clansmen, having attracted attention, was passed round the long table for inspection. By and by it was missing. All attempts to trace it were in vain, and the party broke up in disgust and distress at the thought that one of their number must be a thief. Some days afterward, the duke, putting on his dress-coat, found the box in his pocket, and immediately sent for the owner and explained the matter. "I knew ye had it," said the owner. "How did ye know it?" said the duke. "Saw ye tak' it." "Then why did n't ye tell me?" asked the duke. "I thocht ye wanted it," was the answer.

Speaking of university life, Froude told the story of an Oxford undergraduate who, on being examined in Paley, was asked to name any instance which he had himself noticed of the goodness and forethought of the Almighty as evidenced in his works: to which the young man answered, "The formation of the head of a bulldog. Its nose is so drawn back that it can hang on the bull and yet breathe freely; but for this, the bulldog would soon have to let go for want of breath."

Walking one day with Froude, I spoke to him regarding his

"Nemesis of Faith," which I had read during my attachéship at St. Petersburg, and which had been greatly objected to by various Oxford dons, one of whom is said to have burned a copy of it publicly in one of the college quadrangles. He seemed somewhat dismayed at my question, and said, in a nervous sort of way, "That was a young man's book—a young man's folly," and passed rapidly to other subjects.

From the stimulus given by the non-resident professors the resident faculty reaped much advantage. It might well be said that the former shook the bush and the latter caught the birds. What is most truthfully stated on the tablet to Professor Agassiz in the Cornell Memorial Chapel of the university might, in great part, be said of all the others. It runs as follows:

"To the memory of Louis Agassiz, LL.D. In the midst of great labors for science, throughout the world, he aided in laying the foundations of instruction at Cornell University, and, by his teachings here, gave an impulse to scientific studies, which remains a precious heritage. The trustees, in gratitude for his counsels and teachings, erect this memorial. 1884."

An incidental benefit of the system was its happy influence upon the resident professors. Coming from abroad, and of recognized high position, the non-residents brought a very happy element to our social life. No veteran of our faculty is likely to forget the charm they diffused among us. To meet Agassiz socially was a delight; nor was it less a pleasure to sit at table with Lowell or Curtis. Of the many good stories told us by Lowell, I remember one especially. During a stay in Paris he dined with Sainte-Beuve, and took occasion to ask that most eminent of French critics which he thought the greater poet, Lamartine or Victor Hugo. Sainte-Beuve, shrugging his shoulders, replied: "Eh bien, charlatan pour charlatan, je préfère Lamartine." This provoked another story, which was that, being asked by an American professor whether in his opinion the Empire of Napoleon III was likely to endure,

Sainte-Beuve, who was a salaried senator of the Empire, answered with a shrug, "Monsieur, je suis payé pour le croire." Agassiz also interested me by showing me the friendly, confidential, and familiar letters which he was then constantly receiving from the Emperor of Brazil, Dom Pedro—letters in which not only matters of science but of contemporary history were discussed. Bayard Taylor also delighted us all. Nothing could exceed, as a provocative to mirth, his recitations of sundry poems whose inspiration was inferior to their ambition. One especially brought down the house—"The Eonx of Ruby," by a poet who had read Poe and Browning until he never hesitated to coin any word, no matter how nonsensical, which seemed likely to help his jingle. In many respects the most charming of all the newcomers was Goldwin Smith, whose stories, observations, reflections, deeply suggestive, humorous, and witty, were especially grateful at the close of days full of work and care. His fund of anecdotes was large. One of them illustrated the fact that even those who are best acquainted with a language not their own are in constant danger of making themselves ridiculous in using it. The Duc d'Aumale, who had lived long in England, and was supposed to speak English like an Englishman, presiding at a dinner of the British Association for the Advancement of Science, gave a toast as follows: "De tree of science, may it shed down pease upon de nations."

Another story related to Sir Allan MacNab, who, while commander of the forces in Canada, having received a card inscribed, "The MacNab," immediately returned the call, and left a card on which was inscribed, "The other MacNab."

As I revise these lines, thirty-six years after his first coming, he is visiting me again to lay the corner-stone of the noble building which is to commemorate his services to Cornell. Though past his eightieth year, his memory constantly brings up new reminiscences. One of these I cannot forbear giving. He was at a party given by Lady Ashburton when Thomas Carlyle was present. During the evening, which was beautiful, the guests went out upon the lawn, and gazed at the starry heavens. All seemed especially impressed by the beauty of the moon, which was at the full, when Carlyle, fastening his eyes upon it, was heard to croak out, solemnly and bitterly, "Puir auld creetur!"

The instruction of the university was at that time divided between sundry general courses and various technical departments, the whole being somewhat tentative. These general courses were mainly three: the arts course, which embraced both Latin and Greek; the course in literature, which embraced Latin and modern languages; and the course in science, which embraced more especially modern languages in connection with a somewhat extended range of scientific studies. Of these general divisions the one most in danger of shipwreck seemed to be the first. It had been provided for in the congressional act of 1862, evidently by an afterthought, and it was generally felt that if, in the storms besetting us, anything must be thrown overboard, it would be this; but an opportunity now arose for clenching it into our system. There was offered for sale the library of Professor Charles Anthon of Columbia, probably the largest and best collection in classical philology which had then been brought together in the United States. Discussing the situation with Mr. Cornell, I showed him the danger of restricting the institution to purely scientific and technical studies, and of thus departing from the university ideal. He saw the point, and purchased the Anthon library for us. Thenceforth it was felt that, with such a means of instruction, from such a source, the classical department must stand firm; that it must on no account be sacrificed; that, by accepting this gift, we had pledged ourselves to maintain it.

Yet, curiously, one of the most bitter charges constantly reiterated against us was that we were depreciating the study of ancient classical literature. Again and again it was repeated, especially in a leading daily journal of the metropolis under the influence of a sectarian college, that I was "degrading classical studies." Nothing could be more unjust; I had greatly enjoyed such studies myself, had found pleasure in them since my graduation, and had steadily urged them upon those who had taste or capacity for them. But, as a student and as a university instructor, I had noticed two things in point, as many other observers had done: the first of these was that very many youths who go through their Latin and Greek Readers, and possibly one or two minor authors besides, exhaust the disciplinary value of such studies, and thenceforward pursue them listlessly and perfunctorily, merely droning over them. On their account it seemed certainly far better to present some other courses of study in which they could take an interest. As a matter of fact, I constantly found that many young men who had been doing half-way mental labor, which is perhaps worse than none, were at once brightened and strengthened by devoting themselves to other studies more in accordance with their tastes and aims.

But a second and very important point was that, in the two colleges of which I had been an undergraduate, classical studies were really hampered and discredited by the fact that the minority of students who loved them were constantly held back by a majority who disliked them; and I came to the conclusion that the true way to promote such studies in the United States was to take off this drag as much as possible, by presenting other courses of studies which would attract those who had no taste for Latin and Greek, thus leaving those who had a taste for them free to carry them much farther than had been customary in American universities up to that time. My expectations in this respect were fully met. A few years after the opening of the university, contests were arranged between several of the leading colleges and universities, the main subjects in the competition being Latin, Greek, and mathematics; and to the confusion of the gainsayers, Cornell took more first prizes in these subjects than did all the older competing institutions together. Thenceforward the talk of our "degrading classical studies" was less serious. The history of such studies at Cornell since that time has fully justified the policy then pursued. Every competent observer will, I feel sure, say that at no other American institution have these studies been pursued with more earnestness or with better results. The Museum of Classical Archæology, which has since been founded by the generous gift of Mr. Sage, has stimulated an increased interest in them; and graduates of Cornell are now exercising a wide influence in classical teaching: any one adequately acquainted with the history of American education knows what the influence of Cornell has been in bettering classical instruction throughout the State of New York. There has been another incidental gain. Among the melancholy things of college life in the old days was the relation of students to classical professors. The majority of the average class looked on such a professor as generally a bore and, as examinations approached, an enemy; they usually sneered at him as a pedant, and frequently made his peculiarities a subject for derision. Since that day far better relations have grown up between teachers and taught, especially in those institutions where much is left to the option of the students. The students in each subject, being those who are really interested in it, as a rule admire and love their professor, and whatever little peculiarities he may have are to them but pleasing accompaniments of his deeper qualities. This is a perfectly simple and natural result, which will be understood fully by any one who has observed human nature to much purpose.

Besides this course in arts, in which classical studies were especially prominent, there were established courses in science, in literature, and in philosophy, differing from each other mainly in the proportion observed between ancient languages, modern languages, and studies in various sciences and other departments of thought. Each of these courses was laid down with much exactness for the first two years, with large opportunity for choice between subjects in the last two years. The system worked well, and has, from time to time, been modified, as the improvement in the schools of the State, and other circumstances have required.

In proposing these courses I was much influenced by an idea broached in Herbert Spencer's "Treatise on Education." This idea was given in his discussion of the comparative values of different studies, when he arrived at the conclusion that a subject which ought to be among those taught at the beginning of every course is human physiology,—that is to say, an account of the structure, functions, and proper management of the human body, on which so much depends for every human being. It seemed to me that not only was there great force in Spencer's argument, but that there was an additional reason for placing physiology among the early studies of most of the courses; and this was that it formed a very good beginning for scientific study in general. An observation of my own strengthened me in this view. I remembered that, during my school life, while my tastes were in the direction of classical and historical studies, the weekly visits to the school by the surgeon who lectured upon the human eye, ear, and sundry other organs, using models and preparations, interested me intensely, and were a real relief from other studies. There was still another reason. For the professorship in this department Professor Agassiz had recommended to me Dr. Burt Wilder; and I soon found him, as Agassiz had foretold, not only a thorough investigator, but an admirable teacher. His lectures were not read, but were, as regards phrasing, extemporaneous; and it seemed to me that, mingled with other studies, a course of lectures given in so good a style, by so gifted a man, could not fail to be of great use in teaching our students, incidentally, the best way of using the English language in communicating their ideas to their fellowmen. I had long deplored the rhetorical fustian and oratorical tall-talk which so greatly afflict our country, and which had been, to a considerable extent, cultivated in our colleges and universities; I determined to try, at least, to substitute for it clean, clear, straightforward statement and illustration; and it seemed to me that a course of lectures on a subject which admitted neither fustian nor tall-talk, by a clear-headed, clear-voiced, earnest, and honest man, was the best thing in the world for this purpose. So was adopted the plan of beginning most courses with an extended course of lectures upon human physiology, in which to real practice in investigation by the class is added the hearing of a first-rate lecturer.

As regards the course in literature, I determined that use should be made of this to promote the general culture of students, as had been done up to that time by very few of our American universities. At Yale in my day, there was never even a single lecture on any subject in literature, either ancient or modern: everything was done by means of "recitations" from text-books; and while young men read portions of masterpieces in Greek and Latin, their attention was hardly ever directed to these as literature. As regards the great fields of modern literature, nothing whatever was done. In the English literature and language, every man was left entirely to his own devices. One of the first professors I called to Cornell was Hiram Corson, who took charge of the department of English literature; and from that day to this he has been a center from which good culture has radiated among our students. Professor H. B. Sprague was also called; and he also did excellent work, though in a different way. I also added non-resident professors. My original scheme I still think a good one. It was to call James Russell Lowell for early English literature, Bishop Arthur Cleveland Coxe for the literature of the Elizabethan and Jacobean periods, Edwin Whipple for the literature of Queen Anne's time, and George William Curtis for recent and contemporary literature. Each of these men was admirable as a scholar and lecturer in the particular field named; but the restricted means of the university obliged me to cut the scheme down, so that it included simply Lowell for early and Curtis for recent literature. Other lectures in connection with the instruction of the resident professors marked an epoch, and did much to remove anything like Philistinism from the student body. Bayard Taylor's lectures in German literature thus supplemented admirably the excellent work of the resident professors Hewett and Horatio White. To remove still further any danger of Philistinism, I called an eminent graduate of Harvard,—Charles Chauncey Shackford, —whose general lectures in various fields of literature were attractive and useful. In all this I was mainly influenced by the desire to prevent the atmosphere of the university becoming simply and purely that of a scientific and technical school. Highly as I prized the scientific spirit and technical training, I felt that the frame of mind engendered by them should be modified by an acquaintance with the best literature as literature. There were many evidences that my theory was correct. Some of our best students in the technical departments developed great love for literary studies. One of them attracted much attention by the literary excellence of his writings; and on my speaking to him about it, and saying that it seemed strange to me that a man devoted to engineering should show such a taste for literature, he said that there was no greater delight to him than passing from one of the studies to the other —that each was a recreation after the other.

The effort to promote that element in the general culture of the student body which comes from literature, ancient and modern, gained especial strength from a source usually unpromising—the mathematical department. Two professors highly gifted in this field exercised a wide and ennobling influence outside it. First of these was Evan William Evans, who had been known to me at Yale as not only one of the best scholars in the class of 1851, but also one of its two foremost writers. Later, he developed a passion for modern literature, and his influence was strongly felt in behalf of the humanities. His successor was James Edward Oliver, a graduate of Harvard, a genius in his chosen field, but always exercising a large influence by virtue of his broad, liberal, tolerant views of life which were promoted by study of the best thoughts of the best thinkers of all times.

The work of organizing and developing the general courses was comparatively easy, and the stimulus given at the outset by the non-resident professors rendered it all the more so. But with the technical departments and special courses there were grave difficulties. The department of civil engineering, of course, went easily enough; there were plenty of precedents for it, and the admirable professor first elected was, at his death, succeeded by another who most vigorously and wisely developed it: Estevan Fuertes, drawn from the most attractive surroundings in the island of Porto Rico to the United States by a deep love of science, and retained here during the rest of his life by a love, no less sincere, for American liberty—a rare combination of the virtues and capabilities of the Latin races with the best results of an American environment. I may mention, in passing, that this combination came out curiously in his views of American citizenship. He was wont to marvel at the indifference of the average American to his privileges and duties, and especially at the lack of a proper estimate of his function at elections. I have heard him say: "When I vote, I put on my best clothes and my top hat, go to the polls, salute the officers, take off my hat, and cast my ballot."

It may be worth mentioning here that, at the election of the first professor in this department, a curious question arose. Among the candidates was one from Harvard, whose testimonials showed him to be an admirable acquisition; and among these testimonials was one from an eminent bishop, who spoke in high terms of the scientific qualifications of the candidate, but added that he felt it his duty to warn me that the young man was a Unitarian. At this I wrote the bishop, thanking him, and saying that the only question with me was as to the moral and intellectual qualifications of the candidate; and that if these were superior to those of other candidates, I would nominate him to the trustees even if he were a Buddhist.

The good bishop at first took some offense at this; and, in one of the communications which ensued, expressed doubts whether laymen had any right to teach at all, since the command to teach was given to the apostles and their successors, and seemed therefore confined to those who had received holy orders; but he became most friendly later, and I look back to my meetings with him afterward as among the delightful episodes of my life.

The technical department which caused me the most anxiety was that of agriculture. It had been given the most prominent place in the Congressional act of 1862, and in our charter from the State in 1865. But how should agriculture be taught; what proportion should we observe between theory and practice; and what should the practice be? These questions elicited all sorts of answers. Some eminent agriculturists insisted that the farm should be conducted purely as a business operation; others that it should be a "model farm"—regardless of balance sheets; others still that it should be wholly experimental. Our decision was to combine what was best in all these views; and several men attempted this as resident professors, but with small success. One day, after a series of such failures, when we were almost desperate, there appeared a candidate from an agricultural college in Ireland. He bore a letter from an eminent clergyman in New York, was of pleasing appearance and manners, gave glowing accounts of the courses he had followed, expatiated on the means by which farming had been carried to a high point in Scotland, and ventured suggestions as to what might be done in America. I had many misgivings. His experience was very remote from ours, and he seemed to me altogether too elegant for the work in hand; but Mr. Cornell had visited English farms, was greatly impressed by their excellence, and urged a trial of the newcomer. He was duly called; and, that he might begin his courses of instruction, an order was given for a considerable collection of English agricultural implements and for the erection of new farm-buildings after English patterns, Mr. Cornell generously advancing the required money.

All this took time—much time. At first great things were expected by the farmers of the State, but gradually their confidence waned. As they saw the new professor walking over the farm in a dilettantish way, superintending operations with gloved hands, and never touching any implement, doubts arose which soon ripened into skepticism. Typical were the utterances of our farm manager. He was a plain, practical farmer, who had taken the first prize of the State Agricultural Society for the excellence of his own farm; and, though he at first indulged in high hopes regarding the new professor, he soon had misgivings, and felt it his duty to warn me. He said: "Yew kin depend on 't, he ain't a-goin' to do nothin'; he don't know nothin' about corn, and he don't want to know nothin' about corn; *and he don't believe in punkins!* Depend on 't, as soon as his new barn is finished and all his new British tackle is brought together, he'll quit the job." I reasoned that, to a farmer brought up among the glorious fields of Indian corn in western New York, and accustomed to rejoice in the sight of golden pumpkins, diffusion of other cultures must seem like treason; but, alas! he was right. As soon as the new buildings and arrangements were ready for our trial of British scientific agriculture, the young foreign professor notified me that he had accepted the headship of an agricultural college in Canada. Still, he met with no greater success there than with us; nor was his reputation increased when, after the foul attacks made upon Mr. Cornell in the legislature, he volunteered to come to the investigation and testify that Mr. Cornell was "not a practical man." In this the career of the young agriculturist culminated. Having lost his professorship in Canada, he undertook the management of a grocery in the oil-regions of western Pennsylvania; and scientific British agriculture still awaits among us a special representative. Happily, since that day, men trained practically in the agriculture of the United States have studied the best British methods, and brought us much that has been of real use.

Fortunately I had found three men who enabled us to tide our agricultural department over those dark days, in which we seemed to be playing "Hamlet" with Hamlet left out. The first of these was the Hon. John Stanton Gould, whom I called as a lecturer upon agriculture. He had been president of the State Agricultural Society, and was eminent, not only for his knowledge of his subject, but for his power of making it interesting. Men came away from Mr. Gould's lectures filled with intense desire to get hold of a spade or hoe and to begin turning the soil.

So, also, the steady work of Professor George C. Caldwell, whom I had called from the State College of Pennsylvania to take charge of the department of agricultural chemistry, won the respect of all leaders in agriculture throughout the State, and, indeed, throughout the country. And with especial gratitude should be named Dr. James Law of the British Royal Veterinary College, whom I had found in London, and called to our veterinary professorship. Never was there a more happy selection. From that day to this, thirty-six years, he has been a tower of strength to the university, and has rendered incalculable services to the State and Nation. His quiet, thorough work impressed every one most favorably. The rudest of the surrounding farmers learned more and more to regard him with respect and admiration, and the State has recently recognized his services by establishing in connection with the university a State veterinary college under his control.

The work of these three men saved us. Apart from it, the agricultural department long remained a sort of slough of despond; but at last a brighter day dawned. From the far-off State Agricultural College of Iowa came tidings of a professor—Mr. J. I. P. Roberts—who united the practical and theoretical qualities desired. I secured him, and thenceforward there was no more difficulty. For more than twenty years, as professor and lecturer, he has largely aided in developing agriculture throughout the State and country; and when others were added to him, like Comstock and Bailey, the success of the department became even more brilliant. Still, its old reputation lasted for a time, even after a better era had been fully ushered in. About a year after the tide had thus turned a meeting of the State "Grange" was held at the neighboring city of Elmira; and the leading speakers made the university and its agricultural college an object of scoffing which culminated in a resolution denouncing both, and urging the legislature to revoke our charter. At this a bright young graduate of Cornell, an instructor in the agricultural department, who happened to be present, stood up manfully, put a few pertinent questions, found that none of the declaimers had visited the university, declared that they were false to their duty in not doing so, protested against their condemning the institution unheard and unseen, and then and there invited them all to visit the institution and its agricultural department without delay. Next day this whole body of farmers, with their wives, sons, and daughters, were upon us. Everything was shown them. Knowing next to nothing about modern appliances for instruction in science and technology, they were amazed at all they saw; the libraries, the laboratories, and, above all, the natural-science collections and models greatly impressed them. They were taken everywhere, and shown not only our successes but our failures; nothing was concealed from them, and, as a result, though they "came to scoff," they "remained to pray." They called a new session of their body, pledged to us their support, and passed resolutions commending our work and condemning the State legislature for not doing more in our behalf. That was the turning-point for the agricultural department; and from that day to this the legislature has dealt generously with us, and the influence of the department for good throughout the State has been more and more widely acknowledged.

Of the two technical departments referred to in the original act of Congress, the second—specified under the vague name of "Mechanic Arts"—went better, though there was at first much groping to find just what ought to be done. First of all, there was a danger which demanded delicate handling. This danger lay in Mr. Cornell's wish to establish, in vital connection with the university, great factories for the production of articles for sale, especially chairs and shoes, thus giving large bodies of students opportunities for self-support. In discussing this matter with him, I pointed to the fact that, in becoming a manufacturing corporation we were making a business venture never contemplated by our charter; that it was exceedingly doubtful whether such a corporation could be combined with an educational institution without ruining both; that the men best fitted to manage a great factory were hardly likely to be the best managers of a great institution of learning; that under our charter we had duties, not merely to those who wished to support themselves by labor, but to others; and I finally pointed out to him many reasons for holding that such a scheme contravened the act of Congress and the legislation of the State. I insisted that the object of our charters from the State and Nation was not to enable a great number of young men to secure an elementary education while making shoes and chairs; that for these the public schools were provided; that our main purpose must be to send out into all parts of the State and Nation thoroughly trained graduates, who should develop and improve the main industries of the country, and, by their knowledge and example, train up skilful artisans of various sorts and in every locality. Mr. Cornell's conduct in this matter was admirable. Tenacious as he usually was when his opinion was formed, and much as it must have cost him to give up what had become a darling project, he yielded to this view.

New questions now opened as to this "Department of Mechanic Arts." It was clear to me, from what I had seen abroad, that not all the models I had sent from Europe would be sufficient to give the practical character which such a department needed; that its graduates must have a direct, practical acquaintance with the construction and use of machinery before they could become leaders in great mechanical enterprises; that they must be made, not only mathematicians and draftsmen, but skilled workmen, practically trained in the best methods and processes. A very shrewd artisan said to me: "When a young mechanical engineer comes among us fresh from college, only able to make figures and pictures, we rarely have much respect for him: the trouble with the great majority of those who come from technical institutions is that they don't know as much about practical methods and processes as we know."

I felt that there was truth in this, but, as things were, hardly dared tell this to the trustees. It would have scared them, for it seemed to open the door to great expenditures demanded by a mere theory; but I laid my views before Mr. Cornell, and he agreed with me so far as to send to us from his agricultural works at Albany sundry large pieces of old machinery, which he thought might be rebuilt for our purposes. But this turned out to be hardly practicable. I dared not, at that stage of the proceedings, bring into the board of trustees a proposal to buy machinery and establish a machine-shop; the whole would have a chimerical look, and was sure to repel them. Therefore it was that, at my own expense, I bought a power-lathe and other pieces of machinery; and, through the active efforts of Professor John L. Morris, my steadfast supporter in the whole matter, these were set up in our temporary wooden laboratory. A few students began using them, and to good purpose. Mr. Cornell was greatly pleased. Other trustees of a practical turn visited the place, and the result was that opinion in the governing board soon favored a large practical equipment for the department.

On this I prepared a report, taking up the whole subject with great care, and brought it before them, my main suggestion being that a practical beginning of the department should be made by the erection and equipment of a small building on the north side of the university grounds, near our main water-power. Then came a piece of great good fortune. Among the charter trustees of the university was Mr. Cornell's old friend and associate in telegraphic enterprise, Hiram Sibley of Rochester; and at the close of the meeting Mr. Sibley asked me if I could give him a little time on the university grounds after the adjournment of the meeting. I, of course, assented; and next morning, on our visiting the grounds together, he asked me to point out the spot where the proposed college of mechanic arts might best be placed. On my doing so, he looked over the ground carefully, and then said that he would himself erect and equip the building. So began Sibley College, which is to-day, probably, all things considered, the most successful department of this kind in our own country, and perhaps in any country. In the hands, first of Professors Morris and Sweet, and later under the direction of Dr. Thurston, it has become of the greatest value to every part of the United States, and indeed to other parts of the American continent.

At the outset a question arose, seemingly trivial, but really serious. Mr. Sibley had gone far beyond his original proposals; and when the lecture-rooms, drafting-rooms, modeling-rooms, foundries, shops for ironwork, woodwork, and the like, had been finished, the question came up: Shall our aim be to produce things having a pecuniary value, or shall we produce simply samples of the most highly finished workmanship, having, generally, no value? Fortunately, Professors Morris and Sweet were able to combine both these purposes, and to employ a considerable number of students in the very best of work which had a market value. The whole thing was thereby made a success, but it waited long for recognition. A result followed not unlike some which have occurred in other fields in our country. At the Centennial Exhibition of 1876, an exhibit was made of the work done by students in Sibley College, including a steam-engine, power-lathes, face-plates, and various tools of precision, admirably finished, each a model in its kind. But while many mechanics praised them, they attracted no special attention from New England authorities. On the other hand, an exhibit of samples of work from the School of Technology of Moscow, which had no merchantable value,—many of the pieces being of antiquated pattern, but of exquisite finish and showily arranged,—aroused great admiration among sundry New England theorists; even the head of the Massachusetts Institute of Technology, in enthusiastic magazine articles, called the attention of the whole country to them, and urged the necessity of establishing machine-shops in connection with schools of science. The fact that this had already been done, and better done, at Cornell, was loftily ignored. Western New York seemed a Nazareth out of which no good could come. That same straining of the mind's eye toward the East, that same tendency to provincialism which had so often afflicted Massachusetts, evidently prevented her wise men in technology from recognizing any new departure west of them.

At a later period I had occasion to make a final comment on all this. Both as commissioner at the Paris Exhibition and as minister to Russia, I came to know intimately Wischniegradsky, who had been the head of the Moscow School of Technology and afterward Russian minister of finance. He spoke to me in the highest terms of what original American methods had done for railways; and the climax was reached when the Moscow methods, so highly praised by Boston critics, proved to be utterly inadequate in training mechanical engineers to furnish the machinery needed in Russia, and men from the American schools, trained in the methods of Cornell, sent over locomotives and machinery of all sorts for the new Trans-Siberian Railway, of which the eastern terminus was that very city of Moscow which enjoyed the privileges so lauded and magnified by the Boston critics! Time has reversed their judgment: the combination of the two systems, so ably and patiently developed by Director Thurston, is the one which has happily prevailed.

Few days in the history of Cornell University have been so

fraught with good as that on which Thurston accepted my call to the headship of Sibley College. At the very outset he gained the confidence and gratitude of trustees, professors, students, and, indeed, of his profession throughout the country, by his amazing success as professor, as author, and as organizer and administrator of that department, which he made not only one of the largest, but one of the best of its kind in the world. The rapidity and wisdom of his decisions, the extent and excellence of his work, his skill in attracting the best men, his ability in quieting rivalries and animosities, and the kindly firmness of his whole policy were a source of wonder to all who knew him. And, at his lamented death in 1903, it was found that he had rendered another service of a sort which such strong men as he are often incapable of rendering—he had trained a body of assistants and students worthy to take up his work.

Another department which I had long wished to see established in our country now began to take shape. From my boyhood I had a love for architecture. In my young manhood this had been developed by readings in Ruskin, and later by architectural excursions in Europe; and the time had now arrived when it seemed possible to do something for it. I had collected what, at that period, was certainly one of the largest, if not the largest, of the architectural libraries in the United States, besides several thousand large architectural photographs, drawings, casts, models, and other material from every country in Europe. This had been, in fact, my pet extravagance; and a propitious time seeming now to arrive, I proposed to the trustees that if they would establish a department of architecture and call a professor to it, I would transfer to it my special library and collections. This offer was accepted; and thus was founded this additional department, which began its good career under Professor Charles Babcock, who, at this present writing, is enjoying, as professor emeritus, the respect and gratitude of a long series of classes which have profited by his teachings, and the cordial companionship of his colleagues, who rejoice to profit by his humorous, but none the less profound, observations upon problems arising in the university and in the world in general.

As regards this illustrative material, I recall one curious experience. While on one of my architectural excursions through the great towns of eastern France, I arrived at Troyes. On visiting the government agent for photographing public monuments, I noticed in his rooms some admirably executed pieces of stone carving,—capitals, corbels, and the like,—and on my asking him whence these came, he told me that they had been recently taken out of the cathedral by the architect who was "restoring" it. After my purchases were made, he went with me to this great edifice, one of the finest in Europe; and there I found that, on each side of the high altar, the architect had taken out several brackets, or corbels, of the best mediæval work, and substituted new ones designed by himself. One of these corbels thus taken out the government photographer had in his possession. It was very striking, representing the grotesque face of a monk in the midst of a mass of foliage supporting the base of a statue, all being carved with great spirit. Apart from its architectural value, it had a historical interest, since it must have witnessed the famous betrothal of the son and daughter of the English and French kings mentioned in Shakspere, to say nothing of many other mediæval pageants.

On my making known to the photographer the fact that I was engaged in founding a school of architecture in the United States, and was especially anxious to secure a good specimen of French work, he sold me this example, which is now in the museum of the Architectural Department at Cornell. I allude to this, in passing, as showing what monstrous iniquities (and I could name many others) are committed in the great mediæval buildings of Europe under pretense of "restoration."

10.

FURTHER DEVELOPMENT OF UNIVERSITY COURSES

1870–1872

IN CLOSE CONNECTION WITH THE TECHNICAL DEPART-
ments were various laboratories. For these, place was at
first made here and there in cellars and sheds; but at last we
were able to erect for them buildings large and complete, and
to the opening of the first of these came Mr. Cleveland, then
Governor of New York, and later President of the United
States. Having laid the corner-stone of the Memorial Chapel
and made an excellent speech, which encouraged us all, he
accompanied me to the new building devoted to chemistry and
physics, which was then opened for the first time. On entering it, he expressed his surprise at its equipment, and showed
that he had seen nothing of the kind before. I learned afterward that he had received a thorough preparation in classics
and mathematics for college, but that, on account of the insufficient means of his father, he was obliged to give up his
university course; and it was evident, from his utterances at
this time, as well as when visiting other colleges and universities, that he lamented this.

Out of this laboratory thus opened was developed, later, a
new technical department. Among my happiest hours were
those spent in visiting the various buildings, collections, and
lecture-rooms, after my morning's work, to see how all were

going on; and, during various visits to the new laboratory I noticed that the majority of the students were, in one way or another, giving attention to matters connected with electricity. There had already been built in the machine-shops, under the direction of Professor Anthony, a dynamo which was used in lighting our grounds, this being one of the first examples of electric lighting in the United States; and on one of my visits I said to him, "It looks much as if, with the rapid extension throughout the country of the telegraph, telephone, electric lighting, and electric railways, we shall be called on, before long, to train men for a new profession in connection with them." As he assented to this, I asked him to sketch out a plan for a "Department of Electrical Engineering," and in due time he appeared with it before the executive committee of the trustees. But it met much opposition from one of our oldest members, who was constitutionally averse to what he thought new-fangled education, partly from conservatism, partly from considerations of expense; and this opposition was so threatening that, in order to save the proposed department, I was obliged to pledge myself to become responsible for any extra expense caused by it during the first year. Upon this pledge it was established. Thus was created, as I believe, the first department of electrical engineering ever known in the United States, and, so far as I can learn, the first ever known in any country.

But while we thus strove to be loyal to those parts of our charter which established technical instruction, there were other parts in which I personally felt even a deeper interest. In my political reminiscences I have acknowledged the want of preparation in regard to practical matters of public concern which had hampered me as a member of the State Senate. Having revolved this subject in my mind for a considerable time, I made, while commissioner to the Paris Exposition of 1878, a careful examination of the courses of study in political and economic science established in European universities, and on my return devoted to this subject my official report.

Like such reports generally, it was delayed a long time in the
Government Printing-office, was then damned with faint praise,
and nothing more came of it until the following year, when,
being called to deliver the annual address at the Johns Hopkins University, I wrought its main points into a plea for
education in relation to politics. This was widely circulated
with some effect, and I now brought a modest proposal in
the premises before our trustees. Its main feature was that
Mr. Frank B. Sanborn, a graduate of Harvard, Secretary of
the Board of Charities of the State of Massachusetts and of
the Social Science Association of the United States, should be
called to give a course of practical lectures before the senior
class during at least one term,—his subjects to be such as
pauperism, crime (incipient and chronic), inebriety, lunacy,
and the best dealing of modern states with these; also that his
instructions should be given, not only by lectures, but by
actual visits with his classes to the great charitable and penal
institutions of the State, of which there were many within
easy distance of the university. For several years, and until
the department took a different form, this plan was carried
out with excellent results. Professor Sanborn and his students,
beginning with the county almshouse and jail, visited the re-
formatories, the prisons, the penitentiaries, and the asylums
of various sorts in the State; made careful examinations of
them; drew up reports upon them, these reports forming the
subject of discussions in which professor and students took
earnest part; and a number of young men who have since
taken influential places in the State legislature were thus in-
structed as to the best actual and possible dealings with all
these subjects. I still think that more should be done in all
our universities to train men by this method for the public
service in this most important and interesting field, and also
in matters pertaining generally to State, county, and city
administration.

Closely connected with this instruction was that in political
economy and history. As to the first of these, I had, some

years before, seen reason to believe that my strong, and perhaps bigoted free-trade ideas were at least not so universal in their application as I had supposed. Down to the time of our Civil War I had been very intolerant on this subject, practically holding a protectionist to be either a Pharisee or an idiot. I had convinced myself not only that the principles of free trade are axiomatic, but that they afford the only means of binding nations together in permanent peace; that Great Britain was our best friend; that, in desiring us to adopt her own system, she was moved by broad, philosophic, and philanthropic considerations. But as the war drew on and I saw the haughtiness and selfishness toward us shown by her ruling classes, there came in my mind a revulsion which led me to examine more closely the foundations of my economical belief. I began to attribute more importance to John Stuart Mill's famous "exception," to the effect that the building up of certain industries may be necessary to the very existence of a nation, and that perhaps the best way of building them up is to adopt an adequate system of protective duties. Down to this time I had been a disciple of Adam Smith and Bastiat; but now appeared the published lectures of Roscher of Leipsic, upon what he called "The Historical System" of political economy. Its fundamental idea was that political economy is indeed a science, to be wrought out by scientific methods; but that the question how far its conclusions are adapted to the circumstances of any nation at any time is for statesmen to determine. This impressed me much. Moreover, I was forced to acknowledge that the Morrill protective tariff, adopted at the Civil War period, was a necessity for revenue; so that my old theory of a tariff for revenue easily developed into a belief in a tariff for revenue with incidental protection. This idea has been developed in my mind as time has gone on, until at present I am a believer in protection as the only road to ultimate free trade. My process of reasoning on the subject I have given in another chapter.

At the opening of the university there was but little instruction in political economy, that little being mainly given by our professor of moral philosophy, Dr. Wilson, a man broad in his views and strong in reasoning power, who had been greatly impressed by the ideas of Friedrich List, the German protectionist. But lectures were also given by free-traders, and I adopted the plan of having both sides as well represented as possible. This was, at first, complained of; sundry good people said it was like calling a professor of atheism into a theological seminary; but my answer was that our university was not, like a theological seminary, established to arrive at certain conclusions fixed beforehand, or to propagate an established creed; that, political economy not being an exact science, our best course was to call eminent lecturers to present both sides of the main questions in dispute. The result was good. It stimulated much thought, and doubtless did something to promote that charity to opposing economical opinions which in my own case had been, through my early manhood, so conspicuously lacking.

The second of these departments—history—was the one for which I cared most. I believed then, and later experience has strengthened my conviction, that the best of all methods in presenting every subject bearing on political and social life is the historical. My own studies had been mainly in this field, and I did what I could to establish historical courses in the university. The lectures which I had given at the University of Michigan were now developed more fully and again presented; but to these I constantly added new lectures and, indeed, new courses, though at a great disadvantage, since my administrative duties stood constantly in the way of my professorial work. At the same time I went on collecting my historical library until it became, in its way, probably the largest and most complete of its kind in the possession of any individual in the United States. Gradually strong men were drawn into the department, and finally there came one on whom I could lay a large portion of the work.

The story is somewhat curious. During the year 1877–1878,

in Germany and France, I had prepared a short course of lectures upon the historical development of criminal law; and while giving it to my senior class after my return, I noticed a student, two or three years below the average age of the class, carefully taking notes and apparently much interested. One day, going toward my house after the lecture, I found him going in the same direction, and, beginning conversation with him, learned that he was a member of the sophomore class; that he had corresponded with me, two or three years before, as to the best means of working his way through the university; had followed out a suggestion of mine, then made, in that he had learned the printer's trade; had supported himself through the preparatory school by means of it, and was then carrying himself through college by setting type for the university press. Making inquiries of professors and students, I found that the young man, both at school and at the university, was, as a rule, at the head of every class he had entered; and therefore it was that, when the examination papers came in at the close of the term, I first took up his papers to see how he had stood the test. They proved to be masterly. There were excellent scholars in the senior class, but not one had done so well as this young sophomore; in fact, I doubt whether I could have passed a better examination on my own lectures. There was in his answers a combination of accuracy with breadth which surprised me. Up to that time, passing judgment on the examination papers had been one of the most tedious of my burdens; for it involved wading through several hundred pages of crabbed manuscript, every term, and weighing carefully the statements therein embodied. A sudden light now flashed upon me. I sent for the young sophomore, cautioned him to secrecy, and then and there made him my examiner in history. He, a member of the sophomore class, took the papers of the seniors and resident graduates, and passed upon them carefully and admirably—better than I should have ever had the time and patience to do. Of course this was kept entirely secret; for had the seniors known that I had intrusted their papers to the tender mercies of a sophomore, they would probably have mobbed me. This mode of examination continued until the young man's graduation, when he was openly appointed examiner in history, afterward becoming instructor in history, then assistant professor; and, finally, another university having called him to a full professorship, he was appointed full professor of history at Cornell, and has greatly distinguished himself both by his ability in research and his power in teaching. To him have been added others as professors, assistant professors, and instructors, so that the department is now on an excellent footing. In one respect its development has been unexpectedly satisfactory. At the opening of the university one of my strongest hopes had been to establish a professorship of American history. It seemed to me monstrous that there was not, in any American university, a course of lectures on the history of the United States; and that an American student, in order to secure such instruction in the history of his own country, must go to the lectures of Laboulaye at the Collège de France. Thither I had gone some years before, and had been greatly impressed by Laboulaye's admirable presentation of his subject, and awakened to the fact that American history is not only more instructive, but more interesting, than I had ever supposed it. My first venture was to call Professor George W. Greene of Brown University for a course of lectures on the history of our Revolutionary period, and Professor Dwight of Columbia College for a course upon the constitutional history of the United States. But finally my hope was more fully realized: I was enabled to call as resident professor my old friend Moses Coit Tyler, whose book on the "History of American Literature" is a classic, and who, in his new field, exerted a powerful influence for good upon several generations of students. More than once since, as I have heard him, it has been borne in upon me that I was born too soon. Remembering the utter want of any such instruction in my own college days, I have especially envied those who have had the good fortune to be conducted by him, and men like him, through the history of our own country.[1]

In some of these departments to which I have referred there were occasionally difficulties requiring much tact in handling. During my professorial days at the University of Michigan I once heard an eminent divine deliver an admirable address on what he called "The Oscillatory Law of Human Progress"— that is, upon the tendency of human society, when reacting from one evil, to swing to another almost as serious in the opposite direction. In swinging away from the old cast-iron course of instruction, and from the text-book recitation of the mere dry bones of literature, there may be seen at this hour some tendency to excessive reaction. When I note in sundry university registers courses of instruction offered in some of the most evanescent and worthless developments of contemporary literature,—some of them, indeed, worse than worthless,—I think of a remark made to me by a college friend of mine who will be remembered by the Yale men of the fifties for his keen and pithy judgments of men and things. Being one day in New Haven looking for assistant professors and instructors, I met him; and, on my answering his question as to what had brought me, he said, "If at any time you want a professor of *horse sense,* call *me.*" I have often thought of this proposal since, and have at times regretted that some of our institutions of learning had not availed themselves of his services. The fact is that, under the new system, "horse sense" is especially called for to prevent a too extreme reaction from the evils which afflicted university instruction during my student days.

While it rejoices my heart to see the splendid courses in modern literature now offered at our larger universities, some of them arouse misgivings. Reflecting upon the shortness of human life and the vast mass of really *great* literature, I see

[1] To my great sorrow, he died in 1900.—A. D. W.

with regret courses offered dealing with the bubbles floating on the surface of sundry literatures—bubbles soon to break, some of them with ill odor.

I would as soon think of endowing restaurants to enable young men to appreciate caviar, or old Gorgonzola, or game of a peculiarly "high" character, as of establishing courses dealing with Villon, Baudelaire, Swinburne, and the like; and when I hear of second-rate critics summoned across the ocean to present to universities which have heard Emerson, Longfellow, Henry Reed, Lowell, Whipple, and Curtis the coagulated nastiness of Verlaine, Mallarmé, and their compeers, I expect next to hear of courses introducing young men to the beauties of absinthe, Turkish cigarettes, and stimulants unspeakable. Doubtless these things are all due to the "oscillatory law of human progress," which professors of "horse sense" like my friend Joe Sheldon will gradually do away with.

As time went on, buildings of various sorts rose around the university grounds, and, almost without exception, as gifts from men attracted by the plan of the institution. At the annual commencement in 1869 was laid the corner-stone of an edifice devoted especially to lecture-rooms and museums of natural science. It was a noble gift by Mr. John McGraw; and amid the cares and discouragements of that period it gave us new heart, and strengthened the institution especially on the scientific side. In order to do honor to this occasion, it was decided to invite leading men from all parts of the State, and, above all, to request the governor, Mr. Fenton, to lay the corner-stone. But it was soon evident that his excellency's old fear of offending the sectarian schools still controlled him. He made excuse, and we then called on the Freemasons to take charge of the ceremony. They came in full regalia, bringing their own orators; and, on the appointed day, a great body of spectators was grouped about the foundations of the new building on the beautiful knoll in front of the upper quadrangle. It was an ideal afternoon in June, and the panorama before and around us was superb. Immediately below us, in front, lay the beautiful valley in which nestles the little city of Ithaca; beyond, on the left, was the vast amphitheater, nearly surrounded by hills and distant mountains; and on the right, Cayuga Lake, stretching northward for forty miles. Few points in our country afford a nobler view of lake, mountain, hill, and valley. The speakers naturally expatiated in all the moods and tenses on the munificence of Mr. Cornell and Mr. McGraw; and when all was ended the great new bell, which had just been added to the university chime in the name of one most dear to me,—the largest bell then swinging in western New York, inscribed with the verse written for it by Lowell,—boomed grandly forth. As we came away I walked with Goldwin Smith, and noticed that he was convulsed with suppressed laughter. On my asking him the cause, he answered: "There is nothing more to be said; no one need ever praise the work of Mr. Cornell again." On my asking the professor what he meant, he asked me if I had not heard the last speech. I answered in the negative—that my mind was occupied with other things. He then quoted it substantially as follows: "Fellow-citizens, when Mr. Cornell found himself rich beyond the dreams of avarice, did he give himself up to a life of inglorious ease? No, fellow-citizens; he founded the beautiful public library in yonder valley. But did he then retire to a life of luxury? No, fellow-citizens; he came up to this height (and here came a great wave of the hand over the vast amphitheater below and around us) and he established this *universe!*"

In reference to this occasion I may put on record Lowell's quatrain above referred to, which is cast upon the great clock-bell of the university. It runs as follows:

> I call as fly the irrevocable hours
> Futile as air, or strong as fate to make
> Your lives of sand or granite. Awful powers,
> Even as men choose, they either give or take.

There was also cast upon it the following, from the Psalter version of Psalm xcii:

To tell of thy loving-kindness early in the morning: and of thy truth in the night season.

While various departments were thus developed, there was going on a steady evolution in the general conception of the university. In the Congressional act of 1862 was a vague provision for military instruction in the institutions which might be created under it. The cause of this was evident. The bill was passed during one of the most critical periods in the history of the Civil War, and in my inaugural address I had alluded to this as most honorable to Senator Morrill and to the Congress which had adopted his proposals. It was at perhaps the darkest moment in the history of the United States that this provision was made, in this Morrill Act, for a great system of classical, scientific, and technical instruction in every State and Territory of the Union; and I compared this enactment, at so trying a period, to the conduct of the Romans in buying and selling the lands on which the Carthaginians were encamped after their victory at Cannæ. The provision for military instruction had been inserted in this act of 1862 because Senator Morrill and others saw clearly the advantage which had accrued to the States then in rebellion from their military schools; but the act had left military instruction optional with the institutions securing the national endowment, and, so far as I could learn, none of those already created had taken the clause very seriously. I proposed that we should accept it fully and fairly, not according to the letter of the act, but to the spirit of those who had passed it; indeed, that we should go further than any other institution had dreamed of going, so that every undergraduate not excused on the ground of conscientious scruples, or for some other adequate cause, should be required to take a thorough course of military drill; and to this end I supported a plan, which was afterward carried out by law, that officers from the United States army should be detailed by the Secretary of War to each of the principal institutions as military professors. My reasons for this were based on my recollections of what took place at the University of Michigan during the Civil War. I had then seen large numbers of my best students go forth insufficiently trained, and in some cases led to destruction by incompetent officers. At a later period, I had heard the West Point officer whom I had secured from Detroit to train those Michigan students express his wonder at the rapidity with which they learned what was necessary to make them soldiers and even officers. Being young men of disciplined minds, they learned the drill far more quickly and intelligently than the average recruits could do. There was still another reason for taking the military clause in the Morrill Act seriously. I felt then, and feel now, that our Republic is not to escape serious internal troubles; that in these her reliance must be largely upon her citizen soldiery; that it will be a source of calamity, possibly of catastrophe, if the power of the sword in civil commotions shall fall into the hands of ignorant and brutal leaders, while the educated men of the country, not being versed in military matters, shall slink away from the scene of duty, cower in corners, and leave the conduct of military affairs to men intellectually and morally their inferiors. These views I embodied in a report to the trustees; and the result was the formation of a university battalion, which has been one of the best things at Cornell. A series of well-qualified officers, sent by the War Department, have developed the system admirably. Its good results to the university have been acknowledged by all who have watched its progress. Farmers' boys,—slouchy, careless, not accustomed to obey any word of command; city boys, sometimes pampered, often wayward, have thus been in a short time transformed: they stand erect; they look the world squarely in the face; the intensity of their American individualism is happily modified; they can take the word of command and they can give it. I doubt whether any feature of instruction at Cornell University has produced more excellent results upon *character* than the training thus given. And this is not all. The effect on the State has been valuable. It has already been felt in the organization and maintenance of the State militia; and during the war with Spain, Cornellians, trained in the university battalion, rendered noble service.

Among the matters which our board of trustees and faculty had to decide upon at an early day was the conferring of degrees. It had become, and indeed has remained in many of our colleges down to the present day, an abuse, and a comical abuse. Almost more than any other thing, it tends to lower respect for many American colleges and universities among thinking men. The older and stronger universities are free from it; but many of the newer ones, especially various little sectarian colleges, some of them calling themselves "universities," have abused and are abusing beyond measure their privilege of conferring degrees. Every one knows individuals in the community whose degrees, so far from adorning them, really render them ridiculous; and every one knows colleges and "universities" made ridiculous by the conferring of such pretended honors.

At the outset I proposed to our trustees that Cornell University should confer no honorary degrees of any sort, and a law was passed to that effect. This was observed faithfully during my entire presidency; then the policy was temporarily changed, and two honorary doctorates were conferred; but this was immediately followed by a renewal of the old law, and Cornell has conferred no honorary degrees since.

But it is a question whether the time has not arrived for some relaxation of this policy. The argument I used in proposing the law that no honorary degree should be conferred was that we had not yet built up an institution whose degrees could be justly considered as of any value. That argument is no longer valid, and possibly some departure from it would now be wise. Still, the policy of conferring no honorary degrees is infinitely better than the policy of lavishing them.

As to regular and ordinary degrees, I had, in my plan of

organization, recommended that there should be but one degree for all courses, whether in arts, science, or literature. I argued that, as all our courses required an equal amount of intellectual exertion, one simple degree should be granted alike to all who had passed the required examination at the close of their chosen course. This view the faculty did not accept. They adopted the policy of establishing several degrees: as, for example, for the course in arts, the degree of A.B.; for the course in science, the degree of B.S.; for the course in literature, the degree of B.L.; and so on. The reason given for this was that it was important in each case to know what the training of the individual graduate had been; and that the true way to obviate invidious distinctions is so to perfect the newer courses that all the degrees shall finally be considered as of equal value and honor. This argument converted me: it seemed to me just, and my experience in calling men to professorships led me more and more to see that I had been wrong and that the faculty was right; for it was a matter of the greatest importance to me, in deciding on the qualifications of candidates for professorships, to know, not only their special fitness, but what their general education had been.

But, curiously enough, within the last few years the Cornell faculty, under the lead of its present admirable president, has reverted to my old argument, accepted it, and established a single degree for all courses. I bow respectfully to their judgment, but my conversion by the same faculty from my own original ideas was so complete that I cannot now agree to the wisdom of the change. It is a curious case of cross-conversion, I having been and remaining converted to the ideas of the faculty, and they having been converted to my original idea. As to the whole matter, I have the faith of an optimist that eventually, with the experience derived from both systems, a good result will be reached.

Another question which at that time occupied me much was that of scholarships and fellowships awarded by competitive examinations *versus* general gratuitous instruction. During the formation of my plans for the university, a number of excellent men urged upon me that all our instruction should be thrown open to all mankind free of charge; that there should be no payment of instruction fees of any kind; that the policy which prevails in the public schools of the State should be carried out in the new institution at the summit of the system. This demand was plausible, but the more I thought upon it the more illogical, fallacious, and injurious it seemed; and, in spite of some hard knocks in consequence, I have continued to dissent from it, and feel that events have justified me.

Since this view of mine largely influenced the plan of the university, this is perhaps as good a place as any to sketch its development. In the first place, I soon saw that the analogy between free education in the public schools and in the university is delusive, the conditions of the two being entirely dissimilar. In a republic like ours primary education of the voters is a practical necessity. No republic of real weight in the world, except Switzerland and the United States, has proved permanent; and the only difference between the many republics which have failed and these two, which, we hope, have succeeded, is that in the former the great body of the citizens were illiterate, while in the latter the great body of voters have had some general education. Without this education, sufficient for an understanding of the main questions involved, no real republic or democracy can endure. With general primary education up to a point necessary for the intelligent exercise of the suffrage, one may have hopes for the continuance and development of a democratic republic. On this account primary education should be made free: it is part of our political system; it is the essential condition of its existence.

The purpose of university education is totally different. The interest of the Republic is, indeed, that it should maintain the very highest and best provision for advanced instruction, general, scientific, and technical; and it is also in the highest interest of the Republic that its fittest young men and women should secure such instruction. No republic, no nation in fact, possesses any other treasure comparable to its young citizens of active mind and earnest purpose. This is felt at the present time by all the great nations of the world, and consequently provision is made in almost all of them for the highest education of such men and women. Next to the general primary education of all voters, the most important duty of our Republic is to develop the best minds it possesses for the best service in all its fields of high intellectual activity. To do this it must supply the best university education, and must smooth the way for those to acquire it who are best fitted for it, no matter how oppressive their poverty.

Now, my first objection to gratuitous university instruction to all students alike is that it stands in the way of this most important consummation; that it not only does not accomplish the end which is desirable, but that it does accomplish another which is exceedingly undesirable. For the real problem to be solved is this: How shall the higher education in different fields be brought within reach of the young men and women best fitted to acquire it, to profit by it, and to use it to best advantage? Any one acquainted with American schools and universities knows that the vast majority of these young people best fitted to profit by higher education come from the families of small means. What does gratuitous instruction in the university offer them? Merely a remission of instruction fees, which, after all, are but a small part of the necessary expenses of a university course. With many of these young persons— probably with most—a mere remission of instruction fees is utterly insufficient to enable them to secure advanced education. I have alluded to the case of President Cleveland, who, having been well fitted for the university, could not enter. His father being a country clergyman with a large family and small means, the future Chief Executive of the United States was obliged to turn aside to a teacher's place and a clerkship which afforded him a bare support. At the Hamilton College commencement a few years since, Mr. Cleveland, pointing to one of the professors, was reported as saying in substance:

"My old school friend by my side is, of all men, the one I have most envied: he was able to buy a good edition of Vergil; I was not."

It would not have been at all difficult for him to secure a remission of instruction fees at various American colleges and universities; but the great difficulty was that he could not secure the means necessary for his board, for his clothing, for his traveling expenses, for his books, for all the other things that go to make up the real cost of life at a university. I can think of but one way, and that is, as a rule, to charge instruction fees upon the great body of the students, but both to remit instruction fees and to give scholarships and fellowships to those who, in competitive examinations and otherwise, show themselves especially worthy of such privileges. This is in conformity to the system of nature; it is the survival of the fittest. This was the main reason which led me to insert in the charter of Cornell University the provision by which at present six hundred students from the State of New York are selected by competitive examinations out of the mass of scholars in the public schools, and to provide that each of these best scholars shall have free instruction for four years.

But this was only a part of the system. From the first I have urged the fact above mentioned, namely, that while remission of instruction fees is a step in the right direction, it is not sufficient; and I have always desired to see some university recognize the true and sound principle of free instruction in universities by *consecrating all moneys received from instruction fees to the creation of competitive scholarships and fellowships, each of which shall amount to a sum sufficient to meet, with economy, the living expenses of a student.* This plan I was enabled, in considerable measure, to carry out by establishing the competitive scholarships in each Assembly district; and later, as will be seen in another chapter, I was enabled, by a curious transformation of a calamity into a blessing, to carry it still further by establishing endowed scholarships and fellowships. These latter scholarships, each, as a general rule, of two hundred and fifty dollars a year, were awarded to those who passed the best examinations and maintained the best standing in their classes; while the fellowships, each of the value of from four to five hundred dollars a year, were awarded to the seniors of our own or other universities who had been found most worthy of them. In the face of considerable opposition I set this system in motion at Cornell; and its success leads me to hope that it will be further developed, not only there, but elsewhere. Besides this, I favored arrangements for remitting instruction fees and giving aid to such students as really showed promising talent, and who were at the time needy. To this end a loan fund was created which has been carefully managed and has aided many excellent men through the university courses.[1] Free instruction, carried out in accordance with the principle and plan above sketched, will, I feel sure, prove of great value to our country. Its effect is to give to the best and brightest young men, no matter how poor, just the chance they need; and not as a matter of charity, but as a matter of wise policy. This is a system which I believe would be fraught with blessings to our country, securing advanced education to those who can profit by it, and strengthening their country by means of it.

On the other hand, the system of gratuitous remission of instruction fees to all students alike, whether rich or poor, I believe to be injurious to the country, for the following reasons: First, it generally cripples the institution which gives it. Two or three large institutions which have thought themselves in possession of endowments sufficient to warrant giving gratuitous instruction have tried it, but as a rule have not been able to go on with it, and have at last come to the principle of charging moderate fees. Secondly, it simply makes a present of a small sum to a large number of young men, most of whom

---

[1] It has since been greatly increased by the bequest of a public-spirited New York merchant.

neither need nor appreciate it, and who would be better for regarding their university instruction as something worth paying for.

But my main objection to the system of indiscriminate gratuitous instruction is that it does the country a positive injury in drawing away from the farms, workshops, and stores large numbers of young persons who would better have been allowed to remain there; that it tends to crowd what have been called "the learned professions" with men not really fitted for them; that it draws masses of men whose good right arms would be of great value in the rural districts, and makes them parasites in the cities. The farmers and the artisans complain of the lack of young men and women for their work; the professional men complain that the cities are overstocked with young men calling themselves lawyers, doctors, engineers, and the like, but really unworthy to exercise either profession, who live on the body politic as parasites more or less hurtful. This has certainly become an evil in other countries: every enlightened traveler knows that the ranks of the anarchists in Russia are swollen by what are called "*fruits secs*"—that is, by young men and young women tempted away from manual labor and avocations for which they are fit into "professions" for which they are unfit. The more *first-rate* young men and young women our universities and technical schools educate the better; but the more young men and women of mediocre minds and weak purpose whom they push into the ranks of poor lawyers, poor doctors, poor engineers, and the like, the more injury they do to the country.

As I now approach the end of life and look back over the development of Cornell University, this at least seems to me one piece of good fortune—namely, that I have aided to establish there the principle of using our means, so far as possible, not for indiscriminate gratuitous higher education of men unfit to receive it; not, as President Jordan has expressed it, in "trying to put a five-thousand-dollar education into a fifty-cent boy"; but in establishing a system which draws out from the community, even from its poorest and lowliest households, the best, brightest, strongest young men and women, and develops their best powers, thus adding to the greatest treasure which their country can possess.

11.

"COEDUCATION" AND AN
UNSECTARIAN PULPIT

1871–1904

S TILL ANOTHER NEW DEPARTURE WAS IN SOME RESPECTS bolder than any of those already mentioned. For some years before the organization of Cornell, I had thought much upon the education of women, and had gradually arrived at the conclusion that they might well be admitted to some of the universities established for young men. Yet, at the same time, Herbert Spencer's argument as to the importance of avoiding everything like "mandarinism"—the attempt to force all educational institutions into the same mold—prevented my urging this admission of women upon all universities alike. I recognized obstacles to it in the older institutions which did not exist in the newer; but I had come to believe that where no special difficulties existed, women might well be admitted to university privileges. To this view I had been led by my own observation even in my boyhood. At Cortland Academy I had seen young men and women assembled in the classrooms without difficulty or embarrassment, and at Yale I had seen that the two or three lecture-rooms which admitted women were the most orderly and decent of all; but perhaps the strongest influence in this matter was exercised upon me by my mother. She was one of the most conservative of women, a High-church Episcopalian, and generally averse to modern reforms; but on my talking over with her some of my plans for Cornell University, she said: "I am not so sure about your other ideas, but as to the admission of women you are right. My main education was derived partly from a boarding-school at Pittsfield considered one of the best in New England, and partly from Cortland Academy. In the boarding-school we had only young women, but in the academy we had both young men and young women; and I am sure that the results of the academy were much better than those of the boarding-school. The young men and young women learned to respect each other, not merely for physical, but for intellectual and moral qualities; so there came a healthful emulation in study, the men becoming more manly and the women more womanly; and never, so far as I have heard, did any of the evil consequences follow which some of your opponents are prophesying."

A conference with Dr. Woolworth, a teacher of the very largest experience, showed me that none of the evil results which were prophesied had resulted. He solemnly assured me that, during his long experiences as principal of two or three large academies, and, as secretary of the Board of Regents, in close contact with all the academies and high schools of the State, he had never known of a serious scandal arising between students of different sexes.

As I drafted the main features of the university charter these statements were in my mind, but I knew well that it would be premature to press the matter at the outset. It would certainly have cost us the support of the more conservative men in the legislature. All that I could do at that time I did; and this was to keep out of the charter anything which could embarrass us regarding the question in the future, steadily avoiding in every clause relating to students the word "man," and as steadily using the word "person." In conversations between Mr. Cornell and myself on this subject, I found that we agreed; and in our addresses at the opening of the university we both alluded to it, he favoring it in general terms, and I developing sundry arguments calculated to prepare the way for future action upon it. At the close of the exercises Mr. John McGraw, who was afterward so munificent toward us, came to me and said: "My old business partner, Henry Sage, who sat next me during the exercises this morning, turned to me during your allusion to Mr. Cornell with tears in his eyes, and said: 'John, we are scoundrels to stand doing nothing while those men are killing themselves to establish this university.'" In the afternoon Mr. Sage himself came to me and said: "I believe you are right in regard to admitting women, but you are evidently carrying as many innovations just now as public opinion will bear; when you are ready to move in the matter, let me know."

The following year came the first application of a young woman for admission. Her case was strong, for she presented a certificate showing that she had passed the best examination for the State scholarship in Cortland County; and on this I admitted her. Under the scholarship clause in the charter I could not do otherwise. On reporting the case to the trustees, they supported me unanimously, though some of them reluctantly. The lady student proved excellent from every point of view, and her admission made a mere temporary ripple on the surface of our affairs; but soon came a peculiar difficulty. The only rooms for students in those days on the University Hill were in the barracks filled with young men; and therefore the young woman took rooms in town, coming up to lectures two or three times a day. It was a hard struggle; for the paths and roads leading to the university grounds, four hundred feet above the valley, were not as in these days, and the electric trolley had not been invented. She bore the fatigue patiently until winter set in; then she came to me, expressing regret at her inability to toil up the icy steep, and left us. On my reporting this to the trustees, Mr. Sage made his proposal. I had expected from him a professorship or a fellowship; but to my amazement he offered to erect and endow a separate college for young women in the university, and for this purpose to give us two hundred and fifty thousand dollars. A committee of trustees having been appointed to examine and report upon this proposal, I was made its chairman; and, in company with Mr. Sage, visited various Western institutions where experiments in the way of what was called "coeducation" had been tried. At Oberlin College in Ohio two serious doubts were removed from my mind. The first of these was regarding the health of the young women. I had feared that in the hard work and vigorous competitions of the university they would lose their physical strength; but here we found that, with wise precautions, the health of the young women had been quite equal to that of the young men. My other fear was that their education with young men might cost some sacrifice of the better general characteristics of both sexes; but on studying the facts I became satisfied that the men had been made more manly and the women more womanly. As to the manliness there could be little doubt; for the best of all tests had been applied only a few years before, when Oberlin College had poured forth large numbers of its young men, as volunteers, into the Union army. As to the good effect upon women, it was easy to satisfy myself when I met them, not only at the college, but in various beautiful Western homes.

Very striking testimony was also given at the University of Michigan. Ten years earlier I had known that institution well, and my professorship there, which lasted six years, had made me well acquainted with the character and spirit of its students; but, since my day, women had been admitted, and some of the results of this change surprised me much. Formerly a professor's lecture- or recitation-room had been decidedly a roughish place. The men had often been slouchy and unkempt. Now all was quiet and orderly, the dress of the students much neater; in fact, it was the usual difference between assemblages of men alone and of men and women together, or, as I afterward phrased it, "between the smoking-car and the car back of it." Perhaps the most convincing piece of testimony came from an old janitor. As I met him I said: "Well, J——, do the students still make life a burden to you?" "Oh, no," he answered; "that is all gone by. They can't rush each other up and down the staircases or have boxing-matches in the lobbies any longer, for the girls are there."

My report went fully into the matter, favored the admission of women, and was adopted by the trustees unanimously—a thing which surprised me somewhat, since two of them, Judge Folger and Mr. Erastus Brooks, were among the most conservative men I have ever known. The general results were certainly fortunate; though one or two minor consequences were, for a year or two, somewhat disappointing. Two or three of the faculty and a considerable number of the students were greatly opposed to the admission of women, a main cause of this being the fear that it would discredit the institution in the eyes of members of other universities, and the number of the whole student body was consequently somewhat diminished; but that feeling died away, the numbers became larger than ever, and the system proved a blessing, not only to the university, but to the State at large. None of the prophecies of evil so freely made by the opponents of the measure have ever been fulfilled. Every arrangement was made in Mr. Sage's building to guard the health of the young women; and no one will say that the manliness of men or the womanliness of women has ever suffered in consequence of the meeting of the two sexes in classrooms, laboratories, chapel, or elsewhere. From one evil which was freely prophesied the university has been singularly free. It was declared that a great deal of "spooning" would result. This has not been the case. Both sexes seem to have been on their guard against it; and, although pleasant receptions have, as a rule, taken place weekly at Sage College, and visits to its residents have been permitted at suitable times, no embarrassing attachments have resulted.

The main difficulties arose from a cause which proved very short-lived. Several of the young women who first applied for admission held high ideas as to their rights. To them Sage College was an offense. Its beautiful parlors, conservatories, library, lecture-rooms, and lawns, with its lady warden who served as guide, philosopher, and friend, were all the result of a deep conspiracy against the rights of women. Again and again a committee of them came to me, insisting that young women should be treated exactly like young men; that there should be no lady warden; that every one of them should be free to go and come from Sage College at every hour in the twenty-four, as young men were free to go and come from their dormitories. My answer was that the cases were not the same; that when young women insisted on their right to come and go at all times of the day and night, as they saw fit, without permission, it was like their right to walk from the campus to the beautiful point opposite us on the lake: the right they undoubtedly had, but insurmountable obstacles were in the way; and I showed them that a firm public opinion was an invincible barrier to the liberties they claimed. Still, they were allowed advisory powers in the management of the college; the great majority made wise use of this right, and all difficulty was gradually overcome.

Closely connected with the erection of Sage College was the establishment of Sage Chapel. From the first I had desired to have every working-day begun with a simple religious service at which attendance should be voluntary, and was glad to see that in the cheerless lecture-room where this service was held there usually assembled a goodly number of professors and students, in spite of the early hour and long walk from town. But for Sunday there was no provision; and one day, on my discussing the matter with Mr. Sage, he said that he would be glad to establish a chapel on the university grounds for the general use of professors and students, if I saw no objection. This proposal I heartily welcomed, but on two conditions: first, that the chapel should never be delivered over to any one sect; secondly, that students should be attracted, but not coerced into it. To these conditions Mr. Sage agreed, and the building was erected.

As it approached completion there came a proposal which opened a new era in our university life. Mr. Dean Sage, the eldest son of him who had given us the women's college and the chapel, proposed to add an endowment for a chaplaincy, and suggested that a clergyman of the Protestant Episcopal Church be appointed to that office. This would have been personally pleasing to me; for, though my churchmanship was "exceeding broad," I was still attracted to the church in which I was brought up, and felt nowhere else so much at home. But it seemed to me that we had no right, under our charter, to give such prominence to any single religious organization; and I therefore proposed to the donor that the endowment be applied to a preachership to be filled by leading divines of all denominations. In making this proposal I had in view, not only the unsectarian feature embodied in our charter, but my observation of university chaplaincies generally. I had noticed that, at various institutions, excellent clergymen, good preachers, thorough scholars, charming men, when settled as chaplains, had, as a rule, been unable to retain their hold upon the great body of the students. The reason was not far to seek. The average parish clergyman, even though he be not a strong preacher or profound scholar or brilliant talker, if he be at all fit for his position, gradually wins the hearts of his congregation. He has baptized their children, married their young men and maidens, buried their dead, rejoiced with those who have rejoiced, and wept with those who have wept. A strong tie has thus grown up. But such a tie between a chaplain and bodies of students shifting from year to year, is, in the vast majority of cases, impossible. Hence it is that even the most brilliant preachers settled in universities have rapidly lost their prestige among the students. I remembered well how, at Geneva and at Yale, my college-mates joked at the peculiarities of clergymen connected with the college, who, before I entered it, had been objects of my veneration. I remembered that at Yale one of my class was wont to arouse shouts of laughter by his droll imitations of the prayers of the leading professors—imitations in which their gestures, intonations, and bits of rhetoric and oratory were most ludicrously caricatured. I remembered, too, how a college pastor, a man greatly revered, was really driven out of the university pulpit by a squib in a students' paper, and how several of his successors had finally retreated into professorships in the Divinity School; and I felt that leading men coming from week to week from the outside world would be taken at the value which the outside world puts upon them, and that they would bring in a fresh atmosphere. My expectations were more than fulfilled. The preachership having been established, I sent invitations to eminent clergymen along the whole gamut of belief, from the Roman Catholic bishop of the diocese to the most advanced Protestants. The bishop answered me most courteously; but, to my sincere regret, declined. One or two bishops of the Protestant Episcopal Church also made some difficulties at first, but gradually they were glad to accept; for it was felt to be a privilege and a pleasure to preach to so large a body of open-minded young men, and the course of sermons has for years deepened and strengthened what is best in university life. The whole system was indeed at first attacked; and while we had formerly been charged with godlessness, we were now charged with "indifferentism"—whatever that might mean. But I have had the pleasure of living to see this system adopted at other leading universities of our country, and it is evidently on its way to become the prevailing system among all of them. I believe that no pulpit in the United States has exercised a more powerful influence for good. Strong men have been called to it from all the leading religious bodies; and they, knowing the character of their audience, have never advocated sectarianism, but have presented the great fundamental truths upon which all religion must be based.

The first of these university preachers was Phillips Brooks, and he made a very deep impression. An interesting material result of his first sermon was that Mr. William Sage, the second son of our benefactor, came forward at the close of the service, and authorized me to secure a beautiful organ for the university chapel.[1] In my addresses to students I urged them to attend for various good reasons, and, if for none of these, because a man is but poorly educated who does not keep himself abreast of the religious thought of his country. Curious was it to see Japanese students, some of them Buddists, very conscientious in their attendance, their eyes steadily fixed upon the preacher.

My selections for the preachership during the years of my presidency were made with great care. So far as possible, I kept out all "sensational preaching." I had no wish to make the chapel a place for amusement or for ground and lofty tumbling by clerical performers, and the result was that its ennobling influence was steadily maintained.

Some other pulpits in the university town were not so well guarded. A revivalist, having been admitted to one of them, attempted to make a sensation in various ways; and one evening laid great stress on the declaration that she was herself a brand plucked from the burning, and that her parents were undoubtedly lost. A few minutes afterward, one of the Cornell students present, thinking, doubtless, that his time would be better employed upon his studies, arose and walked down the aisle to the door. At this the preacher called out, "There goes a young man straight down to hell." Thereupon the student turned instantly toward the preacher and asked quietly, "Have you any message to send to your father and mother?"

Our list of university preachers, both from our own and other countries, as I look back upon it, is wonderful to me. Becoming acquainted with them, I have learned to love very many men whom I previously distrusted, and have come to see more and more the force of the saying, "The man I don't like is the man I don't know." Many of their arguments have not appealed to me, but some from which I have entirely dissented, have suggested trains of profitable thought; in fact,

[1] Sunday, June 13, 1875.

no services have ever done more for me, and, judging from the numbers who have thronged the chapel, there has been a constant good influence upon the faculty and students.

In connection with the chapel may be mentioned the development of various religious associations, the first of these being the Young Men's Christian Association. Feeling the importance of this, although never a member of it, I entered heartily into its plan, and fitted up a hall for its purposes. As this hall had to serve also, during certain evenings in the week, for literary societies, I took pains to secure a series of large and fine historical engravings from England, France, and Germany, among them some of a decidedly religious cast, brought together after a decidedly Broad-church fashion. Of these, two, adjoining each other, represented—the one, Luther discussing with his associates his translation of the Bible, and the other, St. Vincent de Paul comforting the poor and the afflicted; and it was my hope that the juxtaposition of these two pictures might suggest ideas of toleration in its best sense to the young men and women who were to sit beneath them. About the room, between these engravings, I placed some bronze statuettes, obtained in Europe, representing men who had done noble work in the world; so that it was for some years one of the attractions of the university.

Some years later came a gift very advantageous to this side of university life. A gentleman whom I had known but slightly—Mr. Alfred S. Barnes of Brooklyn, a trustee of the university—dropped in at my house one morning, and seemed to have something on his mind. By and by he very modestly asked what I thought of his putting up a building for the religious purposes of the students. I welcomed the idea joyfully; only expressing the hope that it would not be tied up in any way, but open to all forms of religious effort. In this idea he heartily concurred, and the beautiful building which bears his honored name was the result,—one of the most perfect for its purposes that can be imagined,—and as he asked me to write an inscription for the corner-stone, I placed on it the words: "For the Promotion of God's Work among Men." This has seemed, ever since, to be the key-note of the work done in that building.

It has been, and is, a great pleasure to me to see young men joining in religious effort; and I feel proud of the fact that from this association at Cornell many strong and earnest men have gone forth to good work as clergymen in our own country and in others.

In the erection of the new group of buildings south of the upper university quadrangle, as well as in building the president's house hard by, an opportunity was offered for the development of some minor ideas regarding the evolution of university life at Cornell which I had deeply at heart. During my life at Yale, as well as during visits to various other American colleges, I had been painfully impressed by the lack of any development of that which may be called the commemorative or poetical element. In the long row of barracks at Yale one longed for some little bit of beauty, and hungered and thirsted for something which connected the present with the past; but, with the exception of the portraits in the Alumni Hall, there was little more to feed the sense of beauty or to meet one's craving for commemoration of the past than in a cotton-factory. One might frequent the buildings at Yale or Harvard or Brown, as they then were, for years, and see nothing of an architectural sort which had been put in its place for any other reason than bare utility.

Hence came an effort to promote at Cornell some development of a better kind. Among the first things I ordered were portraits by competent artists of the leading nonresident professors, Agassiz, Lowell, Curtis, and Goldwin Smith. This example was, from time to time, followed by the faculty and trustees, the former commemorating by portraits some of their more eminent members, and the latter ordering portraits of some of those who had connected their names with the university by benefactions or otherwise, such as Mr. Cornell, Senator Morrill, Mr. Sage, Mr. McGraw, and others. The alumni and undergraduates also added portraits of professors. This custom has proved very satisfactory; and the line of portraits hanging in the library cannot fail to have an ennobling influence on many of those who, day after day, sit beneath them.

But the erection of these new buildings—Sage College, Sage Chapel, Barnes Hall, and, finally, the university library—afforded an opportunity to do something of a different sort. There was a chance for some effort to promote beauty of detail in construction, and, fortunately, the forethought of Goldwin Smith helped us greatly in this. On his arrival in Ithaca, just after the opening of the university, he had seen that we especially needed thoroughly trained artisans; and he had written to his friend Auberon Herbert, asking him to select and send from England a number of the best he could find. Nearly all proved of value, and one of them gave himself to the work in a way which won my heart. This was Robert Richardson, a stone-carver. I at first employed him to carve sundry capitals, corbels, and spandrels for the president's house, which I was then building on the university grounds; and this work was so beautifully done that, in the erection of Sage College, another opportunity was given him. Any one who, to-day, studies the capitals of the various columns, especially those in the porch, in the loggia of the northern tower, and in some of the front windows, will feel that he put his heart into the work. He wrought the flora of the region into these creations of his, and most beautifully. But best of all was his work in the chapel. The tracery of the windows, the capitals of the columns, and the corbels supporting the beams of the roof were masterpieces; and, in my opinion, no investment of equal amount has proved to be of more value to us, even for the moral and intellectual instruction of our students, than these examples of a conscientious devotion of genius and talent which he thus gave us.

The death of Mr. Cornell afforded an opportunity for a further development in the same direction. It was felt that his remains ought to rest on that beautiful site, in the midst of the institution he loved so well; and I proposed that a memorial chapel be erected, beneath which his remains and those of other benefactors of the university might rest, and that it should be made beautiful. This was done. The stone vaulting, the tracery, and other decorative work, planned by our professor of architecture, and carried out as a labor of love by Richardson, were all that I could desire. The trustees, entering heartily into the plan, authorized me to make an arrangement with Story, the American sculptor at Rome, to execute a reclining statue of Mr. Cornell above the crypt where rest his remains; and citizens of Ithaca also authorized me to secure in London the memorial window beneath which the statue is placed. Other memorials followed, in the shape of statues, busts, and tablets, as others who had been loved and lost were laid to rest in the chapel crypt, until the little building has become a place of pilgrimage. In the larger chapel, also, tablets and windows were erected from time to time; and the mosaic and other decorations of the memorial apse, recently erected as a place of repose for the remains of Mr. and Mrs. Henry Sage, are a beautiful development of the same idea.

So, too, upon the grounds, some effort was made to connect the present with the past. Here, as elsewhere in our work, it seemed to me well to impress, upon the more thinking students at least, the idea that all they saw had not "happened so," without the earnest agency of human beings; but that it had been the result of the earnest life-work of men and women, and that no life-work to which a student might aspire could be more worthy. In carrying out this idea upon the "campus" Goldwin Smith took the lead by erecting the stone seat which has now stood there for over thirty years. Other memorials followed, among them a drinking-fountain, the stone bridge across the Cascadilla, the memorial seat back of the library, the entrance gateway, and the like; and, at the lamented death of Richardson, another English stone-carver put his heart into some of the details of the newly erected library.

Meanwhile, the grounds themselves became more and more beautiful. There was indeed one sad mistake; and I feel bound, in self-defense, to state that it was made during an absence of mine in Europe: this was the erection of the chemical laboratory upon the promontory northwest of the upper quadrangle. That site afforded one of the most beautiful views in our own or any other country. A very eminent American man of letters, who had traveled much in other countries, said to me, as we stood upon it, "I have traveled hundreds of miles in Europe to obtain views not half so beautiful as this." It was the place to which Mr. Cornell took the trustees at their first meeting in Ithaca, when their view from it led them to choose the upper site for the university buildings rather than the lower. On this spot I remember once seeing Phillips Brooks evidently overawed by the amazing beauty of the scene spread out at his feet—the great amphitheater to the south and southwest, the hills beyond, and Cayuga Lake stretching to the north and northwest. But though this part of the grounds has been covered by a laboratory which might better have been placed elsewhere, much is still left, and this has been treated so as to add to the natural charm of the surroundings. With the exception of the grounds of the State University of Wisconsin and of the State University and Stanford University in California, I know of none approaching in beauty those of Cornell. I feel bound to say, however, that there is a danger. Thus far, though mistakes have been made here and there, little harm has been done which is irremediable. But this may not always be the case. In my view, one of the most important things to be done by the trustees is to have a general plan most carefully decided upon which shall be strictly conformed to in the erection of all future buildings, no matter what their size or character may be. This has been urged from time to time, but deferred.[1] The experience of other universities in the United States is most instructive in this respect. Nearly every one of them has suffered greatly from the want

[1] It has now—1904—been very intelligently developed.

of some such general plan.   One has but to visit almost any
one of them to see buildings of different materials and styles—
classical, Renaissance, Gothic, and nondescript—thrown together in a way at times fairly ludicrous.   Thomas Jefferson,
in founding the University of Virginia, was wiser; and his
beautiful plan was carried out so fully, under his own eyes,
that it has never been seriously departed from.   At Stanford
University, thanks to the wisdom of its founders, a most
beautiful plan was adopted, to which the buildings have been
so conformed that nothing could be more satisfactory; and
recently another noble Californian—Mrs. Hearst—has devoted
a queenly gift to securing a plan worthy of the University of
California.   At the opening of Cornell, as I have already said,
a general plan was determined upon, with an upper quadrangle
of stone, plain but dignified, to be at some future time archi-
tecturally enriched, and with a freer treatment of buildings on
other parts of the grounds; but there is always danger, and I
trust that I may be allowed to remind my associates and successors in the board of trustees, of the necessity, in the future
development of the university, for a satisfactory plan, suitable
to the site, to be steadily kept in mind.

12

ROCKS, STORMS, AND PERIL

1868–1874

THUS FAR I HAVE DWELT ESPECIALLY UPON THE STEADY development of the university in its general system of instruction, its faculty, its equipment, and its daily life; but it must not be supposed that all was plain sailing. On the contrary, there were many difficulties, some discouragements, and at times we passed through very deep waters. There were periods when ruin stared us in the face—when I feared that my next move must be to close our doors and announce the suspension of instruction. The most serious of these difficulties were financial. Mr. Cornell had indeed endowed the institution munificently, and others followed his example: the number of men and women who came forward to do something for it was astonishing. In addition to the great endowments made by Mr. Cornell, Mr. Sage, Mr. McGraw, Mr. Sibley, and others, which aggregated millions, there were smaller gifts no less encouraging: Goldwin Smith's gift of his services, of his library, and of various sums to increase it, rejoiced us all; and many other evidences of confidence, in the shape of large collections of books and material, cheered us in that darkest period; and from that day to this such gifts have continued.

Some of the minor gifts were especially inspiring, as showing the breadth of interest in our work. One of them warmed my heart when it was made, and for many years afterward cheered me amid many cares. As Mr. Sage and myself were one day looking over matters upon the grounds, there came along, in his rough wagon, a plain farmer from a distant part of the county, a hard-working man of very small means, who had clearly something upon his mind. Presently he said: "I would very much like to do something for the university if I could. I have no money to give; but I have thought that possibly some good elm-trees growing on my farm might be of use to you, and if you wish them I will put them in the best condition and bring them to you." This offer we gladly accepted; the farmer brought the trees; they were carefully planted; they have now, for over twenty years, given an increasing and ever more beautiful shade to one of the main university avenues; and in the line of them stands a stone on which are engraved the words, "Ostrander Elms."

But while all this encouraged us, there were things of a very different sort. Could the university have been developed gradually, normally, and in obedience to a policy determined solely by its president, trustees, and faculty, all would have gone easily. But our charter made this impossible. Many departments must be put into operation speedily, each one of them demanding large outlay for buildings, equipment, and instruction. From all parts of the State came demands—some from friends, some from enemies—urging us to do this, blaming us for not doing that, and these utterances were echoed in various presses, and reëchoed from the State legislature. Every nerve had to be strained to meet these demands. I remember well that when a committee of the Johns Hopkins trustees, just before the organization of that university, visited Cornell and looked over our work, one of them said to me: "We at least have this in our favor: we can follow out our own conceptions and convictions of what is best; we have no need of obeying the injunctions of any legislature, the beliefs of any religious body, or the clamors of any press; we are free to do what we really believe best, as slowly, and in such manner, as we see fit." As this was said a feeling of deep envy came over me: our condition was the very opposite of that. In getting ready for the opening of the university in October, 1868, as required by our charter, large sums had to be expended on the site now so beautiful, but then so unpromising. Mr. Cornell's private affairs, as also the constant demands upon him in locating the university lands on the northern Mississippi, kept him a large part of the time far from the university; and my own university duties crowded every day. The president of a university in those days tilled a very broad field. He must give instruction, conduct examinations, preside over the faculty, correspond with the trustees, address the alumni in various parts of the country, respond to calls for popular lectures, address the legislature from time to time with reference to matters between the university and the State, and write for reviews and magazines; and all this left little time for careful control of financial matters.

In this condition of things Mr. Cornell had installed, as "business manager," a gentleman supposed to be of wide experience, who, in everything relating to the ordinary financial management of the institution, was all-powerful. But as months went on I became uneasy. Again and again I urged that a careful examination be made of our affairs, and that reports be laid before us which we could clearly understand; but Mr. Cornell, always optimistic, assured me that all was going well, and the matter was deferred. Finally, I succeeded in impressing upon my colleagues in the board the absolute necessity of an investigation. It was made, and a condition of things was revealed which at first seemed appalling. The charter of the university made the board of trustees personally liable for any debt over fifty thousand dollars, and we now discovered that we were owing more than three times that amount. At this Mr. Cornell made a characteristic proposal. He said: "I will pay half of this debt if you can raise the other half." It seemed impossible. Our friends had been called upon so constantly and for such considerable sums that it seemed vain to ask them for more. But we brought together at

Albany a few of the most devoted, and in fifteen minutes the whole amount was subscribed: four members of the board of trustees agreed to give each twenty thousand dollars; and this, with Mr. Cornell's additional subscription, furnished the sum needed.

Then took place one of the things which led me later in life, looking back over the history of the university, to say that what had seemed to be our worst calamities had generally proved to be our greatest blessings. Among these I have been accustomed to name the monstrous McGuire attack in the Assembly on Mr. Cornell, which greatly disheartened me for the moment, but which eventually led the investigation committee not only to show to the world Mr. Cornell's complete honesty and self-sacrifice, but to recommend the measures which finally transferred the endowment fund from the State to the trustees, thus strengthening the institution greatly. So now a piece of good luck came out of this unexpected debt. As soon as the subscription was made, Mr. George W. Schuyler, treasurer of the university, in drawing up the deed of gift, ended it with words to the following effect: "And it is hereby agreed by the said Ezra Cornell, Henry W. Sage, Hiram Sibley, John McGraw, and Andrew D. White, that in case the said university shall ever be in position to repay their said subscriptions, then and in that case the said entire sum of one hundred and sixty thousand dollars *shall be repaid into a university fund for the creation of fellowships and scholarships* in the said university." A general laugh arose among the subscribers, Mr. McGraw remarking that this was rather offhand dealing with us; but all took it in good part and signed the agreement. It is certain that not one of us then expected in his lifetime to see the university able to repay the money; but, within a few years, as our lands were sold at better prices than we expected, the university was in condition to make restitution. At first some of the trustees demurred to investing so large a sum in fellowships and scholarships, and my first effort to carry through a plan to this effect failed; but at the next meeting I was successful; and so, in this apparently calamitous revelation of debt began that system of university fellowships and scholarships which has done so much for the development of higher instruction at Cornell.

So far as the university treasury was concerned, matters thenceforth went on well. Never again did the university incur any troublesome debt; from that day to this its finances have been so managed as to excite the admiration even of men connected with the most successful and best managed corporations of our country. But financial difficulties far more serious than the debt just referred to arose in a different quarter. In assuming the expenses of locating and managing the university lands, protecting them, paying taxes upon them, and the like, Mr. Cornell had taken upon himself a fearful load, and it pressed upon him heavily. But this was not all. It was, indeed, far from the worst; for, in his anxiety to bring the university town into easy connection with the railway system of the State, he had invested very largely in local railways leading into Ithaca. Under these circumstances, while he made heroic efforts and sacrifices, his relations to the comptroller of the State, who still had in his charge the land scrip of the university, became exceedingly difficult. At the very crisis of this difficulty Mr. Cornell's hard work proved too much for him, and he lay down to die. The university affairs, so far as the land-grant fund was concerned, seemed hopelessly entangled with his own and with those of the State: it seemed altogether likely that at his death the institution would be subjected to years of litigation, to having its endowment tied up in the courts, and to a suspension of its operations. Happily, we had as our adviser Francis Miles Finch, since justice of the Court of Appeals of the State, and now dean of the Law School—a man of noble character, of wonderfully varied gifts, an admirable legal adviser, devoted personally to Mr. Cornell, and no less devoted to the university. He set at work to disentangle the business relations of Mr. Cornell with the university, and of both with the State. Every member of the board, every member of Mr. Cornell's family,—indeed, every member of the community,—knew him to be honest, faithful, and capable. He labored to excellent purpose, and in due time the principal financial members of the board were brought together at Ithaca to consider his solution of the problem. It was indeed a dark day; we were still under the shadow of "Black Friday," the worst financial calamity in the history of the nation. Mr. Finch showed us that the first thing needful was to raise about two hundred and fifty thousand dollars, which could be tendered to the comptroller of the State in cash, who, on receiving it, would immediately turn over to the trustees the land scrip, which it was all-important should be in our possession at the death of Mr. Cornell. He next pointed out the measures to be taken in separating the interests of the university from Mr. Cornell's estate, and these were provided for. The sum required for obtaining control of the land scrip was immediately subscribed as a loan, virtually without security, by members of the board then present; though at that depressing financial period of the country strong men went about with the best of securities, unable to borrow money upon them. In a few days Mr. Cornell was dead; but the university was safe. Mr. Finch's plan worked well in every particular; and this, which appeared likely to be a great calamity, resulted in the board of trustees obtaining control of the landed endowment of the institution, without which it must have failed. But the weeks while these negotiations were going on were gloomy indeed for me; rarely in my life have I been so unhappy. That crisis of our fate was the winter of 1874. The weather was cold and depressing, my family far off in Syracuse. My main refuge then, as at sundry other times of deep personal distress, was in work. In the little southwest room of the president's house, hardly yet finished and still unfurnished, I made my headquarters. Every morning a blazing fire was lighted on the hearth; every day I devoted myself to university work and to study for my lectures. Happily, my subject interested me deeply. It was "The Age of Discovery"; and, surrounded with my books, I worked on, forgetful, for the time, of the December storms howling about the house, and of the still more fearful storms beating against the university. Three new lectures having been thus added to my course on the Renaissance period, I delivered them to my class; and, just as I was finishing the last of them, a messenger came to tell me that Mr. Cornell was dying. Dismissing my students, I hurried to his house, but was just too late; a few minutes before my arrival his eyes had closed in death. But his work was done—nobly done. As I gazed upon his dead face on that 9th of December, 1874, I remember well that my first feeling was that he was happily out of the struggle; and that, wherever he might be, I could wish to be still with him. But there was no time for unavailing regrets. We laid him reverently and affectionately to rest, in the midst of the scenes so dear to him, within the sound of the university chimes he so loved to hear, and pressed on with the work.

A few years later came another calamity, not, like the others, touching the foundations and threatening the existence of the university, yet hardly less crushing at the time; indeed, with two exceptions, it was the most depressing I have ever encountered. At the establishment of the university in Ithaca, one of the charter trustees who showed himself especially munificent to the new enterprise was Mr. John McGraw. One morning, while I was in the midst of the large collection of books sent by me from Europe, endeavoring to bring them into some order before the opening day, his daughter, Miss Jenny McGraw, came in, and I had the pleasure of showing her some of our more interesting treasures. She was a woman of kind and thoughtful nature, had traveled in her own country and abroad to good purpose, and was evidently deeply interested. Next day her father met me and said: "Well, you are pressing us all into the service. Jenny came home yesterday, and said very earnestly, 'I wish that I could do something to help on the university'; to which I replied, 'Very well. Do anything you like; I shall be glad to see you join in the work.'"

The result was the gift from her of the chime of bells which was rung at the opening of the university, and which, with the additions afterward made to it, have done beautiful service. On the bells she thus gave were inscribed the verses of the ninety-fifth chant of Tennyson's "In Memoriam"; and some weeks afterward I had the pleasure of placing in her hands what she considered an ample return for her gift—a friendly letter from Tennyson himself, containing some of the stanzas written out in his own hand. So began her interest in the university—an interest which never faltered.

A few years later she married one of our professors, an old friend of mine, and her marriage proved exceedingly happy; but, alas, its happiness was destined to be brief! Less than two years after her wedding day she was brought home from Europe to breathe her last in her husband's cottage on the university grounds, and was buried from the beautiful residence which she had built hard by, and had stored with works of art in every field.

At the opening of her will it was found that, while she had made ample provision for all who were near and dear to her, and for a multitude of charities, she had left to the university very nearly two millions of dollars, a portion of which was to be used for a student hospital, and the bulk of the remainder, amounting to more than a million and a half, for the university library. Her husband joined most heartily in her purpose, and all seemed ready for carrying it out in a way which would have made Cornell University, in that respect, unquestionably the foremost on the American continent. As soon as this munificent bequest was announced, I asked our leading lawyer, Judge Douglas Boardman, whether our charter allowed the university to take it, calling his attention to the fact that, like most of its kind in the State of New York, it restricted the amount of property which the university could hold, and reminding him that we had already exceeded the limit thus allowed. To this he answered that the restriction was intended simply to prevent the endowment of corporations beyond what the legislature might think best for the commonwealth; that if the attorney-general did not begin proceedings against us to prevent our taking the property, no one else could; and that he would certainly never trouble us.

In view of the fact that Judge Boardman had long experience and was at the time judge of the Supreme Court of the State, I banished all thought of difficulty; though I could not but regret that, as he drew Mrs. Fiske's will, and at the same time knew the restrictions of our charter, he had not given us a hint, so that we could have had our powers of holding property enlarged. It would have been perfectly easy to have the restrictions removed, and, as a matter of fact, the legislature shortly afterward removed them entirely, without the slightest objection; but this action was too late to enable us to take the McGraw-Fiske bequest.

About a fortnight after these assurances that we were perfectly safe, Judge Boardman sent for me, and on meeting him I found that he had discovered a decision of the Court of Appeals—rendered a few years before—which might prevent our accepting the bequest.

But there was still much hope of inducing the main heirs to allow the purpose of Mrs. Fiske to be carried out. Without imputing any evil intentions to any person, I fully believe—indeed, I may say I *know*—that, had the matter been placed in my hands, this vast endowment would have been saved to us; but it was not so to be. Personal complications had arisen between the main heir and two of our trustees which increased the embarrassments of the situation. It is needless to go into them now; let all that be buried; but it may at least be said that day and night I labored to make some sort of arrangement between the principal heir and the university, and finally took the steamer for Europe in order to meet him and see if some arrangement could be made. But personal bitterness had entered too largely into the contest, and my efforts were in vain. Though our legal advisers insisted that the university was sure of winning the case, we lost it in every court—first in the Supreme Court of the State, then in the Court of Appeals, and finally in the Supreme Court of the United States. To me all this was most distressing. The creation of such a library would have been the culmination of my work; I could then have sung my *Nunc dimittis*. But the calamity was not without its compensations. When the worst was known, Mr. Henry W. Sage, a lifelong friend of Mr. McGraw and of Mrs. Fiske, came to my house, evidently with the desire to console me. He said: "Don't allow this matter to prey upon you; Jenny shall have her library; it shall yet be built and well endowed." He was true to his promise. On the final decision against us, he added to his previous large gifts to the university a new donation of over six hundred thousand dollars, half of which went to the erection of the present library building, and the other half to an endowment fund. Professor Fiske also joined munificently in enlarging the library, adding various gifts which his practised eye showed him were needed, and, among these, two collections, one upon Dante and one in Romance literature, each the best of its kind in the United States. Mr. William Sage also added the noted library in German literature of Professor Zarncke of Leipsic; and various others contributed collections, larger or smaller, so that the library has become, as a whole, one of the best in the country. As I visit it, there often come back vividly to me remembrances of my college days, when I was wont to enter the Yale library and stand amazed in the midst of the sixty thousand volumes which had been brought together during one hundred and fifty years. They filled me with awe. But Cornell University has now, within forty years from its foundation, accumulated very nearly three hundred thousand volumes, many among them of far greater value than anything contained in the Yale library of my day; and as I revise these lines comes news that the will of Professor Fiske, who recently died at Frankfort-on-the-Main, gives to the library all of his splendid collections in Italian history and literature at Florence, with the addition of nearly half a million of dollars.

Beside these financial and other troubles, another class of difficulties beset us, which were, at times, almost as vexatious. These were the continued attacks made by good men in various parts of the State and Nation, who thought they saw in Cornell a stronghold—first, of ideas in religion antagonistic to their own; and secondly, of ideas in education likely to injure their sectarian colleges. From the day when our charter was under consideration at Albany they never relented, and at times they were violent. The reports of my inauguration speech were, in sundry denominational newspapers, utterly distorted; far and wide was spread the story that Mr. Cornell and myself were attempting to establish an institution for the propagation of "atheism" and "infidelity." Certainly nothing could have been further from the purpose of either of us. He had aided, and loved to aid, every form of Christianity; I was myself a member of a Christian church and a trustee of a denominational college. Everything that we could do in the way of reasoning with our assailants was in vain. In talking with students from time to time, I learned that, in many cases, their pastors had earnestly besought them to go to any other institution rather than to Cornell; reports of hostile sermons reached us; bitter diatribes constantly appeared in denominational newspapers, and especially virulent were various addresses given on public occasions in the sectarian colleges which felt themselves injured by the creation of an unsectarian institution on so large a scale. Typical was the attack made by an eminent divine who, having been installed as president over one of the smaller colleges of the State, thought it his duty to denounce me as an "atheist," and to do this especially in the city where I had formerly resided, and in the church which some of my family attended. I took no notice of the charge, and pursued the even tenor of my way; but the press took it up, and it recoiled upon the man who made it.

Perhaps the most comical of these attacks was one made by a clergyman of some repute before the Presbyterian Synod at Auburn in western New York. This gentleman, having attended one or two of the lectures by Agassiz before our scientific students, immediately rushed off to this meeting of his brethren, and insisted that the great naturalist was "preaching atheism and Darwinism" at the university. He seemed about to make a decided impression, when there arose a very dear old friend of mine, the Rev. Dr. Sherman Canfield, pastor of the First Presbyterian Church in Syracuse, who, fortunately, was a scholar abreast of current questions. Dr. Canfield quietly remarked that he was amazed to learn that Agassiz had, in so short a time, become an atheist, and not less astonished to hear that he had been converted to Darwinism; that up to that moment he had considered Agassiz a deeply religious man, and also the foremost—possibly, indeed, the last—great opponent of the Darwinian hypothesis. He therefore suggested that the resolution denouncing Cornell University brought in by his reverend brother be laid on the table to await further investigation. It was thus disposed of, and, in that region at least, it was never heard of more. Pleasing is it to me to chronicle the fact that, at Dr. Canfield's death, he left to the university a very important part of his library.

From another denominational college came an attack on Goldwin Smith. One of its professors published, in the Protestant Episcopal "Gospel Messenger," an attack upon the university for calling into its faculty a "Westminster Reviewer"; the fact being that Goldwin Smith was at that time a member of the Church of England, and had never written for the "Westminster Review" save in reply to one of its articles. So, too, when there were sculptured on the stone seat which he had ordered carved for the university grounds the words, "Above all nations is humanity," there came an outburst. Sundry pastors, in their anxiety for the souls of the students, could not tell whether this inscription savored more of atheism or of pantheism. Its simple significance—that the claims of humanity are above those of nationality—entirely escaped

them. Pulpit cushions were beaten in all parts of the State
against us, and solemn warnings were renewed to students by
their pastors to go anywhere for their education rather than
to Cornell. Curiously, this fact became not only a gratuitous,
but an effective, advertisement: many of the brightest men
who came to us in those days confessed to me that these attacks first directed their attention to us.

We also owed some munificent gifts, to this same cause.
In two cases gentlemen came forward and made large additions to our endowment as their way of showing disbelief in
these attacks or contempt for them.

Still, the attacks were vexatious even when impotent. In-
genius was the scheme carried out by a zealous young clergyman settled for a short time in Ithaca. Coming one day into
my private library, he told me that he was very anxious to
borrow some works showing the more recent tendencies of
liberal thought. I took him to one of my book-cases, in which,
by the side of the works of Bossuet and Fénelon and Thomas
Arnold and Robertson of Brighton, he found those of Channing, Parker, Renan, Strauss, and the men who, in the middle
years of the last century, were held to represent advanced
thought. He looked them over for some time, made some
excuse for not borrowing any of them just then, and I heard
nothing more from him until there came, in a denominational
newspaper, his eloquent denunciation of me for possessing
such books. Impressive, too, must have been the utterances
of an eminent "revivalist" who, in various Western cities,
loudly asserted that Mr. Cornell had died lamenting his inability to base his university on atheism, and that I had fled
to Europe declaring that in America an infidel university was,
as yet, an impossibility.

For a long time I stood on the defensive, hoping that the
provisions made for the growth of religious life among the
students might show that we were not so wicked as we were
represented; but, as all this seemed only to embitter our adversaries, I finally determined to take the offensive, and having

been invited to deliver a lecture in the great hall of the Cooper Institute at New York, took as my subject "The Battle-fields of Science." In this my effort was to show how, in the supposed interest of religion, earnest and excellent men, for many ages and in many countries, had bitterly opposed various advances in science and in education, and that such opposition had resulted in most evil results, not only to science and education, but to religion. This lecture was published in full, next day, in the "New York Tribune"; extracts from it were widely copied; it was asked for by lecture associations in many parts of the country; grew first into two magazine articles, then into a little book which was widely circulated at home, reprinted in England with a preface by Tyndall, and circulated on the Continent in translations, was then expanded into a series of articles in the "Popular Science Monthly," and finally wrought into my book on "The Warfare of Science with Theology." In each of these forms my argument provoked attack; but all this eventually created a reaction in our favor, even in quarters were it was least expected. One evidence of this touched me deeply. I had been invited to repeat the lecture at New Haven, and on arriving there found a large audience of Yale professors and students; but, most surprising of all, in the chair for the evening, no less a personage than my revered instructor, Dr. Theodore Dwight Woolsey, president of the university. He was of a deeply religious nature; and certainly no man was ever, under all circumstances, more true to his convictions of duty. To be welcomed by him was encouragement indeed. He presented me cordially to the audience, and at the close of my address made a brief speech, in which he thoroughly supported my positions and bade me Godspeed. Few things in my life have so encouraged me.

Attacks, of course, continued for a considerable time, some of them violent; but, to my surprise and satisfaction, when my articles were finally brought together in book form, the opposition seemed to have exhausted itself. There were even indications of approval in some quarters where the articles composing it had previously been attacked; and I received letters thoroughly in sympathy with the work from a number of eminent Christian men, including several doctors of divinity, and among these two bishops, one of the Anglican and one of the American Episcopal Church.

The final result was that slander against the university for irreligion was confined almost entirely to very narrow circles, of waning influence; and my hope is that, as its formative ideas have been thus welcomed by various leaders of thought, and have filtered down through the press among the people at large, they have done something to free the path of future laborers in the field of science and education from such attacks as those which Cornell was obliged to suffer.

13.

CONCLUDING YEARS

1881–1885

THIS WORK OF PRESSING ON THE DEVELOPMENT OF the leading departments in the university, establishing various courses of instruction, and warding off attacks as best I could, was added the daily care of the regular and steady administration of affairs, and in this my duty was to coöperate with the trustees, the faculty, and the students. The trustees formed a body differently composed from any organization for university government up to that time. As a rule, such boards in the United States were, in those days, self-perpetuating. A man once elected into one of them was likely to remain a trustee during his natural life; and the result had been much dry-rot and, frequently, a very sleepy condition of things in American collegiate and university administration. In drawing the Cornell charter, we provided for a governing body by first naming a certain number of high State officers —the governor, lieutenant-governor, speaker, president of the State Agricultural Society, and others; next, a certain number of men of special fitness, who were to be elected by the board itself; and, finally, a certain proportion elected by the alumni from their own number. Beside these, the eldest male lineal descendant of Mr. Cornell, and the president of the university, were trustees *ex officio*. At the first nomination of the charter trustees, Mr. Cornell proposed that he should name half the

number and I the other half. This was done, and pains were
taken to select men accustomed to deal with large affairs. A
very important provision was also made limiting their term
of office to five years.

During the first nine years the chairmanship of the board
was held by Mr. Cornell, but at his death Mr. Henry W. Sage
was elected to it, who, as long as he lived, discharged its
duties with the greatest conscientiousness and ability.   To
the finances of the university he gave that shrewd care which
had enabled him to build up his own immense business.
Freely and without compensation, he bestowed upon the
institution labor for which any great business corporation
would have gladly paid him a very large sum.   For the immediate management, in the intervals of the quarterly meetings of the board, an executive committee of the trustees was
created, which also worked to excellent purpose.

The faculty, which was at first comparatively small, was
elected by the trustees upon my nomination. In deciding on
candidates, I put no trust in mere paper testimonials, no matter
from what source; but always saw the candidates themselves,
talked with them, and then secured confidential communications regarding them from those who knew them best.   The
results were good, and to this hour I cherish toward the faculty, as toward the trustees, a feeling of the deepest gratitude.
Throughout all the hard work of that period they supported
me heartily and devotedly; without their devotion and aid,
my whole administration would have been an utter failure.

To several of these I have alluded elsewhere; but one should
be especially mentioned to whom every member of the faculty
must feel a debt of gratitude—Professor Hiram Corson. No
one has done more to redress the balance between the technical side and the humanities. His writings, lectures, and
readings have been a solace and an inspiration to many of us,
both in the faculty and among the students. It was my re-
membrance of the effect of his readings that caused me to
urge, at a public address at Yale in 1903, the establishment not

only of professorships but of readerships in English literature
in all our greater institutions, urging especially that the readers
thus called should every day present, with little if any note
or comment, the masterpieces of our literature. I can think
of no provision which would do more to humanize the great
body of students, especially in these days when other branches
are so largely supplanting classical studies, than such a continuous presentation of the treasures of our language by a
thoroughly good reader. What is needed is not more talk
about literature, but the literature itself. And here let me
recall an especial service of Professor Corson which may
serve as a hint to men and women of light and leading in the
higher education of our country. On sundry celebrations of
Founder's Day, and on various other commemorative occasions, he gave in the university chapel recitals from Milton,
Wordsworth, Tennyson, and other poets of the larger inspiration, while organ interludes were given from the great masters
of music. Literature and music were thus made to do beautiful service as yokefellows. It has been my lot to enjoy in
various capitals of the modern world many of the things which
men who have a deep feeling for art most rejoice in, but
never have I known anything more uplifting and ennobling
than these simple commemorations.

From one evil which has greatly injured many American
university faculties, especially in the middle and western
States, we were virtually free. This evil was the prevalence
of feuds between professors. Throughout a large part of the
nineteenth century they were a great affliction. Twice the
State University of Michigan was nearly wrecked by them;
for several years they nearly paralyzed two or three of the
New York colleges; and in one of these a squabble between
sundry professors and the widow of a former president was
almost fatal. Another of the larger colleges in the same State
lost a very eminent president from the same cause; and still
another, which had done excellent work, was dragged down
and for years kept down by a feud between its two foremost

professors. In my day, at Yale, whenever there was a sudden influx of students, and it was asked whence they came, the answer always was, "Another Western college has burst up"; and the "burst up" had resulted, almost without exception, from faculty quarrels.

In another chapter I have referred to one of these explosions which, having blown out of a Western university the president, the entire board of trustees, and all the assistant professors and instructors, convulsed the State for years. I have known gifted members of faculties, term after term, substitute for their legitimate work impassioned appeals to their religious denominations, through synods or conferences, and to the public at large through the press,—their quarrels at last entangling other professors and large numbers of students.

In my "Plan of Organization" I called attention to this evil, and laid down the principle that "the presence of no professor, however gifted, is so valuable as peace and harmony." The trustees acquiesced in this view, and from the first it was understood that, at any cost, quarrels must be prevented. The result was that we never had any which were serious, nor had we any in the board of trustees. One of the most satisfactory of all my reflections is that I never had any ill relations with any member of either body; that there was never one of them whom I did not look upon as a friend. My simple rule for the government of my own conduct was that I had *no time* for squabbling; that life was not long enough for quarrels; and this became, I think, the feeling among all of us who were engaged in the founding and building of the university.

As regards the undergraduates, I initiated a system which, so far as is known to me, was then new in American institutions of learning. At the beginning of every year, and also whenever any special occasion seemed to require it, I summoned the whole body of students and addressed them at length on the condition of the university, on their relations to it, and on their duties to it as well as to themselves; and in all these addresses endeavored to bring home to them the idea that under our system of giving to the graduates votes in the election of trustees, and to representative alumni seats in the governing board, the whole student body had become, in a new sense, part of the institution, and were to be held, to a certain extent, responsible for it. I think that all conversant with the history of the university will agree that the results of thus taking the students into the confidence of the governing board were happy. These results were shown largely among the undergraduates, and even more strongly among the alumni. In all parts of the country alumni associations were organized, and here again I found a source of strength. These associations held reunions during every winter, and at least one banquet, at which the president of the university was invited to be present. So far as possible, I attended these meetings, and made use of them to strengthen the connection of the graduates with their alma mater.

The administrative care of the university was very engrossing. With study of the various interests combined within its organization; with the attendance on meetings of trustees, executive committee, and faculty, and discussion of important questions in each of these bodies; with the general oversight of great numbers of students in many departments and courses; with the constant necessity of keeping the legislature and the State informed as to the reasons of every movement, of meeting hostile forces pressing us on every side, of keeping in touch with our graduates throughout the country, there was much to be done. Trying also, at times, to a man never in robust health was the duty of addressing various assemblies of most dissimilar purposes. Within the space of two or three years I find mention in my diaries of a large number of addresses which, as president of the university, I could not refuse to give; among these, those before the legislature of the State, on Technical Education; before committees of Congress, on Agriculture and Technical Instruction; before the Johns Hopkins University, on Education with Reference to Political Life;

before the National Teachers' Association at Washington, on
the Relation of the Universities to the State School Systems;
before the American Social Science Association of New York,
on Sundry Reforms in University Management; before the
National Association of Teachers at Detroit, on the Relations
of Universities to Colleges; before four thousand people at
Cleveland, on the Education of the Freedmen; before the
Adalbert College, on the Concentration of Means for the
Higher Education; before the State Teachers' Association at
Saratoga, on Education and Democracy; at the Centennial
banquet at Philadelphia, on the American Universities; and
before my class at Yale University, on the Message of the
Nineteenth Century to the Twentieth; besides many public
lectures before colleges, schools, and special assemblies.
There seemed more danger of wearing out than of rusting out,
especially as some of these discourses provoked attacks which
must be answered. Time also was required for my duties as
president of the American Social Science Association, which
lasted several years, and of the American Historical Society,
which, though less engrossing, imposed for a time much responsibility. Then, too, there was another duty, constantly
pressing, which I had especially at heart. The day had not
yet arrived when the president of the university could be
released from his duties as a professor. I had, indeed, no
wish for such release; for, of all my duties, that of meeting my
senior students face to face in the lecture-room and interesting
them in the studies which most interested me, and which
seemed most likely to fit them to go forth and bring the influence of the university to bear for good upon the country at
large, was that which I liked best. The usual routine of administrative cares was almost hateful to me, and I delegated
minor details, as far as possible, to those better fitted to take
charge of them—especially to the vice-president and registrar
and secretary of the faculty. But my lecture-room I loved.
Of all occupations, I know of none more satisfactory than
that of a university professor who feels that he is in right

relations with his students, that they welcome what he has to give them, and that their hearts and minds are developed, day by day, by the work which he most prizes. I may justly say that this pleasure was mine at the University of Michigan and at Cornell University. It was at times hard to satisfy myself; for next to the pleasure of directing younger minds is the satisfaction of fitting one's self to do so. During my ordinary working-day there was little time for keeping abreast with the latest and best in my department; but there were odds and ends of time, day and night, and especially during my frequent journeys by rail and steamer to meet engagements at distant points, when I always carried with me a collection of books which seemed to me most fitted for my purpose; and as I had trained myself to be a rapid reader, these excursions gave me many opportunities.

But some of these journeys were not well suited to study. During the first few years of the university, being obliged to live in the barracks on the University Hill under many difficulties, I could not have my family with me, and from Saturday afternoon until Monday morning was given to them at Syracuse. In summer the journey by Cayuga Lake to the New York Central train gave me excellent opportunity for reading and even for writing. But in winter it was different. None of the railways now connecting the university town with the outside world had then been constructed, save that to the southward; and, therefore, during those long winters there was at least twice a week a dreary drive in wagon or sleigh, sometimes taking all the better hours of the day, in order to reach the train from Binghamton to Syracuse. Coming out of my lecture-room Friday evening or Saturday morning, I was conveyed through nearly twenty-five miles of mud and slush or sleet and snow. On one journey my sleigh was upset three times in the drifts which made the roads almost impassable, and it required nearly ten hours to make the entire journey. The worst of it was that, coming out of my heated lecture-room and taking an open sleigh at Ithaca, or coming out of the heated cars and taking it at Cortland, my throat became affected, and for some years gave me serious trouble.

But my greater opportunities—those which kept me from becoming a mere administrative machine—were afforded by various vacations, longer or shorter. During the summer vacation, mainly passed at Saratoga and the seaside, there was time for consecutive studies with reference to my work, my regular lectures, and occasional addresses. But this was not all. At three different times I was summoned from university work to public duties. The first of these occasions was when I was appointed by President Grant one of the commissioners to Santo Domingo. This appointment came when I was thoroughly worn out with university work, and it gave me a chance of great value physically and intellectually. During four months I was in a world of thought as different from anything that I had before known as that wonderful island in the Caribbean Sea is different in its climate from the hills of central New York swept by the winds of December. And I had to deal with men very different from the trustees, faculty, and students of Cornell. This episode certainly broadened my view as a professor, and strengthened me for administrative duties.

The third of these long vacations was in 1879–80–81, when President Hayes appointed me minister plenipotentiary in Berlin. My stay at that post, and especially my acquaintance with leaders in German thought and with professors at many of the Continental universities, did much for me in many ways.

It may be thought strange that I could thus absent myself from the university, but these absences really enabled me to maintain my connection with the institution. My constitution, though elastic, was not robust; an uninterrupted strain would have broken me, while variety of occupation strengthened me. Throughout my whole life I have found the best of all medicines to be travel and change of scene. Another example of this was during my stay of a year abroad as commissioner at the Paris Exposition. During that stay I prepared several additions to my course of general lectures, and during my official stay in Berlin added largely to my course on German history. But the change of work saved me: though minor excursions were frequently given up to work with book and pen, I returned from them refreshed and all the more ready for administrative duties.

As to the effect of such absences upon the university, I may say that it accorded with the theory which I held tenaciously regarding the administration of the university at that formative period. I had observed in various American colleges that a fundamental and most injurious error was made in relieving trustees and faculty from responsibility, and concentrating all in the president. The result, in many of these institutions, had been a sort of atrophy,—the trustees and faculty being, whenever an emergency arose, badly informed as to the affairs of their institutions, and really incapable of managing them. This state of things was the most serious drawback to President Tappan's administration at the University of Michigan, and was the real cause of the catastrophe which finally led to his break with the regents of that university, and his departure to Europe, never to return. Worse still was the downfall of Union College, Schenectady, from the position which it had held before the death of President Nott. Under Drs. Nott and Tappan the tendency in the institutions above named was to make the trustees in all administrative matters mere ciphers, and to make the faculty more and more incapable of administering discipline or conducting current university business. That system concentrated all knowledge of university affairs and all power of every sort in the hands of the president, and relieved trustees and faculty from everything except nominal responsibility. From the very beginning I determined to prevent this state of things at Cornell. Great powers were indeed given me by the trustees, and I used them; but in the whole course of my administration I constantly sought to keep ample legislative powers in the board of trustees and in the faculty. I felt that the university, to be successful, should not depend on the life and conduct of any one man; that every one of those called to govern and to manage it, whether president or professor, should feel that he had powers and responsibilities in its daily administration. Therefore it was that I inserted in the fundamental laws of the university a provision that the confirmation by the trustees of all nominations of professors should be by ballot; so that it might never be in the power of the president or any other trustee unduly to influence selections for such positions. I also exerted myself to provide that in calling new professors they should be nominated by the president, not of his own will, but with the advice of the faculty and should be confirmed by the trustees. I also provided that the elections of students to fellowships and scholarships and the administration of discipline should be decided by the faculty, and by ballot. The especial importance of this latter point will not escape those conversant with university management. I insisted that the faculty should not be merely a committee to register the decrees of the president, but that it should have full legislative powers to discuss and to decide university affairs. Nor did I allow it to become a body merely advisory: I not only insisted that it should have full legislative powers, but that it should be steadily trained in the use of them. On my nomination the trustees elected from the faculty three gentlemen who had shown themselves especially fitted for administrative work to the positions of vice-president, registrar, and secretary; and thenceforth the institution was no longer dependent on any one man. To the first of these positions was elected Professor William Channing Russel; to the second, Professor William Dexter Wilson; to the third, Professor George C. Caldwell; and each discharged his duties admirably.

Of the last two of these I have already spoken, and here some record should be made of the services rendered by Dr. Russel. He was among those chosen for the instructing body at the very beginning. Into all of his work he brought a perfect loyalty to truth, with the trained faculties of a lawyer in seeking it and the fearlessness of an apostle in announcing it. As to his success in this latter field, there may be given, among other testimonies, that of an unwilling witness—a young scholar of great strength of mind, who, though he had taken deep offense at sundry acts of the professor and never forgiven them, yet, after a year in the historical lecture-rooms of the University of Berlin, said to me: "I have attended here the lectures of all the famous professors of history, and have heard few who equal Professor Russel and none who surpass him in ascertaining the really significant facts and in clearly presenting them."

In the vice-presidency of the faculty he also rendered services of the greatest value. No one was more devoted than he to the university or more loyal to his associates. There was, indeed, some friction. His cousin, James Russell Lowell, once asked me regarding this, and my reply was that it reminded me of a character in the "Biglow Papers" who "had a dre'dful winnin' way to make folks hate him." This was doubtless an overstatement, but it contained truth; for at times there was perhaps lacking in his handling of delicate questions something of the *suaviter in modo*. His honest frankness was worthy of all praise; but I once found it necessary to write him: "I am sorry that you have thought it best to send me so unsparing a letter, but no matter; write me as many as you like; they will never break our friendship; only do not write others in the same strain." This brought back from him one of the kindest epistles imaginable. Uncompromising as his manner was, his services vastly outweighed all the defects of his qualities; and among these services were some of which the general public never dreamed. I could tell of pathetic devotion and self-sacrifice on his part, not only to the university, but to individual students. No professor ever had a kindlier feeling toward any scholar in need, sickness, or trouble. Those who knew him best loved him most;

and, in the hard, early days of the university, he especially made good his title of the gratitude of every Cornellian, not only by his university work, but by his unostentatious devotion to every deserving student.

As to my professorial work, I found in due time effective aid in various young men who had been members of my classes. Of these were Charles Kendall Adams, who afterward became my successor in the presidency of Cornell, and George Lincoln Burr, who is now one of my successors in the professorship of history.

Thus it was that from time to time I could be absent with a feeling that all at the university was moving on steadily and securely; with a feeling, indeed, that it was something to have aided in creating an institution which could move on steadily and securely, even when the hands of those who had set it in motion had been removed.

There was, however, one temporary exception to the rule. During my absence as minister at Berlin trouble arose in the governing board so serious that I resigned my diplomatic post before my term of service was ended, and hastened back to my university duties. But no permanent injury had been done; in fact, this experience, by revealing weaknesses in sundry parts of our system, resulted in permanent good.

Returning thus from Berlin, I threw myself into university work more heartily than ever. It was still difficult, for our lands had not as yet been sold to any extent, and our income was sadly insufficient. The lands were steadily increasing in value, and it was felt that it would be a great error to dispose of them prematurely. The work of providing ways and means to meet the constantly increasing demands of the institution was therefore severe, and the loss of the great library bequest to the university also tried me sorely; but I labored on, and at last, thanks to the admirable service of Mr. Sage in the management of the lands, the university was enabled to realize, for the first time, a large capital from them. Up to the year 1885 they had been a steady drain upon our resources; now the sale of a fraction of them yielded a good revenue. For the first time there was something like ease in the university finances.

Twenty years had now elapsed since I had virtually begun my duties as president by drafting the university charter and by urging it upon the legislature. The four years of work since my return from Berlin had tried me severely; and more than that, I had made a pledge some years before to the one who, of all in the world, had the right to ask it, that at the close of twenty years of service I would give up all administrative duties. To this pledge I was faithful, but with the feeling that it was at the sacrifice of much. The new endowment coming in from the sale of lands offered opportunities which I had longed for during many weary years; but I felt that it was best to put the management into new hands. There were changes needed which were far more difficult for me to make than for a new-comer—especially changes in the faculty, which involved the severing of ties very dear to me.

At the annual commencement of 1885, the twenty years from the granting of our charter having arrived, I presented my resignation with the declaration that it must be accepted. It was accepted in such a way as to make me very grateful to all connected with the institution: trustees, faculty, and students were most kind to me. As regards the first of these bodies, I cannot resist the temptation to mention two evidences of their feeling which touched me deeply. The first of these was the proposal that I should continue as honorary president of the university. This I declined. To hold such a position would have been an injury to my successor; I knew well that the time had come when he would be obliged to grapple with questions which I had left unsettled from a feeling that he would have a freer hand than I could have. But another tender made me I accepted: this was that I should nominate my successor. I did this, naming my old student at the University of Michigan, who had succeeded me there as professor of history—Charles Kendall Adams; and so began a second and most prosperous administration.

In thus leaving the presidency of the university, it seemed to me that the time had come for carrying out a plan formed long before—the transfer to the university of my historical and general library, which had become one of the largest and, in its field, one of the best private collections of books in the United States. The trustees accepted it, providing a most noble room for it in connection with the main university library and with the historical lecture-rooms; setting apart, also, from their resources, an ample sum, of which the income should be used in maintaining the library, in providing a librarian, in publishing a complete catalogue, and in making the collection effective for historical instruction. My only connection with the university thenceforward was that of a trustee and member of its executive committee. In this position it has been one of the greatest pleasures and satisfactions of my life to note the large and steady development of the institution during the two administrations which have succeeded my own. At the close of the administration of President Adams, who had especially distinguished himself in developing the law department and various other important university interests, in strengthening the connection of the institution with the State, and in calling several most competent professors, he was succeeded by a gentleman whose acquaintance I had made during my stay as minister to Germany, he being at that time a student at the University of Berlin,—Dr. Jacob Gould Schurman, whose remarkable powers and gifts have more than met the great expectations I then formed regarding him, and have developed the university to a yet higher point, so that its number of students is now, as I revise these lines, over three thousand. He, too, has been called to important duties in the public service; and he has just returned after a year of most valuable work as president of the Commission of the United States to the Philippine

Islands, the university progressing during his absence, and showing that it has a life of its own and is not dependent even on the most gifted of presidents.

On laying down the duties of the university presidency, it did not seem best to me to remain in its neighborhood during the first year or two of the new administration. Any one who has ever been in a position similar to mine at that period will easily understand the reason. It is the same which has led thoughtful men in the churches to say that it is not well to have the old pastor too near when the new pastor is beginning his duties. Obedient to this idea of leaving my successor a free hand, my wife and myself took a leisurely journey through England, France, and Italy, renewing old acquaintances and making new friends. Returning after a year, I settled down again in the university, hoping to complete the book for which I had been gathering materials and on which I had been working steadily for some years, when there came the greatest calamity of my life,—the loss of her who had been my main support during thirty years,—and work became, for a time, an impossibility. Again I became a wanderer, going, in 1888, first to Scotland, and thence, being ordered by physicians to the East, went again through France and Italy, and extended the journey through Egypt, Greece, and Turkey. Of the men and things which seemed most noteworthy to me at that period I speak in other chapters. From the East I made my way leisurely to Paris, with considerable stops at Buda-Pesth, Vienna, Ulm, Munich, Frankfort-on-the-Main, Paris, London, taking notes in libraries, besides collecting books and manuscripts.

Returning to the United States in the autumn of 1889, and settling down again in my old house at Cornell, I was invited to give courses of historical lectures at various American universities, especially one upon the "Causes of the French Revolution," at Johns Hopkins, Columbian University in Washington, the University of Pennsylvania, Tulane University in New Orleans, and Stanford University in California. Excursions to these institutions opened a new epoch in my life; but of this I shall speak elsewhere.

During this period of something over fifteen years, I have been frequently summoned from these duties, which were especially agreeable to me—first, in 1892, as minister to Russia; next, in 1896, as a member of the Venezuelan Commission at Washington; and, in 1897, as ambassador to Germany. I have found many men and things which would seem likely to draw me away from my interest in Cornell; but, after all, that which has for nearly forty years held, and still holds, the deepest place in my thoughts is the university which I aided to found.

Since resigning its presidency I have, in many ways, kept in relations with it; and as I have, at various times, returned from abroad and walked over its grounds, visited its buildings, and lived among its faculty and students, an enjoyment has been mine rarely vouchsafed to mortals. It has been like revisiting the earth after leaving it. The work to which I had devoted myself for so many years, and with more earnestness than any other which I have ever undertaken, though at times almost with the energy of despair, I have now seen successful beyond my dreams. Above all, as I have seen the crowd of students coming and going, I have felt assured that the work is good. It was with this feeling that, just before I left the university for the embassy at Berlin, I erected at the entrance of the university grounds a gateway, on which I placed a paraphrase of a Latin inscription noted by me, many years before, over the main portal of the University of Padua, as follows:

"So enter that daily thou mayest become more learned
    and thoughtful;
So depart that daily thou mayest become more useful
    to thy country and to mankind."

I often recall the saying of St. Philip Neri, who, in the days of the Elizabethan persecutions, was wont to gaze at the students passing out from the gates of the English College at Rome, on their way to Great Britain, and to say: "I am feasting my eyes on those martyrs yonder." My own feelings are like his, but happier: I feast my eyes on those youths going forth from Cornell University into this new twentieth century to see great things that I shall never see, and to make the new time better than the old.

During my life, which is now extending beyond the allotted span of threescore and ten, I have been engaged, after the manner of my countrymen, in many sorts of work, have become interested in many conditions of men, have joined in many efforts which I hope have been of use; but, most of all, I have been interested in the founding and maintaining of Cornell University, and by the part I have taken in that, more than by any other work of my life, I hope to be judged.